FROM DE

THE STORY OF FOOT

FROM DELHI TO THE DEN
THE STORY OF FOOTBALL'S MOST TRAVELLED COACH

Stephen Constantine with Owen Amos

deCoubertin
BOOKS

First published by deCoubertin Books Ltd in 2017.

First Edition

deCoubertin Books, Studio I, Baltic Creative Campus, Liverpool, L1 OAH
www.decoubertin.co.uk

ISBN: 978-1-909245-47-1

A CIP catalogue record for this book is available from the British Library.

Typeset by Thomas Regan | Milkyone Creative.

Cover Design by Dave Williams

Printed and bound by Opolgraf.

To my Lucy, who has suffered with me, stood by me,
and raised our three beautiful children.

STEPHEN CONSTANTINE
CV

1990 – 1991: Assistant Manager, CW Post, USA

1992 – 1994: Assistant Reserve Team Manager, Apollon Limassol, Cyprus

1994 – 1995: Manager, Agios Therapon, Cyprus

1995 – 1996: Reserve Team Manager / First Team Manager, APEP, Cyprus

1996 – 1998: Director of Youth, AEL, Cyprus

1998 – 1999: Manager, APEP, Cyprus

1999 – 2001: Manager, Nepal National Team

2001 – 2002: Youth Coach, AFC Bournemouth, England

2001 – 2002: Head Coach, Chichester College, England

2002 – 2005: Manager, India National Team

2005 – 2006: First Team Coach, Millwall, England

2007 – 2008: Manager, Malawi National Team

2009: Manager, Sudan National Team

2010: Manager, APEP, Cyprus

2010 – 2012: Manager, Nea Salamina, Cyprus

2012 – 2013: Manager, Ethnikos Achna, Cyprus

2013 – 2014: Assistant Manager, Apollon Smyrnis, Greece

2014 – 2015: Manager, Rwanda National Team

2015 – Manager, India National Team

CONTENTS

FOREWORD
BY FIFA PRESIDENT, GIANNI INFANTINO

FIFA'S MISSION IS TO DEVELOP FOOTBALL WORLDWIDE AND TO assist all our member associations according to their specific needs and challenges.

In order to achieve this goal, FIFA needs a tailor-made approach that can only be implemented thanks to technical experts like Stephen Constantine. His commitment and dedication to our sport is exemplary and he does not hesitate to accept any appointment wherever the mission goes in order to help promoting and further developing football around the world. He is one of those precious experts who brings our philosophy to the pitch and convert it into reality.

FIFA is very happy to know Stephen, a highly skilled, knowledgeable, experienced and professional football enthusiast who contributed and still contributes to the development of our sport across the globe. We truly hope that his motivation, commitment and passion will further guide him, as these are much-needed elements in football development.

Particularly, we wish him much success in his current role as head coach of the India national football team, a challenging and exciting mission in one of the fastest growing football countries in the world, where all ingredients are reunited for a bright future for our sport.

FIFA would sincerely like to thank Stephen for his contribution to the development of football and we wish him all the best for the future.

Gianni Infantino
Zurich, May 2017

1
GROWING UP
1962–82

NOMADIC. THAT'S WHAT PEOPLE CALL ME.

I've coached six national sides. Worked in four continents. I've taken my teams to Zimbabwe, North Korea, and most places in between.

I've lived in Khartoum and Kathmandu. New York and New Delhi. Brighton and Blantyre.

I've been on countless flights. Stayed in countless hotel rooms. Spent countless nights on my own, looking forward to seeing my wife and three children.

So yes, I'm a nomad. I go from place to place. But here's what people don't know: it's always been like this.

I went to eight schools. Moved homes. Moved countries. Moved continents. At one point, I was a refugee, fleeing my home as bombs fell from the sky.

And when I was a teenager, I left home with nothing. I never went back.

I WAS SIXTEEN YEARS OLD. DAD AND I WERE ARGUING. THIS TIME, it was about football.

I'd just moved to Cyprus, where he lived with my brothers and sister. We lived in a village just outside Limassol, a city on the south coast.

I'd started training with the reserves of a first-division team, AEL. Two other teams in the city – Aris and Apollon – also wanted me to sign.

At the time, I was a striker. Quite quick. Aggressive. Good in the air. At AEL they called me Jordan, after the Scotland striker Joe Jordan. I used to get stuck in.

The problem was, Dad wanted me to move to the village team, Kolossi. They were non-league. Amateur. They trained twice a week and, if I signed for them, I would never have to leave the village. That suited Dad. He never thought I would amount to much.

'You'll never make a living playing football,' he told me, over and over again.

Kolossi were small time. AEL were big time. Playing for them meant travelling to the city every day. It meant leaving the village behind. It meant my dream – playing professional football – was alive.

Dad wouldn't have it.

'It's my house, my rules,' he said. 'When I say jump, you don't ask why – you ask how high.'

I said no. I wanted to sign for AEL or Apollon. I wanted to play in the first division.

'If you don't like it,' he told me, 'there's the door.'

I thought about the arguments. The years of yelling. The lack of any father–son relationship.

I thought about his boozing. His temper. And most of all, I thought about Mum. She died on 15 September 1975 – a month short of my thirteenth birthday.

Dad and I didn't get on before she died. Afterwards, it was much worse. There was nothing, and no one, to stop the arguments.

So I looked at the door. I said bye to my brothers and sister, and left home for good.

IT WAS TEN-THIRTY AT NIGHT. ALL I HAD WERE THE CLOTHES ON my back. We lived six or seven miles outside Limassol, so I started walking.

The road was half-built. There were no streetlights. I stuck to the edge of the tarmac, so I didn't get run over. The night seemed darker than normal.

Eventually, I reached a set of traffic lights. On the corner was a club called Traffic. I knew the owners, and I knew AEL players went there, so I went in. I had nowhere else to go.

I told the guys what happened. They let me sleep on a couch. The next day, I hung out: coffee shops, street corners, anywhere. Being on your own isn't too bad in daylight. At night, it's different.

I couldn't go back to the club – my pride wouldn't let me – so I went to my great-grandmother's house. I didn't knock on the door. I didn't want my dad's grandma to know I'd left home.

Instead, I went round the back. She had a shed, so I tried the door. It was locked, but somehow I forced it open. The next morning, she found me.

'Why don't you go back to your father?' she asked me.

'No,' I replied.

'You should make up,' she said.

'I'm not doing it,' I replied. It wasn't much of a discussion.

I said bye to my great-grandmother, left the shed, and spent most of the day walking round Limassol. When it was dark, I saw an abandoned car in a field.

I tried the door. Unlike my great-grandmother's shed, it opened first time.

I climbed in, lay down, and slept on the back seat. It was the longest night of my life.

The next day was match day. AEL were playing in Larnaca, forty miles up the coast.

In those days, the reserve teams played immediately before the first team. If the punters turned up early, they got two games for the price of one. I wasn't playing for the reserves – I hadn't been in Cyprus long, and I wasn't registered – but they wanted me to come watch. I went to AEL's clubhouse, as I'd been told, and waited.

The reserves coach was Costas Pambou, a former AEL player. He was affectionately known as Mavrokolos, which literally meant 'black arse'. He was old-school. Sometimes, he'd pass me on his motorbike on his way to training. Instead of giving me a lift, he would whizz past.

'Hurry up, you English bastard,' he'd shout. 'You'll be late!'

If that wasn't bad enough, his nickname for me was Kavlintiri. Loosely translated, it means 'hard-on'.

Despite that, he took a shine to me. He liked my aggression. When I was waiting outside the clubhouse, he opened the door.

'Faggot English boy – what are you doing outside?'

At the time, my Greek wasn't great. Perhaps there'd been a mistake. Perhaps I wasn't meant to travel with the team.

'You told me to come,' I replied, almost whispering.

'I told you to come inside!' he said. 'Not hang around out here!'

I went inside and had steak and chips with the reserves. For a starving kid who'd spent the night in an abandoned car, it was heaven.

I went to Larnaca and watched the reserves, followed by the first team. On the way home, the team manager, Mr Fodis, asked where I wanted to be dropped off.

'It doesn't matter,' I said. 'Anywhere.'

I had nowhere to go. I probably would have tried Traffic again, or slept on the beach.

'But you must have somewhere,' Mr Fodis said.

'Honestly,' I repeated, 'anywhere will do.'

He must have asked six times. Eventually he got pissed off.

'I don't have anywhere,' I finally told him. 'I left home three nights ago.'

Mr Fodis took me to his house and let me sleep in a shack in his back garden. Back then, a lot of houses in Cyprus had them: they were made from corrugated iron, usually with a bed, a hob and not much else.

The next day, he went to the house three doors down, where they had a spare shack. He spoke to the owners and gave them a month's rent. It was basic, but it was better than staying with Dad. The shower was a hose that hung from a lemon tree. When I built my house in Cyprus in 2006, I stuck a lemon tree in the garden. It always reminds me of the shack on Mr Fodis's street.

As well as the shack, AEL got me a job in a hotel: first as a doorman, then by the pool. I was sixteen years old, and football had saved me.

I WAS BORN IN MARYLEBONE, LONDON, ON 16 OCTOBER 1962. My mum, Paula, was a hairdresser with her own salon called Vogue. The customers loved her, apparently. I've still got her business card.

She met dad when he was selling dresses from a van. He was Cypriot, but moved to England when he was young. They went into business, running clothes shops around north London. We moved about the suburbs: Muswell Hill in the beginning, then Mill Hill and Hadley Wood.

Mum was English, but there was Irish there too. Her maiden name was Shine. She was a proper ginger, covered head to foot in freckles. When she lay in the sun they used to join up.

She was really smart, with a great sense of humour. But she was tough. I remember when I was eleven, I used the F-word. Mum was horrified.

'If you need to use that word to express yourself, you're not worth listening to,' she said, before taking me upstairs to wash my mouth out with soap. Literally.

There were six of us: Mum, Dad, me, my two brothers and my sister. Costa is two years younger than me, Monica's three years younger, and Anthony's eight years younger.

From an early age, I was obsessed with football. I'd organise Subbuteo leagues on my dad's snooker table. I'd listen to the scores on the radio. And I'd play in the garden, or the park, or – more dangerously – in the front room.

Once, I smashed the glass in Dad's office door with a tennis ball. Another time, when playing in the garden with my Uncle Spyro, I hit a volley towards the top corner of the living-room window.

I fell to my knees. Not in recognition of the wonder strike, but because I was going to get a beating. As the ball hit the window, a crack raced from one side of the glass to the other. I went to bed at 6 p.m., before Mum and Dad got back from the shop, to delay the hiding. I got a proper telling-off the next day, but my life was spared.

When I wasn't breaking windows, I'd watch the best team in north London. My first live game was on 3 May 1971: Spurs v Arsenal at White Hart Lane. It was the last game of the season: Arsenal needed a win or a goalless draw to be champions. I went with my dad, who was a Tottenham fan. Perhaps that was another reason we didn't get on. Or perhaps it was a symptom.

Dad and I stood on the terraces. I couldn't see anything, but I remember the nonstop noise; the atmosphere; the sense of everyone being on edge. I fell in love.

At the time, I was leaning towards Arsenal, but I hadn't picked them. With three minutes left, Ray Kennedy headed past Pat Jennings – 1–0. Arsenal were champions and I was hooked. Five days later, I watched the FA Cup final against Liverpool. Charlie George's wonder strike won us the double.

I often went to Highbury as a boy. Back then, you could turn up, pay your money, and walk in. Once, I went with Dad and my younger brother, Costa. We sat on a scoreboard by a corner flag in the North Bank. It had barbed wire on to stop people sitting on it and, at the end of the game, my coat got caught. By the time Dad freed it, Costa had wandered off. We couldn't find him anywhere.

We spent hours looking. We even told the police. Eventually, we walked past a chip shop and there he was, sitting on the counter, eating a bag of chips. He was happy as Larry.

Around that time, Dad drove home from the pub after a few drinks. He was nicked and banned from driving. The business relied on him going shop to shop, dropping off stock, so without a licence, he was stuck. He decided to start again. He told us we were moving to Cyprus.

I think the move had been on the cards; the ban just made up his mind. To be honest, I didn't mind. It was exciting. We were moving to a holiday island, and I couldn't wait. Even then, I liked adventure.

We moved to Famagusta, which was the place to be in Cyprus. Mum and Dad opened two shops: one on Kennedy Avenue, the main street, and another on a roundabout nearby. They were called Hot Pants boutique. They were the first to do print-your-own T-shirts, which became the big fad.

At first I went to school in Famagusta. It was all in Greek and I couldn't understand a word. Not only that, I was the new kid. The foreign boy. I played football, which helped in the playground, but really, it was a nightmare. After three months I was sent to boarding school in Nicosia, forty-odd miles away.

Terra Santa College was a Catholic school. On the up side, the lessons were mainly in English. On the down side, the school was run by priests who beat the living daylights out of us. One Sunday morning, we were being served breakfast in the classroom. A boy called Sotiris was sitting in the row in front. When we finished the meal, a priest asked him to collect the trays.

'That's a job for women,' said Sotiris. 'I'm not doing it.'

The priest approached Sotiris from behind, then whacked him so hard he flew out of his chair. As Sotiris lay on the floor, the priest kicked him to bits. We sat there in shock. Sotiris, bloody and bruised, begged him to stop. He didn't argue with the priest again. None of us did.

When we walked to the dorms after our evening meal, we weren't allowed to speak. But there was this one kid – Paul, the youngest of us all – who had an infectious laugh. Once he started, we all went. One time, Paul laughed. We all cracked up. The priest didn't say a word but, when we were outside the dorm, he got his ruler out. We held our palms out, waiting to be whacked.

Instead, the priest told us to clench our fists. He turned the ruler on its side and smacked our knuckles with the sharp side. I ran to bed to stick my hand under the pillow, where the coolness took the pain away. The pillowcase turned blood-red.

Another time, someone farted in the dormitory as we were being put to bed. I started laughing, so one of the sisters slapped me round the face until I stopped. There was another priest who carried a plastic whip in the sleeve of his cassock. He wasn't afraid to use it, either. It was brutal.

We went home every other weekend. I used to count the days. One day – a Thursday, I think – my mum turned up at school. It was strange: I never saw her at school.

'There's something wrong with me,' she said. 'They don't know what it is, so I'm going to England to get some tests. But don't worry. Everything will be fine.'

Of course, I did worry, although Mum came back after the tests were done. And later that year, 1974, there was more to worry about.

A military coup deposed the elected president of Cyprus, Archbishop Makarios. The Turkish community thought the new rulers, backed by Greece, would ignore their rights. Mum and Dad must have known something was coming, because they had already begun packing. But on 20 July, before we could return to England, Turkey invaded Cyprus. Our island became a war zone.

The invasion began on the north coast, about fifty miles away from our home. On the horizon, we could see bombs falling from the sky. We were told to stay in the basement.

Two days into the war, a ten-ton truck came down the street. We heard British accents. A voice from a loudspeaker said anyone with a UK passport should grab a suitcase and come out.

I remember climbing on the back of the army lorry. You needed a ladder to get there. As we waited to leave, I realised I'd left my football and autograph book in the house. I had loads of big names in that book, as the England team used to stay in a hotel near Hadley Wood before matches. I jumped from the lorry and sprinted into the house. The soldiers went mad. So did my mum.

We were taken to Anzio, a camp at the British base of Dhekelia in eastern Cyprus. We slept in a huge tent with loads of other families. We were lucky: some people slept in cars and buses.

One day, I was kicking a ball around with some other lads when I heard a noise. I looked up and saw a dozen Turkish tanks roll past the base. The Turkish commander was standing behind the gun turret, shouting. The British squaddies cocked their guns.

The British soldiers were yelling: 'This is British sovereign land; you are not coming in here.' A British officer, accompanied by some of his soldiers, spoke to the Turks. They turned round. I breathed a sigh of relief and went back to my football.

After three days, the fighting stopped. We were allowed to visit Famagusta. As we reached the town, you could smell burning flesh. There were bodies in the street.

We went to the beachfront. There was a famous hotel called the Salaminia Tower, which was in the shape of an H – two towers connected by a walkway. I saw a boy on a balcony, hanging by his legs. He was dead. The firemen were trying to saw through his leg to retrieve the body.

Of our two shops, one was damaged but standing. A rocket had gone through the top of the building: everything above was destroyed, but the shop was intact. But the other store, on Kennedy Avenue, was ruined. It had taken a direct hit, despite being surrounded by blocks of flats. As we looked at the rubble, my dad said the strangest thing.

'Crawl in there and get some stuff out,' he said, meaning the dresses.

I don't know what he was thinking. The place was a bomb site, but he thought it was important to save a dress or two. Of course, if you're eleven years old, you do what your dad says. And – in truth – it was quite exciting. But I wouldn't send my son into a place that had been hit by a 200lb bomb.

Like most people, Dad didn't realise how terrible the war would become. When we went back to England – on a Hercules into Brize Norton in Oxfordshire – he stayed in Cyprus. He wanted to salvage the business and, if he was out of the country, he couldn't do that. The rest of us stayed with my mum's sister, Aunty Kay. She lived in Staines, just west of London. We stayed for four or five months. I went to the Matthew Arnold secondary school.

In 1975, when I was twelve, we moved from Aunty Kay's in Staines to a house in Hadley Wood, which we'd rented out. Things were getting back to normal. Except by then, we knew Mum had cancer.

It started in her stomach. She was in and out of Barnet General, so we went to see her most days. At one point, she went to Greece on holiday with Dad and some friends, while Aunty Rose – Mum's other sister – looked after us. We thought she was out of the woods. You don't go on holiday if you're ill, do you?

We were wrong. Dad, who had moved back to England, called me into his office. 'Your mum's dying,' he said, bluntly.

Mum got worse every day. She went from an energetic 35-year-old – running her own business, raising four kids – to a dying woman. By the end, she was unable to do anything. For a boy, to see his mother die… I can't tell you what it's like. I would leave the hospital and cry.

I went to see her the day before she died. She could barely speak. For a twelve-year-old boy, it was agonising. Even now, I think about it. The next day, I was in the play room in Hadley Wood. My Uncle John – who was Aunty Kay's husband – came in and spoke to me.

'Your mum's gone,' he said. And that was it. On 15 September 1975, I lost my mother.

She was cremated a week later. Her ashes are in Trent Park cemetery in Cockfosters, north London. On the day of the funeral, it rained. Mum loved the rain.

For months, I couldn't believe she'd gone. I didn't want to believe it. My young mind thought it was a joke. A test. I thought – or hoped – that she would walk in and say: 'That was to see how you'd cope without me.' But she never came back. And, from then on, something was missing.

Aunty Rose was a massive help. Every family has someone who makes things better, and she was that person. If you can have two mothers, I did. After Mum died, she told my dad: 'I'll look after the two older boys. Go to Cyprus with the younger ones, do what you've got to do.'

But Dad didn't want to split us up, and he didn't want to stay in England. He was worried social services might look at him – widower, four kids – and think he couldn't cope. Eight or nine months after Mum died, we all moved to Limassol.

To begin with, we didn't have a proper home: Dad rented a shop and we slept on the marble floor. We had to leave by eight o'clock, so my brother and I would play football on the beach all day. After a while we found a house in Pentadromos in

Limassol, and I went to the nearby grammar school.

It was a fee-paying school – for all his faults, Dad wanted the best for us – and it was where I met my two best friends, Deme and Nick Gregoriou. Their dad founded the school. Deme was my age and in the same class; Nick was three years younger. It was the start of a special friendship.

My relationship with Nick and Deme was one of the few things I could count on. To this day, they are fantastic friends. Even if we haven't seen each other for months, within a few minutes it's like we've never been apart. They are both godfathers to my first two girls. Their school is one of the best in Cyprus, and my daughters all went there. As I can testify, they work them bloody hard.

Despite meeting those two, I was unhappy. I was thirteen years old and, when Dad was working, I was looking after my brothers and sister. I was cleaning, trying to cook. But I couldn't even look after myself. And if Dad came home in a bad mood, who was he going to take it out on? Me.

I know it wasn't easy for my dad. He lost his wife to cancer, and his house and business to the war. But it's hard to feel sympathetic. We never got on.

I wrote letters to Aunty Rose, saying I wanted to come home. I missed England, and I missed my mum. I wanted to be with her or – at least – her side of the family. Dad and I kept arguing and so, after nine months of begging, he flew me back to live with Aunty Rose.

After dad lost his driving licence, I moved from England to Cyprus, then back to England after the invasion, back to Cyprus after Mum died, and back to England again. Like I said: I have always been nomadic.

Aunty Rose was divorced and lived in a three-bedroom house in New Barnet, near Hadley Wood in north London. Her daughter, my cousin Sue, was married and lived in Milton Keynes, so Aunty Rose used to rent her spare rooms to lodgers. With me there, it meant one fewer room to rent.

I went to Southgate secondary school and was soon picked for their football team. I started at left-back but I bombed forward, scoring nine goals in a season, so they put me up front.

Pretty soon, I was playing for the school on Saturday mornings, a junior side called Hinton Youth on Saturday afternoons, and a men's side from the Home Office on Sundays. The games were usually played on Hackney Marshes. Afterwards I'd go back to Aunty Rose's for Sunday dinner, followed by The Big Match with Brian Moore on TV. I'd have tea and Jaffa Cakes, then run to the park for a kickabout. No wonder I was fit.

One Saturday, I was playing for Hinton when our keeper broke his thumb. I was charging round up front, about to get sent off, so they stuck me in goal. I stayed there for the next six weeks and was pretty good. A Millwall scout noticed me and invited me for a trial.

I headed south to the Old Den on Cold Blow Lane. There were thirty other kids, including four keepers, so we only got a half each. I made a couple of saves, let one in, did OK. After the game, I was kept behind. A couple of lads fired shots at me from the edge of the box. I made some decent saves and was told to see the youth-team manager.

I stood outside his office for ten minutes. I was given a cup of tea but I was so nervous, most of it went in the saucer. Eventually, he came out.

'Right, son,' he said. 'Our next game is away at Crystal Palace. Make sure you're at the Den for nine a.m.'

I went to Palace but didn't get on. The next game was against Fulham: I played one half and let two in. Afterwards, they said they didn't want me. My unplanned career in goal was over.

My other trial in England was with Chelsea, this time as an outfield player. We had to be at RAF Uxbridge in north-west London for 9 a.m. I had to set off about six: a bus to Oakwood station, then two or three trains from there. I arrived at Uxbridge station at 8.55 with no clue where to go.

There was another kid on the train with a football bag. As we got off, we looked at each other.

'Are you going to the trial?' I asked. He was, so we sprinted to the ground together.

The lad, it turned out, was Turkish-Cypriot. Despite the invasion, I never had a problem with Turks. There were lots at school and we got on fine. It was pretty simple, really: it wasn't them who bombed Cyprus. They were as innocent as me.

The guy in charge of the trial was Ken Shellito, who played over a hundred times for Chelsea. As we burst through the changing room door, we heard him say: '. . . and two chickens haven't turned up.' We got changed in record time and started on the bench. The match was blues versus reds.

We were losing 1–0, so Ken told me to come on, right side of midfield. Being a cocky bugger, I told him I was a striker.

'Do you want to play or not?' he replied. Point taken.

I played midfield and had the game of my life, scoring a hat-trick and clearing one off the line. We won 4–1. All the other parents congratulated me, so I thought I was in. That night, I went to a party at Uncle Ted's, who was mum's older brother.

'Well done, son!' he said, when I told him about the hat-trick. 'You're going to the Bridge!'

I waited ages to hear from Chelsea. Then after six weeks, a letter came through the door. I didn't meet their standard. Honestly, I must have cried for six months.

In hindsight, it wasn't a surprise. They had five different games that weekend, and they might have been looking for one player. But the trial influenced me as a coach, one million per cent.

At senior level, you get a feel for a player after five minutes. But at youth level, you need to give players time. You need to see them in their own environment. These days, clubs have six-week trials, which means they have a proper chance. It's fairer than judging thirty or forty kids in one afternoon.

Although I kept playing, I never got another chance in England. The problem was, I didn't have a Plan B. I finished school at sixteen – I can't remember what qualifications I got, if any – and worked at Datsun in Whetstone, learning to service cars. At the same time, I started to get into trouble.

In England in the 1970s, there were a lot of fights. Going to Arsenal matches was a risk – I've been chased through King's Cross station by Chelsea and West Ham fans – but, thankfully, I avoided most of the bother. I would have the occasional scrap – most boys did – but, if there was a top ten of fighters in school, I wasn't in it. I was a decent footballer, so people left me alone.

But one day, a kid from our school went to a youth club in Cockfosters – rival turf, if you like – and had the crap kicked out of him. The hard nuts of Southgate school weren't having it. They teamed up and said, 'Steve – are you coming with us?' Being sixteen and daft, I thought, why not?

There must have been 200 of us. Some of them were tooled up – bats, chains – and I began to think, oh no – what have I done? But I couldn't turn round. It would have been shameful.

We got to Cockfosters station. Our boys stormed into the youth club, but the lads who beat up our mate weren't there. Our boys came out, and it looked like the whole thing would peter out. But, after hearing about our mob, the coppers turned up. Twelve people were hooked. I was one.

I was taken to the station with the other lads. The police phoned Aunty Rose, who was absolutely livid. She didn't need to say anything. I'd let her down. It went to court but, because no one was hurt, and no property damaged, the case was dismissed. But for my aunty, it was a warning.

As I said, I wasn't a fighter. But I was cheeky, bordering on disrespectful, and Aunty Rose was worried I'd go down the wrong path. Who knows: I might have. To her, the answer was obvious.

'You need a man in your life,' she said.

She wanted me to move back to Cyprus and live with Dad. I wanted to stay in England, but I couldn't argue. I'd let her down so, in the summer of 1979, I flew back to Limassol.

Within two hours, I was mixing cement, helping my dad build his house in the refugee village. As the sun beat down, and sweat poured off me, one thought kept me going. I had to become a professional footballer.

I WALKED OUT SIX WEEKS LATER. THANKFULLY I HAD AEL, WHERE Mr Fodis found me the shack, and two first-teamers took me under their wing.

Pambos Pamboulis was a big name; a striker who'd played for the national team and Olympiakos in Greece. When he returned to Cyprus he was like a god. He used to teach me things – body shape, holding the ball up, things like that. I was trying to take his place, yet he still helped me.

He runs a betting shop in Cyprus now, so, when I was on the island recently, I said hello. He recognised me straight away. I thanked him for helping a sixteen-year-old English kid all those years ago.

The other guy was Nikos Japonas: a big, strong, battering-ram centre-forward. He also played for Cyprus, but he wasn't appreciated back then. For me, he was a great player. Along with the reserves' manager Costas Pambou, Nikos and Pambos were my first 'coaches'. Perhaps then, a seed was planted.

AEL trained in the afternoons, so in the daytime they got me that job in a hotel. I was a doorman, then a lifeguard; the manager was an AEL supporter who let me eat in the restaurant on my days off. One day by the pool, I met a guy called Gus. He was a London toughie – late fifties, grey hair, tall – and ran a furniture business. We got on well so I told him my story. I said I wanted to move back to England.

'I could buy your ticket right now,' Gus said. 'But if you really want it, you'll save up, and buy your own. Here's my number if you make it back.'

By now, I was part of the AEL senior squad. The manager, a Bulgarian called Chemely Tomov, liked me and wanted to play me in the top division. But the club didn't pay much – Cypriot football was part-time – and when the summer ended, so did the hotel job.

I worked on a building site, pushing wheelbarrows of cement along planks of wood ten feet in the air, but it wasn't regular. AEL tried to get me something full-time but most winter jobs in Cyprus were in the government, or in the banks, and my Greek wasn't good enough.

As autumn set in, I decided to move back to England. Flights were expensive, so I planned to catch a ferry to Greece, then get the bus across Europe. As I went to buy my ticket, I bumped into my old man. I hadn't seen him since I'd left home. If I'd noticed him in time, I would have crossed the road.

He asked where I was going. I told him. He reached into his pocket and gave me fifty quid. I took his money and never looked back.

When we reached Piraeus in Greece, there were huge strikes taking place in France. It meant I had to wait three days before I could catch a bus. Even then, we went via Belgium, rather than Calais. The delay ate up my fifty quid. I went sightseeing, seeing the Acropolis for the first time, and had to pay for three nights' accommodation. By the time I got on the coach, I was skint.

I met a Canadian lad on the bus who was also broke. At one stop-off, he pinched a loaf of bread and I nicked some marmalade. Other times, we used to go into takeaways and ask for kebabs with no meat – just pitta, salad and sauce.

Eventually, I made it to Victoria bus station with 50p in my pocket. I didn't know whether to call Aunty Rose, who I'd left months earlier, or Gus.

I called Gus. Thankfully, he remembered me.

'Get in a cab to Catford,' he said. 'I'll pay.'

When I arrived, he told me there were two choices. Move back in with Aunty Rose, or stay with him and go to work at six o'clock the next morning. I told him I'd work for him.

'Right answer,' he replied.

I worked in a factory in Hackney that made three-piece suites. When the guys wanted anything, I ran off to get it. It was simple work. After a while, I moved from Catford to one of Gus's houses in Maidstone, which doubled as a furniture showroom. But that caused a problem: most people bought suites at the weekend, meaning I didn't have time to play football.

I worked with Gus for a year or two, but the football thing was coming to a head. In 1982, I moved back to Aunty Rose's house and started training with Enfield, which was a good standard. They won the Alliance Premier League that season, the highest level of semi-professional football in England, but I never played in the first team.

At the time, my brother Costa was studying at Queens College in New York, living with another aunt. He invited me to stay for a few weeks over Christmas. I overpacked, just in case, and ended up staying ten years. It was the seventh time I'd moved from one country to another. I was twenty years old.

In America, my life changed. I turned from a boy into a man. I also fulfilled my dream: for a short time only, I became a professional footballer.

2
LIVING IN AMERICA
UNITED STATES, 1982–92

WHEN MOST FOOTBALL MANAGERS WERE TWENTY, THEY PLAYED
the game for a living. Me? I pumped gas at a petrol station near La Guardia airport
in New York.

La Guardia is a waterfront airport. In winter, the wind whips off the bay and
freezes anyone stupid enough to stand outside. I worked eight-hour shifts putting
petrol in people's cars. When it was quiet, you sat inside and stayed warm by the fire.
But when a customer arrived, you ran into the New York winter. My body shivered
and my fingers went numb. I longed for quiet shifts.

The owner of the petrol station was a football fan from Greece. He had a team
called AO Crete in the Hellenic League, which was a strong local competition.
When my brother – who also worked at the station – told him I was coming to visit,
the owner said, 'Tell him to train with us.'

In January, the team played in a tournament in Upstate New York. It was indoor
five-a-side – football was barely played outdoors in winter – and there were teams
from all over the East Coast. I ended up top scorer. In between games, some guys
introduced themselves. They were from a pro team, the Pennsylvania Stoners, and
invited me for a trial. I extended my visa, cancelled my return trip to England, and

waited for the try-out in spring. Thank goodness I overpacked.

At the time, early 1983, the NASL was the top league in America. The second tier was the American Soccer League, where the Stoners played. There were only six teams, stretching from Detroit to Dallas, and the crowds weren't huge – a few thousand if you were lucky. But it was full-time football: my first glimpse of it since the reds-versus-blues Chelsea trial at RAF Uxbridge.

The Stoners' try-out was held over a weekend. In the first game, I scored a couple of goals and knocked some people about. They must have been impressed because when, on the second day, I told them my hamstring was tight, the physio worked on me for half an hour to make sure I could play.

I didn't have the touch to be a top player, but I was aggressive. A pain in the arse. I wouldn't score 25 goals a season, but I would run all day. Those weekends on Hackney Marshes did me good. After day two, the Stoners coach – a Hungarian called Kalman Csapo – said, 'We're going to bring you in.'

Teams in the ASL were allowed to pick four foreigners, and I was the fifth in the squad, so I knew I wouldn't get many games. I only had an eight-month contract and the wages weren't great – $800 a month, I think. But I had done it. After years of practice, and years of knockbacks, I was a professional footballer. It wasn't England but, to me, it was the big time. It felt amazing.

The Stoners – named after the Keystone State of Pennsylvania, by the way – were based in Allentown, 100 miles from New York. I said bye to my brother, bye to the petrol station, and moved west. My days were simple: train in the morning, eat lunch, then come back for more training.

My first game was a friendly against the big name in the NASL, the New York Cosmos. Pele had moved on but they were full of tough, hardened pros who wouldn't take shit from a skinny twenty-year-old. I played the last twenty minutes on the right of midfield. Andranik Eskandarian, who played 29 times for Iran, gave me a kicking. Boris Bandov, the American international, elbowed me in the throat.

I came off bruised but inside I was buzzing. I was making my way in pro football. My teammates were guys like Solomon Hilton, Michael Collins – who went on to play for the US national team – and Jeff Tipping, our Liverpool-born captain who became a highly respected coach in America.

In the local paper, the Globe Times, Coach Csapo called me 'a good runner with pretty good skills', which summed me up nicely. I wasn't physically strong, but I put myself about. Soon after, Csapo picked me for a fundraising friendly against a team from Cleveland. We won 5–3 and I scored twice. I thought it was a turning point. It was actually the high point. The league, and the team, were in trouble. There wasn't enough money to pay the bills. No wonder we were fundraising.

I lived in a room above a bar, which the Stoners paid for. One day, I came home to find a padlock on the door. The club hadn't paid the rent. With nowhere else to go, I shimmied up a flagpole to the roof of my flat. From there I climbed through a window, but after three days, the owners put a lock on that, too. The whole thing summed up US soccer in the mid-80s. It was a farce.

The club and the league limped to the end of the season before going bust (the Stoners actually made the final, but were beaten by the Jacksonville Tea Men). I left halfway through the year without playing a league game. After working my whole life to be a pro, it was over within months.

I went back to New York and enrolled at Queensborough Community College, which was near my aunt's house in Queens. I wasn't there to study – I can't even remember the course I signed up for – but I knew the soccer coach, Bob Ritchie, and he wanted me in the team. Bob – who helped me pass the SATs I needed to enrol – used to call me Soccer Whore. One day, I asked him why.

'Because you'll go anywhere for a game,' he replied. Spot on, I thought.

At Queensborough I met Andy Nicolaou, an English-Cypriot guy who became one of my best friends. Andy was a couple of years older and grew up in Wood Green, just down the road from Aunty Rose's house in New Barnet. For the best part of ten years, we were inseparable.

We played up front together: if someone nailed me, he would run fifty yards to fight for me, and I mean that literally. They called us the Gold Dust Twins, which is an American nickname for a sporting partnership. I don't know how many goals we scored, but we got plenty of red and yellow cards. Andy still lives in New York, and we still speak.

I enjoyed my time at Queensborough. It was a worse standard than the Stoners, but we trained every day and became one of the best college sides in America. At one point, we were ranked eighth in the country, which was a big deal for a community college. But the season was only sixteen games, and when it finished I left. I should have got a degree, but the Soccer Whore just wanted to play.

After college, I trained with the Pancyprian Freedoms, a club formed by Cypriot immigrants after the Turkish invasion in 1974. At the time, they were huge. They played in the Hellenic League, before joining the Cosmopolitan League – which had teams from across the East Coast – followed by the Northeastern Super Soccer League. They also entered the US Open Cup, which was a national version of the FA Cup (although NASL teams didn't enter). They won it three times in 1980, 1982 and 1983. In 1984, they even made the semi-finals of the Concacaf Champions' Cup.

Really, they were a team of superstars. They had a coach, Mimis Papaioannou, who had scored more than 200 goals for AEK Athens and had 60-odd Greece caps. Some of their players had been in the Cyprus national team. I was good enough, but when they registered players for the 1984 season, I was injured. So I went to a Hellenic League club called Hermes, which was also based in Astoria, Queens.

The owner of Hermes was a guy called Christos Rizos. He was a jeweller with a workshop on the junction of 47th Street and 5th Avenue in Manhattan – the Diamond District, right by the Rockefeller Center. As part of the Hermes deal, he got me a job in the workshop. At first I swept floors, but after six months they taught me how to set diamonds. There are three or four different methods, and I used to practise by bending an old penny. As a kid, I was into military models – I still am, actually – so I was pretty good. If my football career ends, I could still set a diamond or two.

Hermes played their home games at the Metropolitan Oval, which, back then, was a dirt pitch surrounded by metal poles. Because I was fit, and didn't score much, I was moved to right-back, before being pushed into centre-midfield, where there were more people to tackle. I loved it.

I had finally found my position. I ran, won the ball, then gave it to someone who could play. In those days, man-to-man marking was normal, as were crunching tackles. Really, I should have been there all along. I ended up as Hermes captain, and to this day I'm proud to call Chris Rizos my friend.

When I wasn't playing football, or setting diamonds, I went to Spanish night-clubs. By then, Nick and Deme were living in New York, but they didn't usually fancy my type of music – merengue or cumbia, both popular in Latin America. I'd go to clubs like Trenta Trenta, Club Broadway or Sounds of Brasil on my own. I told Nick and Deme to call the police if I wasn't home by 1 p.m. the next day. You couldn't be too careful: some of those clubs weren't designed for skinny white boys with a ponytail.

I loved Latin clubs. Great music, great atmosphere, and if you put your hand out, a girl would dance with you. In other clubs, they'd tell you to get lost. Of course, if you couldn't dance, the Latinas would tell you to get lost, too. In fact, they'd walk off and leave you in the middle of the dancefloor. But I learned some basic steps, so I got by. I also learned a little Spanish, which I still use.

You have to be confident to survive in New York. After leaving the jewellery trade, I sold flowers at Flatbush Avenue subway station in Brooklyn. I went to the market in the morning, spent $150–$200 on fresh flowers, then sold them outside a kiosk in a space rented from the Indian owner. I must have done it for a year or so and – on a good day – I made a killing.

Valentine's Day was fantastic, as was St Patrick's Day. I'd buy all the white flowers I could, then stick them in water dyed green. By the afternoon they were as green as the Irish hills. I look back at those days and laugh. I was a hustler.

When I stopped selling flowers, Andy Nicolaou and I sold watches on the street in the Bronx, Spanish Harlem, Queens… anywhere we didn't get chased by cops, basically. I also worked for a building firm, installing kitchens and bathrooms, or putting together pre-fabricated houses. Really, I did anything to survive. I earned a few dollars playing football, but it wasn't enough to get by.

After two years playing for Hermes in the Hellenic League I moved to Pontos, a Greek team in the same league. Andy was there too. I won promotion with Pontos, helped keep them in the top division, then moved to a new team called Eleftheria, which means 'freedom' in Greek. They were rivals with the Freedoms: the first time they met, every Greek in Astoria turned up. It was brutal. We lost 2–1, but my reputation in New York was growing.

While I was at Eleftheria, the Freedoms asked me to sign. It was an easy decision: they were a bigger club and paid more. One of their players was Pambos Haralambos, a really good midfielder. He was so happy to see me. 'Now I've got someone to look after me!' he said. 'You won't kick me any more!'

I was known for being fit and aggressive. To some, I was dirty, but I never tried to injure another player. If I was going to hurt anyone, it was me. I was sore before most games, but that didn't stop me. One weekend, I even played with a broken hand, despite my arm being in plaster up to kick-off.

I had been to Cyprus on holiday. While I was away, I told my brother to look after my apartment – including the saltwater fish tank – and not to use my car. Before I came back, Nick and Deme called. My car had been broken into, after my brother used it, and my fish tank had overflowed, flooding my apartment. I punched the nearest thing which, unfortunately, was a solid wood wardrobe.

Back in the States, an X-ray revealed my hand was broken. I trained in a cast all week but when match day arrived the coach, Marios Laoutas, said the referee wouldn't let me play. I was furious, so I ran outside, found the team doctor, and got the plaster removed. I ran back, played the game, and had a replacement fitted the next day. Another time, I injured my ankle. I had cortisone injections for six Friday nights in a row, just so I could finish the season. Like I said: anything to play.

The Freedoms were part-time, but the owner, Philip Christopher, ran a business called Audiovox which sold car phones and stereos. He offered me a job as part of the deal, and I became sales manager for New York state. It was nice to have a guaranteed wage.

By this point, I had been in the US for six or seven years. I had a grown-up job – more grown-up than selling watches on the streets of Spanish Harlem, anyway – and was playing for one of the best teams in New York. After years of hustling, things were coming together.

Despite that, I couldn't be a salesman forever. I also knew my playing career wouldn't last. I was 26 or 27 so had ten years left. I started thinking about the future, and realised one thing: football had to be involved. It was the only thing that excited me. The only thing that inspired me. When I woke up on match days, I jumped out of bed. When I woke up to sell car phones, it took a little longer.

While I was full-time with the Stoners, the young pros helped run football courses for kids in the area. It was PR for the club more than anything – the kids were only six or seven years old – but I loved it. I enjoyed seeing the kids improve and, when I thought about the future, I remembered those sessions. Coaching could keep me in football for the rest of my life. I decided to get qualified.

My first badge was the US Soccer Federation D Licence, which taught us the basics over a weekend. I enjoyed it, so I enrolled for the C Licence, which lasted a week. That course was a revelation. I remember thinking, why haven't I been taught this before? What a player I would have been!

Remember: I was brought up in Britain in the 1970s, where most coaches made you run ten laps of a muddy field before kicking a ball. I became a decent player despite that. The C Licence was the first time I learned about technique and training sessions. For the first time, I learned what a good coach looked like. I was desperate to give other players the knowledge, and the chance, that I never had.

It wasn't just technique; it was tactics, too. As a midfielder, I thought about myself: my opponent, my area, my runs. Now I thought about the team. If the centre-half drops deep, where should the right-back go? I was fascinated. It made me think about the game in a way I hadn't before.

Also, there was no doubt that coaching suited my personality. On the pitch, I saw things happen before other people. I always told other players where they should be. And – when I'm in the mood – I'm good with people. I can walk into a room of strangers and walk out knowing five people.

With my D and C Licences under my belt, I thought a coaching career was possible. But I wasn't in a rush. I loved playing for the Freedoms and presumed I had plenty of years left. Then, one Saturday afternoon, I snapped the anterior cruciate ligament in my right knee. Pop goes the playing career.

We were playing an Italian side (at Queensborough College, funnily enough). I was in centre-midfield. The ball bounced, so I planted my right foot, and tried to pass with the outside of my left. I heard a noise and went down. In those days, you didn't go down. At least, I didn't.

Shit, I thought. I'm hurt.

I thought one of their players had kicked me. I was going to kill someone. Nikos Andreou, our centre-half, came to pick me up. He could see I was angry. 'Steve,' he said, 'you were by yourself.'

I tried to stand up and my kneecap slid out. That doesn't look good, I thought.

I went to the doctor on Monday, but it was so swollen, they couldn't see anything.

After a week or two, when the swelling had gone down, I decided to go training. There was no pain, so I started the usual routine of running laps. After ten yards, I felt my kneecap slide forward. It was time to see the orthopaedic surgeon.

A few days later I had an arthroscopic operation, where the surgeon looked at my knee. I woke up freezing, but felt OK. When the doctor came to see me, I was quite chirpy.

He looked serious.

'You've suffered a complete tear of the ACL,' he said.

'How long?' I asked.

'I've never seen a tear like it,' he said. 'You need major surgery. I'm afraid you won't play again.'

I couldn't believe it. Nikos and my teammates, who picked me up from the hospital, kept asking what happened, but I couldn't reply. If I spoke, I would have cried. I was heartbroken.

I'd played football all my life. I had never missed a session. I had gone through cortisone injections and broken bones and now, after a mis-step on a field in New York, it was over. The lads dropped me off at my apartment in Kew Gardens in Queens. Once they were gone, I cried like a baby.

I had surgery a few weeks later at Lenox Hill Hospital in Manhattan. The surgeon had operated on Bo Jackson – the famous baseball and American football player – so I was in good hands. To begin with, I was awake, and watched the operation on a monitor. But I asked too many questions, so the surgeon gave me a general anaesthetic. The last words I heard were, 'For God's sake – put him out.'

When I came round, I was in plaster for six weeks. They don't do that now, as you need flexibility, and because of that my knee never felt right. I needed another three arthroscopies over the next ten months – and three to four hours of rehab, six days a week – before I was able to flex fully.

My former club Eleftheria knew I had my badges, so they asked if I wanted to coach their under-16s while I wasn't playing. I limped to training in my knee brace. Again, I loved it.

We had four or five Puerto Rican boys who were really quick. I taught them simple things: when to pass and when to take their man on, when to pull wide, things like that. I was then asked to help with the New York state under-17 side. It wasn't regular – we met two or three times – but it was more experience.

If you want to coach, you need to practise. You have to coach kids, reserve sides, anything. You have to show you're keen but – more importantly – you have to learn. I soon realised what type of session the players enjoyed, and what kept them motivated. You will make mistakes, even if you're a natural. But it's better to make them with Eleftheria under-16s than at senior level.

I get emails all the time from young coaches: 'I've done two seasons with the under-15s, now I want to work at national level.' Or: 'I've just done my B Licence – can you give me a job?' With respect, you have to learn your trade. Sure, some guys will progress quicker than others. But you can't skip the early stages. They're too important. That's where you lay the foundations to build a career on.

One of my friends in New York was a guy from Liverpool called Paul Riley, who played all over the north-eastern US. Paul was a clever player – short and quick – and I used to enjoy kicking him, when I could catch him. In 1991, he became head coach of CW Post, which was part of Long Island University. By this time I had my B licence, so he asked me to become his assistant.

'Stephen is as tough as they come,' he told the university magazine. 'You would always want him on your side.'

I loved the coaching, but most of it was at the start of the academic year. They wanted me back the following season – but what would I do before then?

I began to realise that America wasn't a good place to start a coaching career. The North American Soccer League folded in 1984 and wasn't replaced by the MLS until 1996. I was trying to climb a ladder that didn't exist. In England, you can see where you're going: non-league, lower league, big league. But in America, there was no structure; just a patchwork quilt of private concerns.

I decided to move to Cyprus. The reason was simple: despite spending ten years in New York, I knew lots of people there. It felt like I'd played with, or against, half the island. Young guys would move from Cyprus to New York and play football while earning their degree. As I'd been in America longer, I'd help them settle. One guy's dad, Michalis Skaboulis, was reserves coach at Apollon in Limassol.

'I appreciate you helping my son,' he told me. 'If you're ever in Cyprus, I'll help you.'

There was another reason I wanted to fly back across the Atlantic. My Aunty Rose – who became my second mother after my mum died – had been diagnosed with cancer. In January 1992, almost ten years after I started pumping gas near La Guardia, I packed my bags and left New York for good.

3
ISLAND LIFE
CYPRUS, 1992–99

I KNEW MY AUNT DIDN'T HAVE LONG. WHEN I SPOKE TO HER ON the phone in New York, she told me to hurry back. My flight was booked for 9 January, but she died suddenly on 2 January. I didn't even make the funeral. She is buried next to Mum. Every time I'm in England, I make sure I visit.

I stayed at Aunty Rose's house for three months and did my FA Preliminary coaching badge. At the time, it was the lowest qualification in England – the equivalent to the Level 1 or 2 badge today. The Luton Town legend Ricky Hill was there too, and we used to hang out. He was a lovely guy, and went on to have a decent coaching career, including almost four years at the Tampa Bay Rowdies.

Although I had my USSF B Licence, I needed to go through the English system to have any chance of working there. When you apply for jobs, you're lucky if clubs even read your CV. If you have only American qualifications, you're giving them another excuse to throw it in the bin. Even now – wherever I am in the world – I fly home for my courses and refreshers.

I looked for work in Britain but it was hopeless. I hadn't played, I hadn't coached, and I'd been in America for ten years. There was no way in. So, as planned, I moved to Cyprus and contacted Mr Skaboulis. He had good news and bad news: yes, I could help; but no, there was no money. At that point, I wasn't bothered. Thanks to Mr Skaboulis – a lovely man – I had a start.

I took a job at Filios Motors in Limassol, selling duty-free cars to the British armed forces on the island. In the evening, I would train Apollon reserves. Officially I was the assistant, but Mr Skaboulis stepped back and let me run the sessions. I was passionate about helping the players reach their potential. When they needed extra work, I didn't ask them to stay behind – I told them.

We had a left-back called Christos Germanos. When he got the ball, too often he would come inside, where the danger is. I told him to open his body, keep his head up, and look down the line or for the striker. He made the first team and ended up winning nine caps for Cyprus. It wasn't just him: every player had things to work on. I replicated parts of the game – for example, pinging passes at them in small grids – until they improved. I loved seeing them get better.

It sounds boastful, but there isn't a player in the world I couldn't improve, if he wanted it. You might say – well, how would you improve Steven Gerrard at his peak? For him, it might be tactical rather than technical: 'Have you thought about sitting deeper in situation X?' But the principle is the same: there is always something to learn. And – as I learned from Inter Milan – that includes coaches.

When big teams came to the island, I watched their sessions to find inspiration. Sometimes I even went to their hotels, to meet the coaches and pick their brains. In October 1992 I saw Wales before their World Cup qualifier against Cyprus. Two years later I watched Arsenal before their European Cup Winners' Cup game against Omonia Nicosia. I told Ian Wright that Omonia's keeper liked to come off his line. In the second half, he dinked one over his head to put Arsenal 2–0 up.

In 1993, Inter came to town to play Apollon in the UEFA Cup. They were managed by Osvaldo Bagnoli, who famously won Serie A with Hellas Verona in 1984/85. I went to the stadium early to watch Inter's warm-up. I was seriously impressed: the sharpness and intensity were a step up from Apollon reserves.

Players like Dennis Bergkamp and Ruben Sosa did everything quicker than my boys, with no mistakes. And when I looked at my stopwatch, the session lasted exactly thirty minutes. Not a second more, not a second less. Right, I thought. I'll have some of that.

For the reserves' next game, I copied Inter's warm-up. I thought I was being super-professional, showing them how Bergkamp and Sosa did things, but after twenty minutes we were 2–0 down. We ended up losing 4–0. One of the first-team lads who played came up to me afterwards.

'Let me ask you something,' he said. 'You watched Inter warm up, right?'

'Yeah,' I replied. 'How good was that?'

'It was good for Inter Milan but not for Apollon reserves,' he said. 'We were knackered after fifteen minutes. You pushed us too hard.'

That was a big lesson for me. What's good for one team isn't always good for another. Today, it's fashionable for coaches to watch other sides train in 'study visits'. That's fine. But I tell them: by all means, watch Arsene Wenger train. Watch Jose Mourinho train. Watch me train, if you like. But you have to know what he's doing, and why. It's no good just copying. You have to know the coach's thought process, and the limitations of your team, before running his sessions.

(Apollon drew 3–3 with Inter and hit the bar twice, which shows what a good team we had. Inter had already won the first leg 1–0 – Bergkamp with the goal – and went on to win the whole tournament.)

By now, Nick and Deme – whose dad had founded the Grammar School in Limassol – were running it themselves. I took a job as football coach, with the aim of setting up an inter-school league for the island. I worked at school in the morning, then coached Apollon reserves in the afternoon. We won the league, finishing above St John's, the school for British military families in Cyprus. One of our players' dad was the president of Cypriot fourth-division team, Agios Therapon.

'I told my dad you're a good coach,' he said. 'He wants to speak to you about running his team.'

I went to the GSO stadium in Limassol, where all the lower-division teams trained. The Therapon players were all in different kit, and the pitch – which was shocking – had another three teams on it.

Welcome to the Cypriot fourth division, I thought.

I met the president and told him my terms. It was a part-time club, so I asked for £350 a month, plus a car. He offered me £250 with no car. I took it. After watching training, it seemed fair enough.

It was 1993/94 and Therapon were second bottom, well adrift of safety. Before the first game I met the committee in Limassol. I walked in the room and could barely see their faces through the smoke.

'We will pick the side for Sunday,' they said, puffing on their cigarettes.

'No chance,' I told them. It was my team now.

'But you don't know the players,' they replied.

'You think I don't,' I said. 'But I do.'

The president gave a piece of paper to six of the committee men. In secret, they wrote down their team. I wrote mine. They were identical, except my sweeper was their defensive midfielder.

'Why are you putting him at the back?' they asked.

'He sees things and he talks,' I said.

Our first game finished 2–2 and the sweeper had a blinder. We would have won, had the referee been fairer. Afterwards, I walked across the pitch to see the referee's assessor.

'A draw – not bad, Steve,' he said.

'The second goal was offside,' I replied.

'Maybe it was, maybe it wasn't,' he replied. 'But tell your president to pay the fees to the referees' committee. You owe fifty pounds for last year and fifty pounds for this.'

On Monday, I went to see one of the referees' committee at his workplace and paid the money myself. After that, we went nine games undefeated, winning five and drawing four.

The characters in our team were unbelievable. One guy was nicknamed (in Greek) 'Knife-puller'. Another was called 'Killer'. I never asked why, but I could guess. Nicknames aside, I thought they were terrific lads. They had bottle. And, with two games left, we had a chance of staying up.

The Cypriot fourth division was spicy. Back then, there was no internet, and no Premier League streaming, so whole villages watched their team play. Some games got a couple of thousand fans, especially at the end of the season. Our penultimate match was away to ATE-PEK Ergaton – a nasty side from a village near Nicosia – who were also in relegation trouble. It was played on a neutral field because of crowd trouble in their previous game.

We took bus-loads of fans. The atmosphere was mad. Players were fighting before kickoff and, after twenty minutes, one of our guys was elbowed while going for a header. He came down with a broken nose so another player ran over, head-butted their guy, and got sent off.

Our keeper played a blinder and, with five minutes left, it was 0–0. Suddenly, our centre-half – Yiorgos Anastasiou, who had a great career with AEL – made a run forward and played a one-two with our lone forward, my former AEL teammate Nikos Japonas. That in itself was a shock. Nikos never passed.

Yiorgos went into the box and time stood still.

He shot. He scored. Our travelling army went mad. But at this point, the ref turned to our boys.

'Why are you getting excited?' he asked. 'You're not leaving here with three points.'

Six minutes into injury time, the ref gave a penalty. It wasn't a foul – and it was two yards outside the box – but apart from that, it was nailed on. As their guy stepped up, one of our players got in his ear. I don't know what he said, but he wasn't inviting him round for tea. The ref marched over and sent him off. The match report – which I still have – said it was for 'anti-athletic behaviour'.

Everyone was on edge. As their player stepped up, the whole ground was silent. He took the kick. It hit the foot of the post and rolled out of play. Reluctantly, the ref blew for full time. We had won.

More fights began. Amid the fists, we escaped back to Limassol, won our final game 3–2, and stayed in the Cypriot fourth division, while ATE-PEK Ergaton went down. Thanks to Killer, Knife-Puller and all the others, my first season in senior football was a success.

The following season, 1994/95, we beat Ermis from the third division 2–1 in the preliminary round of the Cypriot FA Cup. In the next round we played Nea Salamina – who qualified for Europe that season, finishing third in the first division – and beat them 2–1 too.

My reputation was growing, but I had problems with the committee and the president. They interfered too much. They thought they knew best. We lost in the second round of the cup over two legs to Apoel Nicosia, and I left the club.

Agios Therapon were the first senior team I managed, and I loved it. In a way, the journey to Nepal, India, and every other country I coached, started there. I learned to deal with men. It made me harder. And I realised that – in senior football – results were everything. Yes, you need a medium-term plan. But if you lose every weekend, you won't have time to implement it. It was the Cypriot fourth division, which was a million miles from where I wanted to be. But I never thought I wouldn't make it. I just kept telling myself: 'This is what you've got to do now. This is how you learn.'

After Therapon, I became reserve-team coach of APEP, a second-division club from Kyperounda in the Troodos mountains. Nikos Andreou, my old friend from New York, was there too. It was great to have a familiar face. Towards the end of the season, 1995/96, the manager was fired. I was given four games in charge; after that, the committee would decide my future.

I won two, drew one, lost in the cup, then lost my fourth league game 4–0. When the vote came, I lost by seven votes to six. Two guys who said they'd vote for me didn't turn up. I still know one of them: he recently said he was told in no uncertain terms to miss the vote. Obviously, the new manager had contacts. My short-lived spell as a second-division manager was over.

The committee asked me to work with the new guy, but I couldn't. At training he would shout, 'Hit the wanker! Fuck them! Drink their blood!' and other nonsense. That's not my style. It might work for a week or two, but eventually you become a joke. And when that happens, you're done.

In a season, I might have two or three rants. But if you do it every session, the players stop listening. They say to themselves, 'Let him go. He'll finish in five minutes.'

I don't treat my players like crap. How does it help me? I can be tough with them, but you have to choose your moments. It's far better to encourage, and help them to improve.

In the same year, 1996, I earned my FA Full Badge. It was the highest qualification in England – similar to the UEFA Pro Licence now – and it was hard. Very hard.

To pass, we had to run thirty-minute sessions on four topics, with professional players doing the drills. The instructors were Dario Gradi and Don Howe, and you got the feeling they didn't want you to pass. The badge was a path to professional football, and they were the gatekeepers. I remember speaking to Arthur Albiston, the former Manchester United and Scotland defender, who was on my course.

'This is the hardest thing I've done,' he told me, 'and I played in a World Cup.'

I was proud to get the Full Badge but, in Cyprus, it didn't seem to matter. Qualifications weren't taken seriously. When I got back from England, I went to see Andreas Michaelides. He managed the national team for five years, and was head of the coaches' association.

'Well done on the qualification,' he said. 'But it's not going to help you get a job in Cyprus. There's no point telling the media. Keep it to yourself.'

My wife Lucy, who was with me, turned red with anger. This was the head of the coaches' association, telling me to keep quiet about my coaching qualifications.

Despite being one of the most highly qualified coaches on the island, I couldn't get a manager's job in the top division. After APEP, I became director of youth at AEL, the club that saved me when I left home. I managed the under-18s and oversaw everything below. I was 33, but I could empathise with the kids. I remembered how it felt to be sixteen and desperate.

The first thing I did at AEL was have a meeting with the parents. Some of them were too close to the coaches. They took them out for dinner, or invited them to weddings, so their son would get a game.

'If your son is any good, he will play,' I told the parents. 'It doesn't matter who you know. Please do not invite me for dinner, tea, coffee, or anything. Let me focus on helping the players. That is what I'm here for.'

The parents didn't like it. An Englishman had turned their social club into a football team. A few complained to the AEL president, a businessman called Dimitris Solomonides. He pulled me in for a meeting. I told him my priority was the players, not the parents. He backed me.

The backing paid off because, in 1997, we won the Cypriot Youth Cup, beating Paralimni 2–1 in the final. We had a wonderful team. Alexis Garpozis went on to play 35 times for Cyprus. Simos Krassas got 17 caps. Yiorgos Konstanti, Pambos Pitakas and Christos Charalambous all had decent careers. I loved sending players into professional football. But in truth, it wasn't enough.

From the mid-1990s onwards, I contacted hundreds of clubs and countries around the world. I was happy in Cyprus but I wanted more: a full-time job in professional football, for a start.

I still worked at the school, so I spent hours by the fax machine, typing in numbers from the FIFA handbook and sending my CV everywhere from Aruba to Zimbabwe. I tried every full-time club in the UK and the US, every English-speaking national association, and most of the non-English ones, too.

Alongside my CV, I faxed covering letters. But they never replied. At most, I had one or two acknowledgments. It was depressing, but what choice did I have? I couldn't sit in Cyprus, waiting for someone to say: 'Mr Constantine! We have heard so much about your work at AEL under-18s!'

I had to keep pushing the door. I had to keep shouting my name, on the off-chance someone was listening. Nick and Deme were very good about the phone bill.

In July 1998, I got in touch with the FA and scouted for England during the UEFA Under-18 Championship, held in Cyprus. England were knocked out in the group stage – Robbie Keane's Ireland won the tournament – but it was good to be involved. Les Reed, the FA's director of technical development, sent me a nice letter afterwards. But, despite working with the national team, I was no closer to working in England. I kept applying, and the clubs kept ignoring me.

Eventually, I got an offer closer to home. APEP – where I'd been caretaker two years earlier – wanted me back as manager. After being promoted under the blood-drinking coach in 1996, they finished bottom in back-to-back seasons, and were now in the third division. I took the job and, in 1998/99, won promotion to the second division. We came third, eight points behind the champions.

Despite that success, I was frustrated. I'd been in Cyprus for seven years but hadn't managed in the top division. I was highly qualified, with a good CV. I kept Agios Therapon up. Won the Youth Cup at AEL. Earned promotion at APEP. But I was banging my head against a brick wall. I soon learned why.

In 1999, I had an interview with a first-division club. The president told me it was between me and another guy.

'You are honest,' he told me. 'Hard-working. Well-qualified. The players like you...

I knew there was a but coming.

'...but if we appoint a big name and it goes wrong, the fans will blame the coach. If we appoint a small name and it goes wrong, they blame us – the board.'

My heart sank. And then it got worse.

'And,' the president said, lowering his voice, 'the other coach knows referees. He gives us fifteen points a season before we kick a ball. He has connections.'

I had suspected there was match-fixing in Cyprus. You would hear rumours, or notice things on the pitch. But I'd never heard it spelled out. I was disgusted.

If football isn't fair, it's pointless. What's the point in working all week, if the referee won't let you win? What's the point in a beautiful goal if it's cancelled out by a non-penalty at the other end? What's the point in staying behind, night after night, if things are being sorted off the pitch?

I came home and told Lucy we were leaving the island. I couldn't stay after that. In Cyprus I was an outsider, trying to break into a secretive world of nods, winks and unspoken alliances. I had to leave to save myself.

If I was going to build a coaching career, I needed to try something different. Somewhere different. Little did I know, as we packed our bags, how different it would be.

4
HIMALAYAN ROYALTY
NEPAL, 1999–2001

I MET LUCY, MY WIFE, IN CYPRUS IN 1993. IT WAS THE LUCKIEST day of my life.

A friend of mine had to join the army. After the swearing-in ceremony he held a party at his house, so I went. As it turned out, Lucy's grandmother lived next door to my friend, and Lucy was there on holiday. Like me, she has a Cypriot background: her parents moved to England when they were sixteen. They ran a popular Greek restaurant in Brighton called the New Athenian, which Lucy managed.

We started chatting and got on really well. But my mate Nikos Andreou – who I knew from New York, and APEP – was playing in Limassol, and I'd promised to watch him. As I said my goodbyes, my friend's wife stopped me.

'You seem to be getting on well,' she said, looking at Lucy.

'Yeah, great,' I said, worried about missing kickoff. 'Get me her number, would you?'

I called her up and arranged a date: Pizza Hut in Limassol. It was going well until, over the deep-pan margherita, I said: 'I've got to tell you something.' She looked worried. As you would, I suppose.

'I have this thing about football,' I started. She laughed.

'How bad can it be?' she asked.

'Well, pretty bad,' I continued. 'If there's a game on TV, I'll watch it. If there's a game within a thousand miles that I want to see, I will. If there's a coaching course anywhere in the world that will benefit my career, I'm there. And if there's a job I want, I will take it. Even in Mongolia.'

She looked at me strangely, got up, and went to the bathroom. I honestly thought she might try to climb out of the window. I knew I sounded strange – obsessed, in fact – but I had to be honest. There was no point wasting her time.

Eventually she came back. She smiled; I sighed with relief. She agreed to a second date – we went to Paphos, in the west of Cyprus, to see the mosaics – but the problem was that Lucy lived in England. After she flew back to Brighton, we kept in touch with letters and phone calls, but we couldn't do that forever. So, a few months later, she moved to Cyprus to see if it would work. It did. We got on brilliantly, which meant I was able to use something I'd bought in New York a decade earlier.

When I worked for Christos Rizos near the Rockefeller Center, I bought a diamond. It was 1.1 carat, and – even though I got a good deal – it cost a lot. I can't remember how much, but it was four figures, easily. I paid it off every month. When I decided to propose I mounted it, put the ring in a cup of tea, and waited for Lucy to notice. She almost swallowed it before she said yes.

We were married in 1995 and have three beautiful girls: Paula, who was born in 1997, Christiana, born in 2000, and Isabel, born in 2006. In fact, Paula is a day older than she could have been.

She was due on 16 October – my birthday, coincidentally – but she was late. The doctor, who was an AEL fan, said they could induce Lucy on Friday or Saturday. He knew I had an AEL youth game on the Saturday, so he arranged it for Friday. Paula was born safely and I made the game. And yes, we won. It was a perfect 24 hours.

I JOINED THE FA COACHES ASSOCIATION IN 1996 AFTER GETTING my Full Badge. A year or two later they sent a letter, saying FIFA and the Asian Football Confederation were looking for coaches to improve standards over there. There was a list of thirty or forty countries, and you had to pick six you were interested in. I ticked the places I fancied going – the Maldives, Philippines, Taiwan, Nepal, a couple of others. To be honest, I didn't give it much thought. For ages I heard nothing about it.

After we left Cyprus in 1999, Lucy and Paula moved in with her parents in Brighton, while I went to America to do my USSF A Licence and look for a job. Since I left the States in 1992, the game had grown. They had hosted the World Cup.

The MLS was up and running. The women's team were considered the best in the world. Soccer was becoming a national sport, on a par with football, ice hockey and basketball. Compared to seven years earlier, when I left New York, it was boom time.

While doing my A licence, I got a call from a nice English-Pakistani guy called Alamgir Kashmiri. He ran a sports agency called Strata, which was following up on the AFC's attempt to find English coaches. He said Cambodia wanted me as their national team manager. I almost dropped the phone.

The offer was a three-year contract on $3,000 a month, paid for by the AFC, plus travel and accommodation paid by the local association – in this case, Cambodia. I was buzzing. From no job to national team manager in one call. I phoned Lucy in Brighton.

'We've been offered a job,' I said, cheerily.

'Great – which state?' she replied, thinking New York or Florida, perhaps.

'Not America,' I said. 'Cambodia. Southeast Asia.' The line went quiet.

'Khmer Rouge?' she said, eventually. 'The Killing Fields? Pol Pot? Mines everywhere? We have a one-year-old daughter – have you lost your mind?'

I heard sniffling down the phone.

I asked her to think about it, but she didn't have to: three days later, Strata said the offer had fallen through. Although the AFC paid the coaches' salary, the association had to pay for accommodation, flights and local transportation. But the offers kept coming. A week or so later, someone from the AFC called and said Mongolia wanted me as their national team manager. Again, I called Lucy.

'Remember that conversation we had on our first date?' I asked.

'How could I forget,' she said.

'Well – you won't believe this – but Mongolia have just called…' I replied.

But in truth, I didn't fancy it. Mongolia only joined the AFC and FIFA in 1998 and barely played games. There was no proper league and the weather – freezing for most of the year, then roasting – made things harder. I couldn't take Lucy and Paula there. I turned them down, and accepted a job in the more temperate climes of Raleigh, North Carolina, as director of a youth football club.

And then, in the dead of night in New York, the phone rang and my life changed.

I was staying in Long Island with Andy Nicolaou, the other Gold Dust twin. He answered the phone and walked half-asleep into my room, not best pleased.

'Someone is calling,' he said, wearily. 'It's three a.m.'

I rubbed my eyes and grabbed the phone. The line was crackly. They weren't calling from Manhattan.

'Stephen!' said the voice from the other side of the world. 'My name is Mr Ganesh Thapa. I am the president of the All Nepal Football Federation. We would like you to coach our team.'

'Are you serious?' I replied.

'Deadly serious!' said Ganesh. 'We got your name from Mr Kashmiri at Strata. We have your CV. We have a tournament, the South Asian Games, in two months. You can come now.'

Unlike Mongolia, this was tempting. Nepal was a beautiful country. They had a tournament coming up. And, most of all, the president called me himself. I was flattered. I called Strata to make sure it was above board, told the club in Raleigh I wasn't coming, then used my return ticket to London.

After catching the bus to Brighton, I told Lucy and her parents about the offer. Her dad, Chris, was my biggest fan. He was also one of the nicest people I ever met. I would have loved a dad like that.

'Whatever you do, don't buy the ticket to Nepal,' said Chris. 'If they're serious, they'll buy it.'

Ganesh called that afternoon, as I'd given him my in-laws' number.

'Catch the next flight from London to Kathmandu,' he told me. 'Buy the ticket, and we'll pay you back when you arrive.'

With my father-in-law's advice in my ears, I told Ganesh I wouldn't. He had to buy the ticket: if they didn't, the deal was off. Ganesh said he'd call back. Later that afternoon, the phone rang.

'Good news, Stephen,' said Ganesh. 'We have found you a ticket.'

'Great – when do I fly?' After three months in the US, I was hoping for a week or two with Lucy and Paula.

'Tonight, Stephen!' said Ganesh, laughing. 'You fly tonight!'

I THREW MY BOOTS, TRAINING KIT AND JEANS INTO A BAG, AND headed for Heathrow. It was less than twelve hours since I'd arrived from New York.

I had spent weeks in America, away from Lucy and Paula, and now I was leaving again. It was painful – very painful – but in truth, staying at home didn't cross my mind. Football was the only thing I wanted to do. It was the only thing I could do. Football was my trade. Moving to Nepal, and continuing my career, was the best way to support the girls.

That's not to say my head wasn't spinning. I had never been to Nepal, I knew no one, and I had no contract – just a promise from the other side of the world. It didn't help that, when I picked up my ticket, the Nepalese had misspelled my name. It took me an hour to get past the check-in desk.

As we descended into Kathmandu, I gazed out of the window. It was monsoon season, so everything was green. But when I looked closely, I saw kids playing football. Every patch of grass had two goals, one ball, and about two hundred players. For a bleary-eyed coach, flying solo into his first national team job, it was an uplifting sight. My mood ticked from nervous to excited.

Two people from ANFA met me at the old-fashioned, red-brick airport, then took me in a jeep to my hotel in Kathmandu. As we got closer to the city, the fields and golf courses gave way to houses. The wide, modern roads became cramped. The mountains, looming on the horizon, grew bigger.

Halfway to the city, the jeep stopped. Ahead, I saw a cow blocking the road. I thought the cars would beep, or drive at the animal. But in Nepal cows are sacred – certainly more sacred than football managers – so we waited. And waited. After twenty minutes, the cow sloped into a field, and the queue of traffic moved towards the city, thinking nothing of it. Welcome to Nepal.

At the hotel, the guys said they'd pick me up at 8 a.m. the next day for training. I thanked them, closed the door, and lay down for the first time since New York, almost 48 hours earlier. I was excited, nervous, but – most of all – knackered. I had travelled 8,000 miles through three continents. I shut my eyes and fell into a deep sleep.

The next morning, the guys took me to the university grounds in Kathmandu for my first session as a national team manager. In truth, it was more Sunday league than big league. The pitch had no lines. The goals had no nets. And the players – up to their ankles in mud – wore their own kit. There was drizzle in the air, and huge dragonflies buzzed round our ears. Then I heard a voice.

'Stephen! Welcome to Nepal!'

Ganesh, in a cream suit and brown shoes, was striding across the muddy pitch. It was the first time I'd seen him. We shook hands, then he spoke in Nepali to my players and coaches. Ganesh – who was a seriously good player in India before becoming ANFA president – had picked 35 players, which I would reduce to 23 before our first game. But first, we needed some bibs.

I marked out a pitch, picked two teams, and played eleven-a-side for half an hour. It sounds basic, but I needed to assess the standard. Next we did some runs, so I could gauge their fitness. Over the next ten days we worked on pretty much everything: the back four, our shape, one-on-ones… you name it, we did it. I ran the sessions in English. The captain, Deepak Amatya, could translate, as could striker Naresh Joshi, and a few other guys. There is a strong British influence in Nepal.

My mind was working overtime: will they understand what I want? What happens if we get beat? How long could I last? But my overriding thought was: I can't believe I'm manager of Nepal.

After ten days' training we flew to Bangladesh for the strangest tournament in football history. The Bangabandhu Cup had twelve teams which – and I looked this up, so I'm not wrong – were as follows:

- *Bangladesh*
- *Nepal*
- *Ghana's Olympic side*
- *Kuwait's Olympic side*
- *Malaysia's Olympic side*
- *Thailand's Olympic side*
- *South Korea under-18*
- *Brazilian league XI*
- *Japanese league XI*
- *Uzbekistan league XI*
- *III Keruleti FC, a club from Hungary*
- *Semen Padang, a club from Indonesia*

There were four groups of three, with our first game against Ghana's Olympic side in the national stadium in Dhaka. It poured with rain, the pitch was a bog, and we lost 2–1. I stood on the touchline in my best suit and tie, a habit I picked up in the Cypriot fourth division. By the end of the game, my trousers and shoes were covered with brown, Bangladeshi mud. But I loved it.

Two days later, we lost 1–0 to the Uzbekistan league XI and were knocked out. The challenge of Semen Padang would have to wait. But my new team impressed me. They did two things every manager wants: they listened and they worked hard. There was no backchat. No ego. They were full of running and full of pride. For a young manager, it was the perfect combination.

Back in Kathmandu, I had my first brush with royalty. The Crown Prince of Nepal, Dipendra, was a keen footballer, so a game was organised between the royal family's staff and the guys from ANFA. It was held at the federation's training centre. The Crown Prince played in midfield for them; the King of ANFA, Ganesh Thapa, was up front for us. To my surprise, I started on the bench. As the game kicked off, I noticed that a goat was tied up behind each goal. Strange, I thought.

After twenty minutes, the royal family went 1–0 up. To mark the occasion, a guard walked behind the goal, whipped out a Kukri knife – the Gurkhas' favourite blade – and chopped the goat's head off. I could barely believe what I'd seen.

'Sacrifice,' whispered the guy next to me on the bench, as the head, oozing with blood, lay on the floor.

In the second half, I came on and scored. As I ran back for the kickoff, I saw the other goat get the same treatment. It didn't feel like a celebration to me. What would happen if we scored again?

We went 2–1 up – thankfully, there were no more goats – before our keeper, the general secretary, threw in a long-range shot.

'What are you doing?' I asked.

'Coach,' he whispered. 'It's the royal team. They must win. Why do you think you didn't start the match?'

We lost 3–2, and afterwards ate freshly cooked goat in a marquee near the pitch. To be honest, the meat tasted great.

I didn't like seeing the goats killed, but who am I to judge a different country's culture? Who am I to tell a Nepali that chopping a goat's head off is unacceptable, but – say – eating a hamburger is fine? I needed to adapt to them – not them to me. If you're a guest in a foreign country, you play by their rules. I try to bring the best of my culture, and work with the best of theirs. Lucy calls me a chameleon, because I would change the colour of my skin to blend in. Of course, she is right.

The South Asian Games, which were being held in Nepal, began at the end of September. The night before I announced the squad, Ganesh called me at my hotel.

'Tell me the squad, and I will inform the players,' he said.

No way, I thought. The players had to know who was in charge. If Ganesh broke the news I'd look like a puppet. He was a powerful man, inside football and outside – his brother, Kamal, was a politician – but I had to stand up to him. I was the manager, not the president's assistant.

'You brought me here to do a job,' I said. 'You can announce the squad to the media. But I'm telling the squad.'

He said we'd discuss it tomorrow, when he picked me up at eight-thirty. I didn't want to wait. During a sleepless night, I decided to leave the hotel early, go to the training ground alone, and tell the players myself. When Ganesh arrived at half-eight, I was long gone.

When he arrived at training, he was fuming. But I had to stand firm. I was Nepal's third manager in twelve months (before me there'd been a German and a South Korean) but I wasn't scared of the sack. I would do things my way, or leave. The players had to respect me. From that moment, they did.

The Games were a massive event in Nepal. They were a mini Olympics, with sports like athletics, swimming and – of course – football. It was only Nepal's second time as host so the country was buzzing. More than $20m was spent getting the venues ready – most of the money provided by China, apparently – and the opening ceremony, which took place in the national stadium, was huge.

Our first game – my first international – took place on 26 September 1999: Nepal versus Bhutan. The Dasarath Rangasala stadium in Kathmandu is a grey concrete bowl, but it came alive that night. The lights were on, and the noise didn't stop. Even the national anthem was deafening.

In Cyprus, I was used to small stadiums with a few hundred fans. Now, I was in the middle of an international tournament with 25,000 people cheering me on. After two minutes we got a penalty, and the crowd cheered like we'd scored a last-minute winner in the World Cup final. Seriously: watch it on YouTube. Hari Khadka tucked the penalty away and sprinted to the corner to celebrate. The whole team joined him. In the stands, it was like a carnival.

Three minutes later, Hari got a second, and it was 3–0 within eighteen minutes. The match finished 7–0. Bhutan were a level below us, but I was buzzing. I had won an international in front of 25,000 fans. Whatever happened, I had that. I went to bed with the fans' noise ringing in my ears.

We were in a group of four alongside India, Pakistan and Bhutan. Two teams went through so, with Bhutan bottom, our game against Pakistan was decisive. They had almost 200 million people to pick from, compared to our 20 million, but we had home advantage. It was another night match, and the atmosphere, if anything, was even better than Bhutan. On the touchline, I tried to stay calm.

After forty minutes, with the score 0–0, we attacked down the left. A low cross came in. There were two Pakistan defenders in the six-yard box. One cleared it off the other, and the ball cannoned into the net. It was a strange goal, but I didn't care. The fans roared, and the players dived on each other. In the corner, the red bulbs on the giant scoreboard told the story. Home 1, Away 0.

Pakistan equalised early in the second half, but Hari Khadka put us 2–1 up soon afterwards. In the 77th minute we made it 3–1. From there, we couldn't lose. The fans wouldn't let us. The match finished 3–1, and Nepal were in the semi-finals. I shook hands with their coach – a Brazilian, Pedro Dias – and looked around. I was very proud. But more than anything, I was ecstatic that we'd earned ourselves another game. Stepping into that stadium, and that atmosphere, was addictive.

For the final group game against India, with qualification confirmed, we rotated the squad. Of course, I didn't want to lose. But for once, it wasn't the end of the world. As I told the players: the only thing that matters is the semi-final. They understood. If we made the final, no one would remember who played against India.

We lost 4–0 to our southern neighbours, which meant we played Maldives in the semi-final. The players didn't fancy their chances. Five months earlier, Nepal had lost twice to Maldives in the South Asian Gold Cup in India – 3–2 in the group stage, and 2–0 in the third-place playoff – and it had an effect. When you lose twice to the same team, there's a mental block. And that's when I had an idea.

For the opening ceremony, I wore the national dress: trousers, cream tunic, blue blazer, and a Nepalese hat. It wasn't my normal gear – people told me I looked like Nepal's prime minister – but the fans loved it. So for the semi-final, I met the players in my normal clothes, did the team talk, then left early and went downstairs.

I slipped into a side room, took off my western clothes, and put on the national dress. I then stood in the tunnel, waiting for the players. The Maldives players saw me first. They thought I was mad. But when the Nepalese boys noticed, they grew.

No one spoke, but their chests swelled and they stood an inch taller. At that moment, I felt we had won the game. To them, my dress was a sign of respect. They marched on to the pitch like soldiers.

I wanted to show that – for one day – I was Nepali, not English. I was one of them, and proud of it. As the players strode across the pitch, I walked round it. At first, the fans didn't notice. But near the corner flag, they saw me, and what I was wearing. A cheer turned into a roar. Within seconds, all 25,000 fans were on their feet. I felt like the most popular man in Kathmandu.

When I think about it, the hairs on my arms stand up. I get tears in my eyes. It was almost twenty years ago but I can still hear the noise. In the record books, it's the semi-final of a regional tournament in Nepal. But to me, it's one of the best days of my life.

We flew at Maldives straight from kickoff. We scored after eleven minutes, then got a second after fifteen. They pulled one back, but we held on. For the last ten minutes, it seemed like the crowd were holding their breath. When the full-time whistle went, they exhaled, then burst on to the pitch. Normally I stay calm, but I couldn't resist. I ran on the field and joined the biggest party in Kathmandu. I couldn't believe I was doing a lap of honour in the shadow of the Himalayas.

In the mayhem, I felt a hand on my shoulder. I turned round and saw a huge guy with an earpiece.

'Palace security,' he said. 'Please come with me.'

Another security guard appeared, and they led me towards the main stands. As they did, I noticed fans falling to their knees, like they were praying. They parted like the Red Sea and, for a second, I thought it was for me. Then I looked up and saw Crown Prince Dipendra striding towards me.

I didn't know what to do. Should I bow? Should I shake his hand? Or should I fall to my knees? As my mind raced, Dipendra stepped forward and hugged me.

The crowd made a shocked noise – 'Whooooa!' – because Nepalese people were forbidden from touching royalty.

'Coach,' said the Prince, 'you have made the whole country very proud.'

From 1996 to 2006, there was a Maoist insurgency in Nepal. The Communists, who wanted to overthrow the monarchy, were targeting the police and government officials. By September 1999, according to the BBC, there had been 900 deaths. The players didn't talk about it – not in English, at least. But the country was tense.

Our team, then, was a bright spot. A bit of good news. A source of national pride. Everywhere you went, people talked about the tournament. People were desperate to see us win. Apparently, even the Sherpas on Mount Everest listened to the semi-final, delaying some people's climbs.

We played Bangladesh in the final in front of another roaring crowd. They went 1–0 up in the 44th minute. We had tons of chances but couldn't score. With ten minutes to go, Hari Khadka had a shot. The ball hit the underside of the bar and bounced down. It crossed the line, I'm sure, but the ref didn't give it. Bangladesh held on. At full time, there was shocked silence. One of our players, Basanta Gauchan, was in tears. There's a picture of me consoling him on the pitch.

I was deflated. It didn't feel right to end the best week of my life as a runner-up. I wanted another pitch invasion; another party. But the Nepalese were more upbeat: we had won three matches and brought the country together. It was the team's best performance in years, and our effort was rewarded: in April 2000, the King honoured the whole squad at the palace.

We were given the Probal Gorkha Dakshin Baahu, which is like a knighthood. At the ceremony, the players were not allowed to touch the King. But when I went forward he shook my hand.

'You have no idea what you've done for this country,' he said.

It was the proudest day of my life. The medal is framed on my wall in Cyprus, and the picture is in my office. Every time I see it, I smile.

LUCY AND PAULA DIDN'T MOVE TO KATHMANDU STRAIGHT away. There was no point: if I was sacked, or didn't get paid, we would have moved straight back. But after the South Asian Games, I was secure. Ganesh was happy, the players respected me, and the AFC paid my wages on time. I expected to see out the three-year contract, at least. Lucy, though, was less keen.

We were on the phone, trying to arrange her arrival, when she told me she had a tooth infection.

'You just don't want to come,' I said.

'You're right, I don't want to come,' she said. 'But I do have a tooth infection.'

I understood her concern. She was taking her two-year-old daughter from her home, and her family, to a strange country on the other side of the world. It was a hard sell. But I knew that, once she came to Kathmandu and met the people, she would love it. Eventually, she booked a flight. I told her I'd meet her at the airport. The next day, I saw Ganesh.

'Good news, Ganesh,' I said happily. 'My family arrives on Friday.'

'One problem,' he replied. 'The Maoists have a bandh from Friday to Sunday.'

A bandh was like a nationwide strike. No one worked, and the Maoists set up road blocks to make sure no one travelled, either. Unless you were manning a barricade, you stayed at home.

'They might let them into the airport terminal,' Ganesh continued. 'Or they might leave them on the plane all weekend. Either way – she cannot travel into Kathmandu.'

Lucy was unhappy anyway. If her first three days in Nepal were spent in Kathmandu airport, she would fly straight home, then divorce me. Or worse.

'You need to fix this,' I told Ganesh. He thought about it, then called Binod Dangol, our goalkeeper.

As well as playing for the national team, Binod worked for the armed police. When Friday came, he arrived at the hotel in full uniform. The sunlight bounced off his machine gun.

'Coach,' he said. 'Come with me.'

Outside was a jeep with eight soldiers, all armed to the teeth. I hopped in and Binod put his foot down. Within minutes we hit a roadblock, where Maoists stopped the traffic. As we approached, the roadblock cleared. A jeep full of AK47s has that effect, I suppose.

We reached the airport and whizzed through the car park. Next thing I know, we're parked by the runway, just yards from the landing strip. After a few minutes, Lucy's plane burst through the clouds and came roaring in to land.

As the plane came to a standstill, Binod jumped out of the jeep. As his colleagues scanned the runway, fingers on their triggers, he walked up the steps of the plane and banged on the big, heavy door. One of the air stewards opened up. Binod addressed the passengers.

'Mrs Constantine and child – please come forward,' he said.

Lucy walked down the stairs with Paula in her arms. They both looked round, bewildered. Binod led them across the runway to the jeep.

'What on earth is going on?' asked Lucy, who had no idea about the bandh.

'Perks of being the national team coach,' I said, smiling. 'We get VIP treatment.'

We zoomed back to the hotel – their bags arrived the next day – and I thanked the boys. It was weeks until I told Lucy the real reason we met her on the runway.

'Coach,' said Binod, after dropping us off, 'do I start the next game?'

'After that,' I replied, 'how could I say no?'

A FEW DAYS LATER, WE MOVED FROM OUR HOTEL TO A NICE house near the British Army's Gurkha barracks. There was a Montessori school nearby, and a grassy lane where goats and pigs ran up and down. We got a dog, and the girls soon settled down. Within days, they loved it like me.

On the pitch, our next matches were qualifiers for the Asian Cup – the equivalent of the European Championships. We were drawn with Kuwait, Turkmenistan, Yemen and Bhutan, with all the games played over one week in Kuwait in February 2000.

Realistically, we had no chance. Kuwait were one of the best teams in Asia – they came fourth in the previous Asian Cup in 1996 – but I couldn't wait to test myself. It was everything I'd dreamed about: big stadiums, big crowds, big competitions.

We lost our first game to Yemen 3–0, then beat Bhutan by the same score. Two days later, Bhutan lost 20–0 to Kuwait. According to the BBC, 'Bhutan's cause was not helped by having two players sent off, as well as conceding four penalties for rugby tackle-style challenges in the area.' But their cause also wasn't helped by Kuwait's players sprinting to the centre circle every time they scored. They didn't need to get twenty. With every goal scored, it became more embarrassing for everyone.

I was asked about the game in my next press conference.

'The game was over after fifteen minutes,' I said. 'They don't need to rub Bhutan's face in it. There is only one team going to win this group, and that's Kuwait. They can score five against anybody.'

The next day, I went to breakfast. The Yemen squad – who were playing Kuwait that day – were there too. I walked past one of their players, who noticed me.

'Fuck you,' he said, behind his newspaper.

I stopped. Was he talking to me? Before I could speak, my players – who were behind me – reacted. They went for the Yemeni. He jumped up and sprinted through the restaurant.

To be fair to the Yemeni, he was quick. He darted past the tables as the Nepal squad gave chase. Eventually, he reached a partition. As he burst through the door, ketchup bottles flew past his head. It was like the Wild West in team tracksuits. My players caught up with him in the lobby: him on one side, us on the other, half a dozen security guards in between. Before long, the police turned up.

'There's no need to speak to my players,' I said, pointing at the Yemeni. 'It was him that caused the problem.'

I told the police and the Yemeni staff what happened, and went into a room with the player and the head coach. I asked why he swore at me.

'You disrespected Yemen,' he said in Arabic. 'You said Kuwait could beat us 5–0.'

I explained that I didn't mean to insult his team. He apologised. Their manager told me I could decide his punishment.

'What are the options?' I asked.

'We send him home,' the manager replied. 'In which case he will be disgraced, and will never play for his country again. Or he apologises and misses the next game.

It's up to you.'

Obviously, I didn't want to end his career. He was a young guy and – apart from anything – he had a nice turn of pace. But he needed to smooth things over. The Nepalese are proud people. They would have been happy to lie under a bush for twelve hours, wait for him, then jump out to slit his throat.

I told him to apologise to my players, which he did. We moved on. Quietly, though, I was proud of my boys. Clearly, they thought my honour was worth defending.

In our remaining games, we lost 5–0 to Turkmenistan and 5–0 to Kuwait. For the first time, I had lost more international games than I'd won. Kuwait went on to reach the quarter-finals of the Asian Cup, beating South Korea on the way – the same South Korea who beat Portugal, Italy and Spain to reach the World Cup semi-final in 2002. It showed what we – and Bhutan – were up against.

I LOVED NEPAL, BUT I SOON LEARNED THE WORST THING ABOUT managing a national team: there aren't enough games. I wanted to work every day, but I went weeks – and sometimes months – without seeing the players. When we didn't have matches, or training camps, I watched games and scouted players. But it wasn't enough, so I also ran our youth sides.

The qualifiers for the AFC Under-17 Championship were held in June 2000. We were in a group with Maldives, Turkmenistan and Uzbekistan. Somehow, Ganesh persuaded them to ignore the bandhs, and the civil war, and play the games in Kathmandu.

Before the tournament, we held camps around the country to look for players. I loved travelling round Nepal. The roads, carved into the sides of mountains, were spectacular, if nerve-wracking. The air was clean, the sky was blue, and the people were fantastic. We also found some real talent. Whether they were under seventeen, though, is another matter.

To me, some of them looked older. I was suspicious. But if they have a birth certificate, and the association says they're good, what can you do? In our first game, we beat Maldives 7–0 in the national stadium, then beat Turkmenistan 5–3. Our final game against Uzbekistan was decisive. If we won or drew, we were through. Even though it was an under-17 match, the stadium in Kathmandu was packed. Nepalese people love football, and their country.

At half-time, I gave the team talk on the pitch. For some reason, the changing rooms were closed. Halfway through, Ganesh came striding down the main stand.

'Coach, it's a tight game,' he said. 'Why don't you…'

'Ganesh,' I said, interrupting him. 'Turn round.'

My team talk obviously worked: the game finished 3–0 and we qualified. It was the first time Nepal had reached the finals of an AFC tournament. The crowd went mad. To them, it was more than an under-17 tournament. It was a chance to show that Nepal – the forgotten kingdom between India and China – was alive and kicking.

The finals were held in Vietnam in September. We flew via Thailand and stayed for a few days' training. The Omani side were in the same hotel in Bangkok. If our boys were pushing seventeen, theirs were pushing seventy. Seriously, half of them had moustaches and I swear one was going grey.

We were staying on the sixth floor. On the third floor was a massage parlour, where you could relax in more ways than one. One evening I got in the lift with the Omani squad. When the lift hit the third floor, they got out. You could see the girls hanging round, waiting for clients.

In the lobby, I met the Omani coach, John Adshead – an Englishman who spent a number of years in New Zealand, taking them to the 1982 World Cup.

'Where are your boys tonight then?' I asked.

'Tucked up in bed, Steve,' he replied, confidently.

'I'm not sure they are,' I said. 'I think they're on the third floor.'

'And what's on the third floor?' he asked, innocently.

'Put it this way, John,' I replied. 'They're not playing table tennis.'

I never saw a coach move so quick.

On the pitch, we played a friendly against Oman in Thailand – which was called off at half-time because the boys kicked lumps out of each other – before flying to Danang on the east coast of Vietnam for the finals. We lost 6–2 to China, 5–0 to Vietnam and 3–0 to both Myanmar and Japan. It hurt, but I wasn't angry: just making the tournament was an achievement. Oman ended up winning it, beating Iran 1–0 in the final. But – as it turned out – they weren't able to defend the trophy.

In 2001, the AFC banned Oman from the next under-17 tournament, after MRI scans of the players' bones from Vietnam showed at least six were overage. Some were as old as nineteen or twenty. Iran, who had five overage players, were also banned, as were Bangladesh, Thailand and – I'm afraid to say – Nepal.

I was so disappointed. I want to win but not at all costs: by age doping, you're cheating both your opponents, and the younger players denied a place in their national team. I don't even know how many of ours were overage: it turned out the federation hadn't allowed them to be tested.

EVEN AT THE LOWEST LEVEL OF INTERNATIONAL FOOTBALL, there is money. Since 1999, FIFA's Goal programme has spent more than $250m on projects, pitches and training centres around the world (almost $2m has been spent in Nepal, according to FIFA's website). There are also grants from confederations – in Nepal's case, the AFC – and from national governments. But where there is money, there is greed.

In 2000 the government accused Ganesh of misusing ANFA's money. He denied the accusation and refused to step down, but the government dug in. They set up their own federation and banned ANFA from using government facilities, including the national stadium. And it soon got worse.

In early 2001, I was told that – as they were no longer the official federation – ANFA could not sponsor my visa. With no visa, I couldn't stay in the country. The national team manager, and his family, faced deportation.

I went to the government directly. They decided that – because of my hard work – we could stay in Nepal until a solution was found. But a solution seemed impossible. I contacted the AFC and FIFA, who said they still recognised ANFA as the official federation. The AFC paid my salary and so, for a while, I tried to work as normal.

Although Ganesh was difficult, he was my boss. I felt some loyalty. He was the one who had called me at 3 a.m. in New York. He was the one who gave me a chance, when hundreds of others threw my faxes into the bin. Thanks to him, I was a national team manager. I didn't realise what he would become.

Nepal were due to play World Cup qualifiers in March 2001. We were in a group with Iraq, Kazakhstan and Macau, with all the games due to be played in Kathmandu. I was desperate to take part. It was only the first round of qualifying, but it was still the biggest tournament in the world. It would have been a huge moment. Which coach wouldn't want 'World Cup' on his CV?

Because of the war between Ganesh and the government, the games were moved to Iraq and Kazakhstan, but Ganesh was clear: I should prepare as normal. I named thirty-eight players in my squad, then watched in horror as the government named sixty in theirs. I didn't even realise we had sixty players.

The boys were in an impossible position. If they played for us, they upset the government. If they played for the government, they upset the AFC and FIFA – who still recognised us, ANFA, as the national federation. We were told that – if we tried to reach Baghdad for the first game – we could be arrested at the airport. And that's when a light bulb went off in Ganesh Thapa's head.

'We will hold a training camp at Chitwan National Park,' he said.

Chitwan was in the lowlands of Nepal, near the border with India.

'At night, we will catch a bus into India. From there, we can drive to the airport, and fly to the game.'

'And how will we cross the Nepali border?' I asked, in a state of shock. 'Bribe the guards?'

'Exactly!' he replied.

Ganesh wasn't thinking straight. His plan had no chance of working – especially as the players, quite rightly, released a statement saying they wouldn't train with either federation.

I decided to resign. I was in the middle of a tug-of-war, and I couldn't coach football teams while my arms were being stretched in different directions. Ganesh told me to stay: he thought he could reach a deal with the government so Nepal could still play in the World Cup qualifiers. But three weeks later, nothing had changed. We had no players and no effective federation. I had to go.

I held a press conference to announce my resignation. Some reporters had tears in their eyes. One columnist in the Nepali Times wrote: 'If there was anyone who could take Nepal's beloved football to a higher plane, it was Stephen Constantine. The national team's remarkable improvement is proof. Nepali football seemed finally to be going somewhere. Now we're back to ground zero.'

The adventure that started with an early-hours call in New York in 1999 had ended less than two years later. It was heartbreaking to leave. I loved Kathmandu, I loved the people, and I loved the players. When I arrived, I was nobody: just a well-qualified English coach from the Cypriot lower leagues. When I left, I was a national team manager: a guy who'd competed in the Asian Cup; who'd won a silver medal in a regional tournament; who'd been carried round the pitch by his own fans.

Nepal welcomed me. It gave me hundreds of happy memories. And – most importantly – it kick-started my career in football. I hope I gave them something back.

AFTER I LEFT, A COMPROMISE WAS REACHED. NEPAL DID PLAY IN the World Cup qualifiers, beating Macau and losing heavily to Iraq and Kazakhstan. But the dispute between the ANFA and the government lasted another two years. When it was resolved, Ganesh remained as president, and became a vice-president of the AFC. To quote the Guardian, he became 'one of the most influential men in Asian football'. But things didn't end well.

In 2014, two ANFA vice presidents asked FIFA to investigate Ganesh. He was accused of embezzling millions of dollars during his nineteen years at ANFA and, in 2015, he was banned from football for ten years. According to FIFA, my old boss 'committed various acts of misconduct over several years, including the solicitation and acceptance of cash payments from another football official, for both personal and family gain'. He appealed, but it was thrown out in 2016.

There were other sad endings, too. In June 2001, eleven members of the royal family – including the King and Crown Prince Dipendra – died in a massacre at the palace. The shooting was blamed on Dipendra, after an argument about his choice of bride. He had, apparently, been drinking.

There are other theories. All I know is that, when I met him, he was a nice guy. I would be amazed if he was involved, but you never know. There was a revolution in 2006, and the monarchy was abolished two years later. The palace, where I had the proudest day of my life, is now a museum.

5
WAKING THE GIANT
INDIA, 2002–05

AFTER LEAVING NEPAL, WE MOVED BACK TO LUCY'S PARENTS'
house in Brighton. I wanted a job in England and thought that, after my spell in
Nepal, there was a good chance.

Being a national team manager had boosted my profile. I had a regular column
on the ESPN website, and I was occasionally mentioned in newspapers and magazines. Don't get me wrong: I could walk through Brighton without being stopped
for autographs. But I wasn't just a youth coach from Cyprus any more.

I signed up for a coach educator's course – where you learn to coach coaches – in
Lilleshall in Shropshire. There, I met a guy called Joe Roach, who was the reserve
and youth-team manager at AFC Bournemouth. He asked if I was interested in
coaching his under-15s and below. It was three nights a week with a game every
weekend. The pay wasn't enough to live on, but it was something. I accepted Joe's
offer.

Soon after, I was introduced to Tony Elkins-Green. He worked at Chichester
College – a huge sixth form in Sussex, not far from Brighton – and wanted me to
run their football teams. I told him about my Bournemouth offer, but there was
time for both jobs, just about.

I left Brighton at seven o'clock, got to Chichester for eight, then worked with the boys until lunchtime. At 3 p.m., I'd drive 65 miles to Bournemouth, work with their youth teams, then drive the 100-odd miles back to Brighton. On a good day, I'd be back home for 11 p.m. It was a comedown from the previous two years.

With Nepal, I coached in sold-out national stadiums across Asia. I picked the best players in the country. I had dozens of journalists at my press conferences, and read about myself on the FIFA website. In England I worked in a sixth form, albeit one with a big football programme. But – honestly – I was just pleased to have work. The money and the standard were less important. I learned from every second on the pitch. And when it came to English boys, there was lots to learn.

Before Bournemouth and Chichester, I had never coached in England. They were great lads – I'm still in touch with one or two, including the captain Steve Sneller – but they were very different to the Nepalese. When I walked in a room in Nepal, the players stood up. In England, half of them would still be tapping their mobile phones. There was a culture of piss-taking; of laddishness.

It wasn't malicious, and it didn't make them bad footballers. But it took some getting used to. If, for example, I told the Nepalese lads to run five laps of the pitch, they did it without blinking. If I told the English boys, they would ask questions: 'Why are we doing this? How is it going to help?'

One time, Chichester had a game at Crawley. I brought Paula along, who was three or four. At half-time, I sat her on top of a cupboard in the changing room – so she wouldn't run off – then started bollocking one of our players who wasn't pulling his weight. As I paused for breath, Paula piped up.

'Daddy,' she said. 'Why are you being so mean to that boy?'

The lads started pissing themselves.

'Yeah, gaffer,' said the player. 'Why are you being so mean to me?'

It was the last time Paula came to a Chichester game.

Although I had two jobs, I wasn't rich. I can't remember how much Bournemouth and Chichester paid, but it wasn't much. I had a wife and two daughters to feed so, when both jobs stopped in mid-December for the holidays, I took a job in Brighton sorting office, dealing with the Christmas mail.

I did the night-shift, which ran from 6 p.m. until midnight or 1 a.m. We'd get a pile of cards and letters then stick them into boxes, depending on their postcode. Some people could do it without looking. It wasn't exciting – and it was a long way from being a national team manager – but I'm happy to do 'normal' jobs, if I need to. I have no divine right to work in football. I needed to support my family, like anyone else. The job lasted a week or two. I can still remember half the postcodes.

In January, I was back on the pitch. I loved both jobs – especially after working nights in the sorting office – but, like when I managed AEL under-18s, I was wary of becoming a full-time youth coach. There is nothing wrong with coaching young players. People like Joe Roach, who's still at Bournemouth, do amazing work. But, back then, it was hard to move from youth football to adult football. I didn't want to be 'Stephen Constantine: youth coach'. I wanted to be 'Stephen Constantine: national team coach' or 'Stephen Constantine: Premier League coach'.

We don't pay youth coaches what they're worth. Across the world, there are senior coaches who can't make their dog sit down getting paid thousands a month. Yet in youth football, super-talented coaches are paid pennies for mining diamonds. It's a crying shame.

After a few months at Bournemouth, Joe asked me to become his assistant. I was tempted, as I loved working there. The first-team manager Sean O'Driscoll and his assistant Peter Grant were very supportive. They respected me. I'd occasionally scout for the first team, which was great experience.

But the pay rise on offer was tiny. I asked for a car, they said no. I asked for a phone, they said no. I needed to get back to senior football. Thankfully, I had an offer from the Indian national team.

THE AGENCY WHO HELPED ME GET THE NEPAL JOB, STRATA, kept in touch after I left Kathmandu. Strata had contacts with the federation in India, so when the Indians were looking for a coach, they put my name forward.

The first email from the All India Football Federation came towards the end of 2001, while I was working at Chichester and Bournemouth. The general secretary, Alberto Colaco, asked if I was interested in the job. I said yes, but there wasn't a vacancy, so I heard nothing for three months.

Alberto's second email said their coach, an Indian called Sukhwinder Singh, was leaving. He asked if I was still interested. Of course, I said yes. I began to get excited, but the cogs turned slowly: three months later I'd heard nothing. Finally, another email arrived from Alberto. He said the position was open. He asked for my passport details and invited me to India to sign a contract.

There wasn't an interview, which may sound strange. But in football, most interviews are a sham. In 95 per cent of cases, the club or country know their new manager before the old one goes. If they hold interviews, they're often for PR reasons. They want to seem open-minded. They want to please the fans by acting professionally. But usually, it's a waste of everyone's time. The Indians had my CV. They knew my qualifications. They had spoken to Nepal. They had everything they needed.

On paper, it seemed like a huge leap. India is twenty times bigger than Nepal. The population is 1.3 billion against 30 million. But really, that didn't matter. Leading someone else's country – whatever the size – is the biggest honour there is. I was ready for the challenge. I couldn't wait to start.

I flew from London to Mumbai and landed late at night. The luggage hall was the busiest place I'd seen, and outside was worse. It was one o'clock in the morning, but it was mayhem. Cars beeped their horns. Yellow headlights illuminated the black night. Everyone was going somewhere, and fast.

All around me, people were shouting. Someone asked if I wanted a taxi. Another person asked if I needed a hotel. I just stood there, blinking. I was due to meet Alberto – who was flying from Goa – at the domestic terminal the following morning. I found a room and waited to meet my new boss.

Straight away, I liked Alberto. Like me, he was desperate to improve Indian football. We flew to Calcutta (which had recently been renamed Kolkata) to meet the AIFF president, Priya Ranjan Dasmunsi, the rest of the board, and the Bengali media. My three-year deal was worth $5,000 a month for two years, rising to $8,000 in the final year. As I signed the contract, I knew it was a career-defining job. If I failed, I would disappear.

Some coaches have a safety net. If you were a big-name player, you can fail in your first two or three jobs and still get offers. Look at – say – Lothar Matthaus. He fails at Rapid Vienna, he goes to Partizan Belgrade. He doesn't qualify with Hungary, he goes to Atletico Paranaense. He quits Brazil after two months, he goes to Red Bull Salzburg. On it goes, job after job, and all because he was a superb player for Germany. And it's not just him. There are so many others like that across Europe.

If I did badly with India, I was gone. My national team career would vanish. I wouldn't get a second chance. No one would say, 'Oh, Stephen Constantine, sacked after three months at India? Let's give him the Bulgaria job.' So when I signed that contract, there was excitement. But there was also fear. A fear of failing. It's been there ever since I left home aged sixteen. If I fall, there's no one to catch me.

DAYS AFTER ARRIVING, WE HELD A FOUR-WEEK TRAINING CAMP in Jamshedpur, a city around 200 miles west of Calcutta. The team's manager – the logistics man, if you like – was a Bengali guy called Santo Mitra, who was a big player in the 1970s. Before we set off, he asked if he should go a day early, to make sure the facilities were OK. 'Great idea, Santo,' I said, pleased at the professionalism.

We took a four-hour train ride to Jamshedpur, arriving late afternoon. I asked Santo if I could see the facilities.

'No need, coach,' he said. 'Wait until tomorrow.'

Fair enough, I thought. It was getting late. It could wait. The next day, we went to see the pitch. It wasn't bad – decent grass, running track, concrete terraces.

'And where are the players staying?' I asked. 'In there,' said Santo, pointing at the main stand.

I went into the stand. There were six or seven rooms with bunk beds in. Water dripped down the walls. The ceilings were stained. The air was sticky.

'Santo,' I said, 'the federation has picked thirty-five players. The camp lasts four weeks. You thought this was OK?'

'The players are used to it,' he replied. 'It was fine in my day.'

'But you played when Noah was building his ark,' I said. I went back to the Tata Football Academy (a team sponsored by the steel conglomerate) in Jamshedpur to phone Alberto Colaco.

'This is the national team,' I said. 'The players can't spend a month living in a stadium.'

Alberto told me I could book new accommodation, if it was within budget. I found a hotel and spoke to the owner. I explained what we needed – nice rooms, light breakfast, healthy lunch – and the next morning, everything was perfect. We came back for lunch, and it was awful. The food was too heavy. You can't train all afternoon with a bellyful of dhal.

'My friend,' I told the owner, 'if the food isn't better tomorrow lunchtime, I will check out all thirty-five players.'

The next day, it was the same: nice breakfast, heavy lunch. We checked out.

It sounds fussy, but I was trying to change the culture. I wanted excellence. I wanted to make the players feel important; to show them that we, the staff, would give them everything they needed to perform well. You can't pick the country's best 35 players then give them basic facilities. On the pitch, I want my players to give me everything. So off the pitch, I look after them.

India's best player was Baichung Bhutia. He was like a home-grown David Beckham; a superstar in the subcontinent. He made his India debut aged nineteen and, when he signed for Bury in 1999, became the first Indian to play professionally in Europe in the modern era. By 2001, he was more famous than the other Indian players put together.

With our permission, he arrived at the camp a day late, as he was tying up loose ends in England. We'd spoken on the phone, but I was wary. Was he a Big Time Charlie? Would he undermine me, and take the players with him? He certainly had the power.

On the second day, while I was training the players, I saw someone in plain clothes in the distance. He noticed me, then started jogging. It was Baichung. He ran into the middle of the pitch.

'Gaffer, gaffer,' he said, as the others watched on. 'I'm really sorry I'm late. I'll get changed straight away.'

I liked it for two reasons. One, he apologised. We knew he was going to be late – it wasn't a problem – but it showed self-awareness. It said: 'You guys were here yesterday. I wasn't on time. I'm aware of that – I'm not above you.' Secondly, he called me gaffer. He was telling the players that I was in charge. Baichung could have been difficult, but he was a dream – off and on the field.

You look at his record in England, and it's average. Three seasons at Bury, twenty league starts, three goals. But he's one of the most under-rated players I know. Great touch, two-footed, quick over ten yards, good finisher. And he's from Sikkim in the north-east, where they're all tough buggers.

I didn't see him at Bury, but he might have been wasted in England. If the ball's in the air, and he's getting it round his neck, it's no good for him. Play it to feet and, you see why he's a superstar.

After the camp we flew to Vietnam for the LG Cup, a tournament organised by Strata. We entered our under-23 team, which I also looked after, along with the under-18s on occasion. For the LG Cup, we were allowed three overage players, so it wasn't a million miles from the first team.

Our first game was a 2–2 draw against Singapore under-23s, which we should have won. Next, we won 3–1 against Vietnam under-23s, with two goals in the last five minutes. We came top of the group – our last-minute goal against Vietnam meant we finished above Singapore on goal difference – and so played an Indonesian side, Petrokimia Putra, in the semi-final. But I was worried.

Indian players – and perhaps Indian people – get too comfortable. They work, they have success, they earn money, they relax. They cruise. They take it easy. After two games in charge, I thought some players were in their comfort zone. The training sessions were too loose. Some players had been in the squad for seven or eight years, and they'd taken their foot off the gas. They thought seven out of ten performances were enough. But there is always room for improvement.

Before the semi-final, I told the players I wanted more aggression. More snap. We couldn't give them time on the ball; we couldn't make it easy. Ten minutes in, Baichung went in for a fifty-fifty. Bang. He got the ball; their player went off injured. Sadly, we later learned he'd broken his leg. Of course, I didn't want the player to get hurt – I know what it's like to suffer a bad injury – but I loved the tackle. Baichung had played in England and it showed. He wanted to win as much as me.

The Indonesians were a good side – six of their team were national players – but after that tackle, they didn't want to know. We won 3–0. Afterwards their coach told the press: 'I haven't seen such a well-organised and fit team from India for a long time.'

I was delighted. Our hard work in Jamshedpur was paying off. But the final could not have been harder: we were up against Vietnam's senior side. To win the trophy, we needed to beat the hosts in front of a full house in Ho Chi Minh City.

After twenty minutes, we were 2–0 down. Vietnam were ranked 108th in the world in 2002 – a good 20 places above our senior team – and, obviously, our under-23s were a level below that. In their semi, Vietnam beat Singapore 3–0, who we only drew with. I had to change something.

After 21 minutes, I brought on Tomba Singh, a midfielder who could beat a man on either side. I don't like making substitutions so early, but there was nothing to lose. Ten minutes later, Baichung pulled one back when their keeper dropped a cross. After 57 minutes he equalised. Game on.

I brought on Abhishek Yadav, a 6ft striker who was good in the air. With two minutes left, Jo Paul Ancheri put in a cross. Abhishek was just behind the penalty spot, but he leaped like a trout and headed it towards goal. For a second, everything stopped. Our bench held its breath. I followed the ball as it left Abhishek's head and flew towards goal. It's going in, I thought. It's going in.

It's in.

As our bench went mad, jumping and cheering, the rest of the stadium fell silent. We'd beaten Vietnam in their own back yard after being 2–0 down inside twenty minutes. I tried to stay calm, but there was an overwhelming feeling of pride, and vindication. To all those who said I couldn't do it, I showed them I could. Nine months earlier, I was doing night-shifts at the sorting office in Brighton.

In the final few seconds, Vietnam tried to kick us off the pitch. Thankfully, we kept our cool. When the full-time whistle went, their coach – a Portuguese guy called Henrique Calisto – went on the pitch to moan at the referee. 'You're right,' I told him. 'The ref was crap.' But the message was lost in translation, and he tried to fight me. I walked away. I saw him two years later and he apologised.

When we arrived in Calcutta there were 10,000 people cheering us at the airport. It took us two hours to reach the bus. Clearly, the LG Cup wasn't a major tournament, but to Indian fans it was huge. It was the first time any Indian side had won a tournament outside the subcontinent since 1974, when the under-19s were joint winners (with Iran) of the Asian Youth Championships.

The senior team hadn't won anything since 1971, when they shared the Pesta Sukan Cup – a tournament in Singapore – with South Vietnam. Even now, the LG Cup is considered one of Indian football's major achievements. To win a tournament outside India, beating the hosts in the final, was massive.

I carried the trophy all the way from Ho Chi Minh to India. It stayed with me on the coach, on the flight to Calcutta, and on the journey to Goa. I even took it home. When I reached Alberto Colaco's office at the Fatorda stadium the next day, I placed it on the table.

'That's for you, boss,' I told him. 'Now the hard work begins.'

TWO WEEKS AFTER THE FINAL AGAINST VIETNAM, WE FLEW TO England for two friendlies against Jamaica. India had been to England twice in the previous two years, but each time they'd mainly played club sides – Fulham and West Bromwich Albion in 2000; Brentford, Nottingham Forest, Leyton Orient and Walsall in 2001. For national teams, that's not good enough.

Club players don't take the games seriously. They don't want to get injured. With all due respect, a nation of one billion people shouldn't be flying halfway round the world to play a friendly against Walsall.

Before the first friendly I took the players and officials to watch Arsenal play West Brom in the Premier League at Highbury. I knew Arsenal's media man, Andy Exley, so I asked for tickets. It was too short notice for the Arsenal seats – there must have been thirty of us – but he phoned West Brom and got tickets for the away end.

It was a strange sight, thirty Indians sitting among the West Brom fans, but it was a great evening. The lights were on – it was a Tuesday night – and Arsenal were 3–0 up inside 24 minutes. After Sylvain Wiltord scored the third, the Albion fans sang: 'We're going to win 4–3.' My players were shocked.

'If this was India,' one of them told me, 'they would be throwing rocks at us by now.'

Our first game was at Vicarage Road, Watford – ten miles from where I grew up in North London. It was my first full international with India, and the first time I'd managed in England, so it was a proud moment. Unfortunately, we lost 3–0. Jamaica were a good, strong side – they'd been to the World Cup four years earlier – but we were too timid. We were pushed around. We moaned at the referee.

Afterwards, I told the boys: 'You played like it was a league match in India.' That wasn't a compliment. In Indian football, too many games are: 'After you. No, I insist, after you.'

The second game, three days later at Molineux in Wolverhampton, was much better. We pressed their players. We snapped into tackles. The game finished 0–0 – Baichung had a goal wrongly disallowed for offside – and afterwards, it was the Jamaicans moaning. I bumped into Luther Blissett, the former England striker, in the tunnel. He was born in Jamaica and was part of their group.

'Bloody hell, Steve,' he said, smiling. 'Your boys were aggressive.' It was just what I wanted to hear.

Later that month, September 2002, we were due in South Korea for the regional Olympics, the Asian Games. But originally, the government didn't want to send a football team. The sports ministry was paying for other athletes, but not us. They thought we would embarrass the nation. A week before the games, we thought we weren't going, but after winning the LG Cup, and drawing against Jamaica, the government changed its mind. We got our suits and flew to Busan.

IN THE CANTEEN IN KOREA, I HEARD A GRUNT. I IGNORED IT AND carried on eating, but the grunting continued.

'Hey, you,' said the voice.

I looked up and saw a guy in a blazer. He was, it turned out, one of the Indian team officials.

'Are you the football coach?' he asked. I said I was.

'You must be at the opening ceremony tomorrow,' he told me.

'No,' I replied, simply.

We'd already played our first game – a 3–0 win against Bangladesh, two days before the ceremony – and our next was against Turkmenistan, the day after. We needed to prepare. Opening ceremonies look nice on telly, but they're boring for athletes: hours of hanging around, waiting to wave at the crowd. I wasn't in the mood to kowtow to the government. We didn't attend the ceremony.

Before the Turkmenistan game, the match commissioner came in to check the players' passports. As he was leaving, he said, matter-of-factly, 'And Stephen, you will sit in the stand.'

'Why would I do that?' I replied, bemused.

'Because you are banned,' he replied, as if I was stupid.

'Why am I banned?' I asked.

He showed me a letter saying I'd been sent off after the Bangladesh game for arguing with the ref. It was news to me. I was livid, but there was no point arguing again.

I watched from the stand and was even more livid at half-time. We were 1–0 down and playing badly. As he walked off the pitch, I went downstairs and grabbed Baichung. As I said earlier, I don't rant often. If you shout too much, it loses its power. But sometimes, it can work.

'Call yourself a captain?' I asked Baichung, angrily. 'You're the superstar of this team, and that's how you play?'

It was the biggest bollocking I'd given him. I love Baichung, but he was going through the motions. To be fair, he knew I was right. Before we reached the dressing room, I spoke to him again.

'I'm going to do that again in front of the players,' I said, calmly. 'Don't react. We're good.'

I tore into Baichung in the dressing room. He sat there, good as gold. Eight minutes into the second half, he equalised. With fifteen minutes left he got another. We won 3–1 and afterwards, the dressing room was buzzing. It was a total transformation from the half-time bollocking.

As we celebrated, there was a knock on the door. I opened it, and saw two huge Punjabi guys. They told me a government minister wanted to congratulate the team. I looked to my assistant, Sukhwinder Singh (the former manager had become my assistant). He said we should let them in.

I disagreed.

'Tell him he can wait,' I said.

After twenty minutes, I let him in, then walked out. It's easy for a government to support a team when they've won two out of two. We needed their support before the tournament.

Our final game was against China, who'd been to the World Cup that summer. We lost 2–0 and finished second in the group. We were on course to reach the quarter-finals as one of the best runners-up but, two days after our China game, Bahrain beat Palestine 5–0 to leapfrog us. I flew home disappointed but satisfied. After three months in the deep end, I hadn't drowned.

LUCY AND THE GIRLS MOVED TO INDIA AFTER THE LG CUP (AT this point we had two children, Paula and Christiana). To begin with, the four of us lived in one room in Club Mahindra, an upmarket beach resort in Goa. Lucy loved it – all the cooking, cleaning and laundry was done for us – but it wasn't big enough, so the federation found us a colonial house nearby. It was in the woods, surrounded by coconut trees. It sounds idyllic, unless you've got young girls.

As soon as we arrived, Paula ran into the garden. Every so often, I heard a thud, so I looked outside and saw big, heavy coconuts falling from the trees. Some were landing just a few yards from her head. I brought her in, then went out to buy two huge bicycle helmets. Every time Paula or Christiana went outside, they stuck them on. There were animals out there too, so the garden was quite a sight: two girls in huge helmets chasing black pigs, while Goan coconuts fell to the earth.

The house was big, but it wasn't homely. The front room was out of bounds because the owners used it for storage. And when the monsoon came, water poured through the windows. Once, Lucy slipped on the stairs while carrying Christiana. They were fine – Lucy bruised her knee and elbow – but we moved soon after. Alberto found us a townhouse close to his office in the Fatorda stadium in Goa. We had a driver, and our bills were taken care of, so everything was good.

Unfortunately for Lucy, I wasn't there much. After we left, she worked out that, of my three years in India, I was on the road for two. If it wasn't matches, it was training camps, or trips to watch league matches. Watching Mohun Bagan or East Bengal play meant a three-hour flight from Goa to Calcutta. I enjoyed seeing new places, meeting new people, and learning about a fantastic country. But that didn't make it easier for Lucy. To be in Goa, on her own, with two kids… I don't know how she coped. A lesser woman would have left. She is the hero of this book.

In January, I was travelling again. The South Asian Football Federation Cup – not to be confused with the South Asian Games – was being held in Bangladesh. It was my worst trip as India manager.

A huge military standoff between India and Pakistan had ended three months earlier. A terrorist attack on the Indian parliament in December 2001 led to both countries massing troops along the border. For months, the Western media talked about the possibility of nuclear war. Thankfully, the troops were stood down after international diplomacy. But it was clear whose side the Bangladeshi public were on.

To them, India was the over-mighty neighbour. An English manager, and a few centuries of colonial resentment, made things worse. After we arrived, I tried to walk from the hotel to a kiosk. I was told I needed two soldiers with me. I literally couldn't cross the road without a machine gun for company.

Our training pitch in Dhaka was littered with glass bottles. When we entered the dressing room before the first game against Pakistan, a cleaner was sweeping clouds of dust into the air. It was enough to give you asthma. As we walked on the pitch, some Bangladesh fans spat at us, and when we lined up for the anthems, Pakistan's was played but ours wasn't. We waited two long, drawn-out minutes and heard nothing. It was embarrassing, so I told the players to sing it themselves.

On the pitch, Pakistan went 1–0 up after fifty minutes and the crowd went mad. We had a young team: four key players were out, including Baichung and Deepak Mondal, our right-back and player of the year for 2002. But that's not an excuse. We should have beaten Pakistan and we didn't.

After that defeat, we beat Afghanistan 4–0, then drew 1–1 against Sri Lanka to make the semi-finals. In front of another hostile crowd, we lost 2–1 to Bangladesh, who scored a golden goal in extra time. To make matters worse, we still had another game: Pakistan in the third-place playoff.

Before the game, I told the players that – no matter what – we would swap shirts with their players. I didn't care if we lost 5–0: we had to show that we, the Indian team, had come in peace. It didn't matter if Pakistan kicked us black and blue for ninety minutes. We represented one billion people, and we had responsibilities. When the crowd booed us, we would kill them with kindness.

In fairness, the Pakistan players were fantastic. There was no trouble. We all knew that one kick, or one punch, could spark something far bigger. Can you imagine if – heaven forbid – a fight had started, and the game was called off? There would be headlines around the world. India versus Pakistan was explosive. We couldn't be the spark. We won 2–1 in extra time and, as promised, the players swapped shirts. The Bangladeshi crowd applauded. It was a good end to a bad fortnight.

THE INDIA JOB WAS TAKING ME ROUND THE WORLD. IN LESS than six months, I'd been to Vietnam, England, South Korea and Bangladesh, as well as all over India. And, two months after we got back from Dhaka, there was another stamp in my passport, one of the rarest in the world: North Korea.

We were drawn against them in the Asian Cup qualifiers. The first leg was in Pyongyang, which meant a long journey: a flight to Japan, then China, then into North Korea on the national carrier, Air Koryo. As I sat down on the plane, I looked up and saw carpet on the ceiling. The food tasted like it came from the 1970s, too. I'm not a nervous flyer, but I made an exception for Air Koryo.

Pyongyang airport was amazing: there was no one there. Apart from the staff, the terminal was empty. There were no passengers, and no planes on the runway. Everything was quiet. The weather was grey. The contrast to India – the colour, the chaos, the nonstop noise – was incredible.

We got off the plane and soldiers led us to the customs area. One of them asked who our leader was. Naturally, I stepped forward.

'Does your team have mobile phones?' the soldier asked. I asked the guys. No one answered.

'No phones,' I told the soldier.

'If we find one, we take it from them, and they don't get it back,' the soldier said. I repeated the information to the boys. They all held out their phones. We didn't see them again for four days.

We went to our hotel, which had a huge car park but no cars. Our rooms were on the sixteenth floor, but we could have had a floor each. I didn't see another guest. There were two North Korea guys with the group at all times, plus a liaison officer. After we arrived, he asked me what time we would shower. Why, I thought, are you scrubbing our backs? Actually, they needed to put the hot water on.

There was a TV in my room, so I switched it on. I knew I wouldn't find Trans World Sport, but I hoped there might be CNN or BBC. In fact, there were three channels: North Korean news, military parades and military songs. I turned it off, went to bed, and was woken at 5 a.m. by the sound of marching. I looked out and saw 400 soldiers goose-stepping in the huge car park. It was a different world.

The month before, North Korea played in a tournament in Bangkok, alongside Thailand, Qatar and Sweden. I knew the Thailand manager Peter Withe – he introduced himself before the Bangabandhu Cup in Bangladesh in 1999 – so I flew over and stayed at his house. I found out where the Koreans trained then watched them from a car by the side of the pitch. It was astonishing.

The Koreans ran and ran and ran. It was like watching marines at boot camp. At one point, they carried each other on their soldiers, and throughout it all, there was no banter. They just worked. But they weren't just fit: they were excellent players, too. We were in for a tough game.

There were at least 40,000 people in the stadium but you could hear a pin drop. It was the opposite of a football match: no noise, no songs and no colour. Everyone wore the same clothes. It was surreal. Afterwards, our left-sided midfield player, Renedy Singh, came up to me.

'Usually I like playing on the far side, because I can't hear you shout at me,' he said. 'Today I heard every word.'

Just before half-time, the Koreans went 1–0 up. The fans stood up, clapped for a minute, then sat down. When they scored a second the same thing happened. It was the most surreal ninety minutes of my life but – apart from the result – I enjoyed it. How many other people have experiences like that?

At the hotel, there were six girls who served our meals. On our last day we tried to give them a $600 tip. Our boys weren't on big money, but they were generous, and they wanted to help these kind people trapped in a strange world. At first, the girls wouldn't accept it, but we pressed it into their hands as we left. They said it was three months' salary. Some were in tears.

We went to the airport, got our phones back, and reboarded our old friend Air Koryo. The view from the window was as grey as the food. On the layover in China, two of our young players knocked on my door to ask if they could go shopping near the hotel. 'No problem – be back for six p.m.,' I said.

That evening, I was reading in the lobby when the front door burst open. I saw one of our best players, Jo Paul Ancheri, weighed down by shopping bags. Behind him were another twenty players. Jo Paul is a legend – fantastic guy, super left foot, strong as you like – but I couldn't have this.

'Where have you been?' I asked him.

'Shopping!' he replied. 'There are so many things to buy in China.'

'And who gave you permission?' I asked. He started smiling.

'I'm not joking,' I continued. 'I gave permission to two players. The rest of you are fined.'

Jo Paul smiled again. 'The assistant coach gave us permission,' he said.

At that point the coach, V.P. Sathyan, piped up. 'That's right – I said they could,' he said.

'Well then, you're fined as well for not telling me,' I said.

I was in charge, and I needed to know where they were. As they walked back to their rooms, I'm sure one of them called me Kim Jong-il.

A week later, we played North Korea at home. We went one up, but they equalised with five minutes left. Our Asian Cup campaign was over after two games.

IN DEVELOPING COUNTRIES, IT'S HARD TO PRIORITISE SPORT. BUT it's even harder when one sport dominates the others.

Indian cricket has been well organised since the British introduced it. The team was successful, winning the World Cup in 1983, and success breeds success. In India, cricket gets a huge amount of sponsorship, television money and attention. Other sports live off scraps. But ambition can make up for a lack of cash.

Our kit was an embarrassment. It was made by a local company and it was awful: bad material, bad design, bad fit. It was out of date; like something bought from a market. Wearing a good kit doesn't make you a good player, but it sends a message. We are professional. We have standards.

Say a young kid is choosing between cricket and football. On the one hand, there is Sachin Tendulkar, beaming from every billboard, looking like a million dollars. On the other hand, there's us, dressed like Raggy Arse Rovers. No contest, is it? So, after the LG Cup, I went to see Alberto Colaco. I must say that, during my time in India, Alberto was brilliant. But he'd heard this one before.

'Who's our kit sponsor?' I asked. He sat there, hands on his belly, and laughed.

'No one is interested,' he said.

'Can I look?' I asked.

'By all means,' he said. 'But they're not interested.'

I contacted all the major manufacturers. Adidas were the only one to reply. They asked what we wanted, so I gave them a list as long as my arm: match kit, training kit, flip flops, everything. Even underwear. We had to choose colours for the shirts, so we went for sky blue and dark blue stripes.

Before the Afro-Asian Games in October 2003, about seventeen huge boxes arrived. The players tore into them like kids. At last, they were being treated like professionals. Some had tears in their eyes.

'No one has fought for us like this before,' our striker I.M. Vijayan told me. He'd been playing for India for a decade.

The Afro Asian Games were a big deal. More than 2,000 athletes from almost 100 countries took part, which made it – at the time – the biggest sporting event held in India (it was surpassed by the Commonwealth Games in 2010). The idea was to bring countries together – the slogan was 'two continents, one spirit' – and give athletes the chance to win medals without Europe and America muscling in. They were like the South Asian Games in Kathmandu, but on a bigger scale.

Before the tournament, some reporters criticised me for picking Vijayan, also known as the Black Pearl. 'He's too old,' they said. 'He's too slow. He drinks.'

These things were all true. The Pearl was at the end of his career. He was 34, looked older, and had already said he was retiring from the national team after the Games. So, no, he wasn't one for the future. But he could play.

I'd first seen him at the South Asian Games in 1999, where he'd finished top scorer. He came from a poor family in Kerala and, on the pitch, was aggressive. He was Indian player of the year three times in the 1990s. In 2001 – before I took the India job – I did an interview with the Hindustan Times, and asked about Vijayan. 'Can he still play?' I asked the reporter. 'Is he still fit?'

The answer was yes. Even though he was retiring, the Pearl was still shining. He was in my team.

Our first game was against Rwanda in Hyderabad. It poured with rain before kickoff so we used our state-of-the-art drying system: dozens of women went on to the pitch with rags and buckets and soaked up the water. It was an incredible sight, and they got the job done.

Despite the weather, the atmosphere was fantastic. Indians get behind their team, especially when they're doing well. Our team had a growing reputation. The fans knew we had a chance. They looked at the other sides in the Afro-Asian Games – teams like Zimbabwe and Burkina Faso – and thought, we might just do this. When we kicked off in Hyderabad, I couldn't hear myself think.

Rwanda were a good side – ranked 104 in the world, almost 30 places above us – but we started well. After thirteen minutes, a cross came in from the right. Vijayan, in his new Adidas shirt, tucked it away, then slid through the puddles to celebrate. He was 34 going on 14. We ended up winning 3–1.

Two days later we won 2–0 against Malaysia under-21s to make the semi-finals, with the Pearl scoring again. The semi-final was against Zimbabwe. They were ranked 48th in the world and went 1–0 up after four minutes. I thought we might get whacked but I needn't have worried. The Black Pearl equalised after 25 minutes, then scored another. I could have kissed him. In fact, I think I did.

We ended up winning 5–3, which was a heck of an achievement. When you're 130th in the world, the FIFA rankings can seem like the longest ladder in history. With all those teams ahead of you, getting in the top 100 looks impossible, never mind the top 50. Then you beat Zimbabwe, ranked 48th, and the ladder seems shorter. If we can beat them, you think, how high could we go?

In the final, Uzbekistan under-21s scored a long-range goal in the last minute to win 1–0. It was disappointing, but the silver medal was a decent result. The fans seemed pleased. We climbed five places in the rankings, to 128, and I was voted the AFC's manager of the month for October.

Overall, I was in a decent position. The senior team were improving and the juniors were doing well. That summer, I coached the under-18s at the Milk Cup in Northern Ireland, where we beat – among others – Dynamo Kiev and Kilmarnock, but lost to Preston North End and River Plate. The youngsters went straight to Wales and won the Ian Rush Trophy, beating Botafogo from Brazil 3–0 in the final.

But I knew the biggest challenge was to come. In 2004, we entered the biggest tournament on earth.

INDIA'S WORLD CUP RECORD IS NOT GLORIOUS. THEY HAVE never reached the finals and, before I took over, had won only seven matches in four qualifying campaigns.

We were drawn against Japan, Oman and Singapore in the first-round group. Only one team goes through and – seeing as Japan were ranked in the top twenty that year – it was impossible to qualify. But in the 2002 qualifiers, the team won three games (two against Brunei, one against the UAE), so we were expected to pick up points.

Our first game, and my first World Cup match, was against Singapore in Goa in February 2004. We won 1–0 – Renedy Singh scored a penalty just after half-time – and I started to dream. Our next game was a month later, at home to Oman in Kochi. If we won, the whole of Asia would notice. It was still impossible to qualify – we weren't ready to beat Japan – but it would send a message. Unfortunately, the Oman game was a disaster.

We prepared well and, for the first time, studied footage of our opponents before the game. In 2004, it wasn't easy to get – there was no YouTube for a start – but I got some DVDs from a contact. Sadly, it didn't work. In fact, I think watching Oman in full flight scared the players. In front of 57,000 people, we lost 5–1. Oman were ranked 68th, so should have beaten us, but not by that many.

We flew to Japan for our third game and I realised that – as a football team – we weren't respected. We stayed in a nice hotel near the ground in Saitama but, for our first meal, there were no tables. The food was laid out, but we were expected to pull up a chair from the edge of the room, sit down, and eat from a plate in our laps. For paying guests, it was unacceptable. For a team representing one billion people, it was far, far worse. I was furious. I asked the waiter to get the manager.

'It will seem like I've lost my temper,' I told my staff. 'But I am in control.'

When the manager arrived, I let rip.

'Who on earth do you think we are?' I yelled. 'You give us chairs but no tables. Do you think we are monkeys? We need tables, napkins, cutlery, bottles of water.'

Within ten minutes, around a dozen waiters – helped by the manager – were making things right.

It may seem like an over-reaction, but I was sick of being treated badly. I was sick of people thinking, it's only India. Let's say Brazil were staying at that hotel. Would they let them eat from their laps? There would be dancing girls in reception and a waiter for each player. We didn't even get a table.

On the pitch, I was planning for the future. There was no chance of reaching the 2006 World Cup so I wanted to build a team that could compete in five or ten years' time. That meant picking youngsters.

I called up a defender called Habibur Rehman Mondal, who was nineteen and still playing for the Tata Academy in Jamshedpur. Another teenager from the academy, Debabrata Roy, came on and did well. Picking young players is risky. They will make mistakes. But football is like any job: if you're not given a chance, you'll never learn. Both players went on to have good careers in Indian football.

Japan won 7–0 and taught my boys a lesson. But in fairness, my players never gave up. They kept running until the last minute. If we'd worked that hard against Oman, we could have won. Japan's manager was the Brazilian legend Zico. Afterwards, he said he was amazed by our spirit, which was nice to hear. But I was gloomy. Getting whacked 7–0 – even with a young team – is embarrassing.

The changing rooms were another reminder of our place in football's pecking order. The benches were fantastic. There was a 70-inch television on the wall. And next to the changing area was a huge space to stretch and warm up. It was built for the 2002 World Cup – England drew their first game against Sweden there – and it showed. Of course, changing rooms don't win you matches. But it showed a level of investment, and professionalism, that was light years ahead of India.

The criticism was growing. India were used to losing, but conceding twelve goals in two games wasn't good enough. It was three months before our next qualifier so in August we flew to Vietnam for the LG Cup – the tournament we had won in 2002.

We beat Myanmar in the first game, then lost 2–1 to the hosts. In the semi-final, we were beaten 4–0 by the South Korean Universities XI. They were a good side – they beat Vietnam in the final – but I flew home from Ho Chi Minh City in a dark mood.

Our next game was home to Japan. I feared a hiding, so I spent a lot of time working on our defence. Technically, we couldn't reach their level – they did everything quicker than us – but we could frustrate them. We had to keep our shape and snap into tackles. The night before, I showed the players Miracle – a film about the United States ice hockey team, made up of amateur players, who beat the Soviet Union in the 1980 Winter Olympics. We were allowed to dream, at least.

The game was in Calcutta, a real football city, and more than 90,000 fans turned up. More were locked outside. It was an amazing sight. I was so pleased that, even after losing to Japan and Oman, the fans came to support us. It was a reminder of India's potential. If almost 100,000 turn up for a dead rubber in the first round of qualifying, what would happen if we reached the World Cup finals?

The fans lifted the players, and we held Japan until the last minute of the first half. The second half was delayed for ten minutes because of floodlight failure, and we ended up losing 4–0. It wasn't a miracle, but it wasn't a disgrace, either. A few fans moaned, but most of the 90,000 knew Japan were on a different level. They had drawn 1–1 against England in Manchester three months earlier.

I picked a young team for our fifth game, which we lost 2–0 away to Singapore, before we flew to Kuwait for a friendly in November. We won 3–2, which was a big upset, and in our final qualifier we drew 0–0 against Oman.

In a way, they were frustrating results. They showed that – if we didn't make mistakes – we were a decent side. The draw in Oman also meant we didn't finish bottom of the group, which was nice. But after beating Singapore in our first game in February, I was dreaming. I thought we could surpass any Indian team in history. Instead, the table looked like this:

	P	W	D	L	Points
Japan	6	6	0	0	18
Oman	6	3	1	2	10
India	6	1	1	4	4
Singapore	6	1	0	5	3

It was – at best – OK. I wanted much more.

SOME YEARS LATER, I SPOKE TO ALBERTO COLACO ABOUT MY first spell as India manager.

'You know,' he said with a smile, 'some of the federation wanted you sacked after a year. You upset too many people. You ruffled too many feathers. I was the one who fought your corner.'

It didn't surprise me. I cared about the team, and the fans they represented. I wasn't interested in charming the blazers.

On our early trips abroad, the federation would often send a 'leader of the delegation' or a 'chef de mission'. To me, they were tourists and nothing more. Some would try to come into the dressing room and speak to the players, which I wouldn't allow. Others would touch down, get whisked away in a nice car, and then reappear for the flight home. Either way, they weren't needed. I'd rather take another player than a politician. If there's money, let's spend it on the squad, not a tourist.

Looking back, it was results that saved me. The federation couldn't sack the manager who lifted the LG Cup, or who won two out of three in the Asian Games, or who won the silver medal at the Afro-Asian Games. And crucially, the players were on my side. One of them, Shanmugam Venkatesh, became my assistant manager in my second spell, while Abhishek Yadav – who headed the winner against Vietnam in the last minute of the LG Cup final – became my director of scouting.

My contract finished in 2005. They asked me to stay but on less money. It wasn't exactly an endorsement. With half the federation against me, it was the right time to leave. To be honest, even if they'd offered the same money, I would have left. I felt I had done my bit. It was time to go.

When I started, the players were expected to sleep in grandstands. We caught the train to training camps. We played in two-dollar shirts. When I left, we stayed in nice hotels, flew to games, and had major brands supplying our kit (Nike took over from Adidas in 2005). I even helped set up a players' trade union, the Football Players' Association of India, getting advice from the PFA in England.

At the start of my career, I sometimes felt like an imposter. Occasionally, I thought someone would wake me up and say: 'National team coach? Stop dreaming, son.' Look, I never doubted my ability. From my first course in the US, I knew I could coach. But I feared things were too good to be true.

By the time I left India, that had gone. I had done five years as a national coach. I had led two countries. I had worked with, and against, some of the best players in Asia. I belonged.

On the day we left, half the Indian team came to our hotel in Mumbai to see us off. It was a lovely touch. As we flew west, I was ready to achieve my ambition: a job in England. I knew I could survive – and thrive – at that level.

Persuading other people was a different matter.

6
INTO THE LIONS' DEN
MILLWALL, 2005–06

WHEN I SPEAK TO A JOURNALIST, OR A FAN, I KNOW A CERTAIN question is coming. Sometimes it's the first question; sometimes it's the last. But it will be asked. I don't mind – it's an obvious question, which I'd ask myself – but I must have heard it two or three thousand times. Maybe more.

'Do you want a job in England?'

After leaving India in 2005, my answer was: where do I sign? There were two reasons.

Firstly: it's home. It's where my roots are. I like the place, I like the people, and I speak the language, just about.

Secondly: the football is fantastic. OK, the national team hasn't done well. But which other country supports five national leagues, with more than a hundred full-time teams? We pay on time (more or less), we don't cheat, and the matches are exciting.

I started applying for English jobs after I got my FA Full Badge in 1996. By the time I left Nepal, I was relentless. If I read that a manager had left a Football League club, that was it: I faxed or emailed my CV. I must have applied to half the full-time teams in England. In 2001, I gave an interview to ESPN, and said I'd applied to Plymouth, Oxford, Southend, Huddersfield, Luton, Brentford, Wolves, Norwich and Barnsley. Only Norwich replied. They said they were appointing Nigel Worthington.

I was fighting for jobs with one arm behind my back. Because I hadn't played in the Football League, I wasn't known, and – as I soon realised – chairmen like appointing people they know. It's human nature: if the manager goes, they give the job to the captain or the popular former centre-half. Most fans won't mind, but they're not recruiting the best. They're recruiting the best that they know.

I spent a long time – and a lot of money – learning my trade. Doing the UEFA Pro Licence, via the FA, cost me £10,000. I flew back four or five times from India at my own expense. I spent ages in the classroom, and even longer on the training pitch (I studied alongside Steve McClaren, Mark Hughes, Peter Reid and Joe Jordan, among others). But not everyone respects the qualification. You wouldn't employ a doctor without a medical degree, but football clubs don't use the same logic.

In 2006, McClaren left Middlesbrough to become England manager. Boro were a Premier League team and could have picked from 99.9 percent of managers around the world. Instead they chose their captain, Gareth Southgate. He didn't even have the Pro Licence, which broke the league's own rules (he was given an exemption).

When you've spent years doing those courses – in my case, flying halfway round the world – that's a kick in the teeth. We're told, over and over again, that they're crucial. We're told we can't work without them. Then an ex-professional player skips the queue.

In 2009, Southgate took Middlesbrough down and was sacked. Afterwards, he admitted he shouldn't have got the job so soon. 'The ideal scenario is that you start with kids,' he said. 'You can learn with a little less pressure and try things in training sessions. There's not a perfect pathway but, in an ideal world, you wouldn't be a first-team manager first time out.' I could have told him that in 2006.

It's not just him. Dozens of players have become managers too soon. In 2008, the former England player Paul Ince was given the Blackburn Rovers job without even the B Licence. Five years later, the ex-England striker James Beattie became manager of Accrington Stanley, despite being similarly unqualified.

I'm not having a go at these guys. They were great players, but coaching is a different skill. You can't wing it, just like you can't wing other professions. The Pro Licence alone involves 240 hours of study. When ex-players get top jobs regardless, you wonder if you're wasting your time.

I became used to hearing 'no'. In May 2005, after leaving India, I applied to Dunfermline Athletic. They were bottom of the Scottish Premier League and had just sacked their manager, David Hay. I was in Greece when their chairman, John Yorkston, called me. He sounded keen, and asked me to fly back for an interview with the director of football, Jim Leishman. I felt a burst of excitement.

After landing at Gatwick, my phone rang. It was Leishman.

'We've just been told we have to tear up our artificial pitch,' he said. 'It's blown a massive hole in our budget for next season. We liked your CV but we're going to have to cancel the interview.'

The next day, Leishman was given the manager's job. I went back to the fax machine.

Before being rejected by Dunfermline, I applied for the Millwall job, where I'd gone on trial as a teenager in the 1970s. They were a good club, comfortable in the second tier, and weren't too far from my family's base in Brighton. It would have been perfect. I wasn't optimistic – would you, after being turned down as often as me? – but in June I got a call from the chairman, Jeff Burnige.

'We're speaking to one other person, and that person is Steve Claridge,' he said. 'So here's a hypothetical question. We give you the job. On Monday morning, six players turn up at your office, and say they want to leave the club. How would you react?'

'If they don't want to play for Millwall, they can get on their bike,' I replied.

'That's interesting,' said Burnige. 'Steve Claridge would persuade them to stay.'

'Perhaps he would,' I replied. 'But I want people who want to play for Millwall.'

Unsurprisingly, Claridge – who had two good seasons as a Millwall player from 2001 to 2003 – got the job. More surprisingly, he was sacked just 36 days into a two-year contract. He was replaced by Colin Lee, but by September, they had one point from six games. Burnige called me again.

'Would you be interested in becoming first-team coach, to help Colin Lee?' he asked.

'Where do I sign?' I replied.

The final decision was Colin's. Jeff gave him my CV and, a few days later, Colin invited me to the training ground. We spoke for five hours about my CV, my experience and my opinions on the game. It went well. When the meeting finished, he told me to watch their next game – at home to Preston on Saturday – then report back on Monday.

I watched the game – Millwall lost 2–1 – and turned up on Monday with my notes.

'Interesting stuff,' said Colin. I smiled. Finally, it seemed, I was getting a job in English football.

'We'll give you a month's trial.'

My heart sank. It is very rare – unheard of, even – for experienced, well-qualified coaches to be given a one-month trial. But I couldn't say no. I was unemployed and desperate for a chance.

Before I left, Colin asked me something else.

'How do you see this working?' he said.

'You're the gaffer,' I replied. 'I'll do what you need me to do.'

It was a strange question. A confident manager with a clear, thought-out strategy would know exactly what he wanted. He was the boss, after all. But still: I was in. Four months after leaving India, and thirteen years after leaving America, I had a full-time job in the top end of English football.

I MUST HAVE BEEN THE WORST-PAID FIRST-TEAM COACH IN THE Championship. My salary was £35,000 a year, so we couldn't afford to move to London. Instead, I drove sixty miles every day from Lucy's parents' house to Bromley, where Millwall trained. I'd leave home at seven in the morning, arrive at eight-thirty, have a slice of toast, plan the session, then wait for the players to arrive at nine-thirty.

At first, I borrowed a car from my old friend Roger Unwin, a former RAF navigator who I met in Cyprus years earlier. Roger was a gem, and a very good coach. Lucy and I spent many happy times with him and his wife, Heather. But the car he lent me was a banger.

Knowing the players would take the piss, I parked the car under a huge oak tree. With the front half covered in branches, only the back end was visible. No one will notice that, I thought.

Some hope.

'What the fuck is that parked in the tree?' asked assistant manager David Tuttle, looking out of his office window.

'Where, Tutts?' I asked, feigning ignorance.

'That thing in the fucking tree!' said Tutts, pissing himself.

'It must be the groundsman's,' I said, while making a mental note to leave Roger's car at home. I got the train for the next couple of days, then bought myself a Volkswagen Passat 1.9.

In the office, there was a good-luck message from an old friend, Chris Kamara. I met Chris in Cyprus in the 1990s. He was Bradford City manager and his assistant, Martin Hunter, had delivered some of my courses. So, when Chris and Martin brought their families to Cyprus on holiday, I showed them round.

We saw the sights, went banana boating, things like that. Chris is fantastic company – he has the same energy in real life as on TV – and his message that morning was a touch of class.

On the pitch, Colin introduced me to the players. He gave me a fantastic build-up, stressing my qualifications and my time in Nepal and India. After watching the Preston game, I knew Millwall had some good, hard-working players, but they weren't organised, and they gave away soft goals. Straight away, I did a four-v-four defensive drill, showing the players when to press and when to drop off. Afterwards, the left-back Jamie Vincent came up to me.

'That was absolutely outstanding,' he said. 'We need more of that.'

Our first game was away to Wolves on the Tuesday. At first, Colin was happy to hear my ideas. I knew Wolves' Darren Anderton used to sit behind the strikers and pull the strings, so I suggested playing a midfield diamond. Alan Dunne, a young Irish defender, could sit deep and hassle Anderton. Jody Morris – who could really pick a pass – could play further forward. Colin agreed.

I'd been to Molineux before, when India played against Jamaica, but this was different. The ground was buzzing. The floodlights were on. The 20,000 fans were noisy. Wolves took the lead after nineteen minutes through Carl Cort, but Jermaine Wright equalised eight minutes later. It looked like ending in a draw, which would have been a good result. Then in the last minute, our big striker Barry Hayles got the winner. Our bench went berserk. After eight games, we had finally won. It was a fantastic moment.

Wolves was the start of a seven-match unbeaten run. We beat Sheffield Wednesday away, won at Yeovil in the League Cup, then drew four in a row in the league. It wasn't until mid-October – five weeks after I arrived – that I saw us lose. Of course, they might have gone seven unbeaten without me. They might have won all seven – who knows? But I think I helped to improve them. Our defence was certainly stronger, and we looked better without the ball. We were harder to break down.

When I started at Millwall, I was nervous. There were some big characters in the squad. Don Hutchison played for Liverpool and Everton and had twenty-odd caps for Scotland. Carl Asaba had been a pro for more than ten years. Dave Livermore and Matty Lawrence weren't afraid to make themselves heard. But if I showed my nerves, I was finished. They would eat me alive. On the training ground, I had to project confidence, then trust the qualifications I'd worked so hard to get.

After most sessions, I would speak to some of the experienced pros, like Hayles or Livermore. 'How was it?' I would ask. 'If you think it's shit, I have to know.' They had no complaints. Some players would always moan – it's the English way – but there was only one bust-up. Lawrence – who was a bright kid, with a degree from Hartwick College in New York state – didn't like one of my drills.

'What the fuck are we doing this for?' he yelled. He had been at Millwall five years and was flexing his muscles. I couldn't back down.

'If you don't like it, fuck off,' I said. So he did. I found him afterwards.

'I am thirty-something,' he told me. 'I have had the life coached out of me. I just want to tick over – not all these bloody sessions.'

Actually, I knew what he meant. In England – compared to other countries – players have the life coached out of them. From the age of six or seven they're being told what to do. 'Do it like this, don't do it like that.' It's continuous. We don't let them play. We don't let them think.

When I worked at Bournemouth, we spent the first twenty minutes of a session coaching technique. The second twenty minutes, we coached them in a game. And the last twenty minutes, we let them play. We wouldn't say a word. I love improving players – it's why the coach is there – but often it needs a word or two, not a lecture. Matty and I shook hands, and there were no problems after that.

At first, I ran 75 per cent of the sessions while Colin and Dave Tuttle watched on. The players knew I was on a month's trial and, if they liked a drill, would shout: 'Sign him up, gaffer!' Colin took the hint and, in mid-October, extended my contract. It was only until the end of May, which was strange – contracts normally run until the end of June – but it was another step forward.

After the unbeaten run, we lost 4–0 to Sheffield United, then 2–0 to Southampton (Theo Walcott got their first, intercepting a back-pass). When we played Burnley away at the start of November, we hadn't won in the league for six weeks. In the hotel before the game, Colin pulled me into his room.

'We've had some complaints about your sessions,' he said. I was amazed.

'Really?' I said. 'From who?'

'I can't tell you that,' he replied. 'But I'm going to take you out of the firing line. From now on, I'll do more of the sessions.'

I never saw it coming: I ran all my sessions past Colin and the players seemed to like them. I have no idea why I was 'taken out of the firing line'. Perhaps he was covering his own back after a bad run.

We had three players sent off at Burnley and lost 2–1. At training on Monday, Colin said he wanted to work with sixteen players. He sent the rest of the first-team squad to train with me.

'What am I supposed to do with five players?' I asked.

'You're the coach – do something technical,' he replied.

Until then, I got on with Colin. I picked him up before training. He took me to an awards night in London. Once, I even stayed at his house. And there's no doubt he was a good coach. He played for Spurs and Chelsea, and managed Wolves, Walsall and Torquay, so he knew what he was doing. I learned plenty from him. But – as I realised after Burnley – his man-management wasn't great.

In my opinion, you should treat every player individually. Some need their confidence building; others you have to keep an eye on. But Colin was abrupt with everyone. There was no rapport with the players. He wasn't admired or feared. Really, there was no relationship at all.

I was in Colin's office when he called our Irish winger, Barry Cogan, in for a chat. Barry wasn't fulfilling his potential – as a youngster he was labelled the next George Best – and Colin wanted to buck his ideas up. But instead of coming into the office, Barry leaned on the doorframe with his hands in his pockets, while Colin spoke. Afterwards, Colin asked how I would have handled it.

'For a start, I wouldn't have let him lean in the doorway,' I said. 'You're the manager. You deserve respect. He can sit down like an adult, or he can clear off.'

Once, I asked Barry if he wanted to stay behind for extra work.

'No thanks, I'm good,' he replied.

'What is it you feel you're good at?' I persisted.

'I'm quick, I can whip a cross in,' he said.

'OK,' I said. 'Let's work on that.' He agreed.

I set up a drill where we played a one-two, then he whipped in a cross. There was a mannequin in front of the six-yard box, and an area marked out behind. He must have put 25 crosses in.

'How many times did you beat the mannequin and hit the area?' I asked him.

'Dunno – seven or eight?' he answered.

'That's why you're not in the first team,' I said.

'Ah, fuck off, Steve,' he replied.

I just laughed. I'm not picking on Barry – he was young, and plenty of his contemporaries had the same attitude – but if you want a long career, you have to put the work in. Barry fell through the divisions and was playing non-league football three years later. I think he could have done better.

A month after the Burnley game we played Birmingham at home in the League Cup fourth round. It was a big match – they were in the Premier League and if we won, we were in the quarter-finals. The club had a new chairman, Peter de Savary, who made his millions in the oil and shipping industries. Before the Birmingham game, he walked into the dressing room and spoke to the players.

'If we win, I will take you to my resort in the Bahamas,' he said. He obviously wanted to impress the boys; to show them the new chairman was a big shot. Then, when he had their attention, he did the strangest thing. He took a bag, tipped it upside down, and emptied £10,000 on to the floor.

'And here's a bit of spending money for the trip!' he said, as the notes fell on to the tiles.

We drew the match 2–2 so it went to penalties. Ben May and Barry Hayles missed, we lost 4–3, and there went our Caribbean holiday. I'm sure the players would have enjoyed the trip, but I doubt they worried about the cash. If you're on £8,000 or £9,000 a week, a few hundred quid is lunch money.

For example: after games, the players had an ice bath. One time, I told Barry

Hayles to get in.

'I'm Jamaican,' he said. 'Jamaicans don't get in ice.'

'Barry,' I said, smiling, 'it's a £250 fine if you don't.'

'Let me get you the money then,' he said. He paid the fine and never got in. The following week, I upped the fine to £500, so he changed his mind.

WE WERE OUT OF THE CUP, BOTTOM OF THE LEAGUE, AND Colin was under pressure. Twice, he cleared his desk and said he was quitting.

While he filled the boot of his car, I took things back to his office and persuaded him to stay. He gave me a chance at Millwall – which I will always be grateful for – and I felt some loyalty. But he couldn't last. At our Christmas party, Colin told us he was quitting to become director of football. Dave Tuttle became Millwall's fourth manager of 2005.

When Colin stepped down, he told the press: 'I'm a perfectionist who finds it difficult to relax at certain times. David is more laid-back.' That was one way of putting it. The Guardian called Colin a sergeant-major, which was more like it. Despite not being manager, Colin kept his office in Bromley, which didn't go down well with Tutts or anyone else. My status was also unclear.

Tuttle's first game as manager was away to Leicester on Boxing Day – we drew 1–1 – but Colin sent me scouting. 'We're changing your role slightly,' he said. For the next game against Watford, two days later, I was sent scouting again. While I was driving to the match, my phone went. It was Tutts.

'Oi,' he said, with his usual bluntness. 'Where the fuck are you?'

'Colin told me to scout a player,' I said.

'I'm the fucking manager and I want you here,' Tuttle replied. 'Turn the car round now. I want you to look at things from up-top.'

The third game of the Christmas period was away to Brighton on New Year's Eve. For me, it was a home game. But Colin had other ideas.

'I want you to watch a player at Brentford,' he said.

'But we're away to Brighton – I live in Brighton,' I replied.

'I want the report on my desk on Monday morning,' he said.

Like a good employee, I did the 130-mile round trip to Brentford, then filed my report first thing on Monday. I'm not sure Colin even read it.

To this day, I don't know why he went off me. Maybe it was the pressure of the job. Perhaps he didn't rate me, even though he appointed me in September, and extended my contract a month later. Either way, life was easier with David Tuttle in charge. With Colin keeping his office, the atmosphere around the building was strange. But on the training pitch, it changed totally.

Tutts was a lovely guy; an old-school character who always cracked jokes (he used to call Colin the Grim Reaper, as he normally wore all black). He was unbeaten after three games and at Brighton – while I was scouting at Brentford – he made a triple substitution at half-time and won 2–1. I was back in the dressing room for the home game against Derby on 2 January and Tutts was buzzing.

After the game, we were due to travel to Bovey Castle in Devon for a team-building break. The castle had been turned into a hotel and was owned by our new chairman Mr de Savary. I sat in the corner of the dressing room, my usual position, and waited for Tutts' team talk.

'Right, lads,' he said. 'You've been brilliant since I took over. We're on a great run. We've got a piss-up in Devon to look forward to, but first we're going to take care of Derby. This is what I want.'

He was standing next to a flip chart and turned over the cover. I was expecting some tactics: a set-piece routine perhaps, or a formation. Instead, in massive letters, was the following:

'SIX CASES OF STELLA. SIX CASES OF BUDWEISER. A BOTTLE OF THE BEST BRANDY.'

And then, in small writing at the bottom:

'And a Coke for the cunt who doesn't drink.'

That was me, by the way.

The players were pissing themselves. Some of them were on the floor. As laughter bounced off the dressing room walls, Tutts came up to me with his hands in his pockets and a grin from ear to ear.

'You don't get that on your Pro Licence, do you, son!' he said, and walked off.

We came from 1–0 down to beat Derby 2–1 and, by the time we hit the M25, the booze was flowing. Although I don't drink, I don't mind the players enjoying themselves. They had played four games in eight days and deserved to relax. As the party bus headed west, I spoke to Matty Lawrence.

'Please be honest,' I said. 'Did you or anyone else complain to Colin about my coaching?'

'There was one drill I didn't like, which I told you about at the time,' said Matty.

'Anything else?' I asked.

'No fucking way,' he replied. 'No one even spoke to the manager.'

After we got back from Devon, we drew 1–1 against Everton in the FA Cup. The replay was ten days later on a Wednesday night at Goodison Park. I remember doing the warm-up under the floodlights. As I watched the stands fill up, and heard the buzz of the crowd, I thought, this is fantastic. For me, it was what dreams were made of. As a boy, this was what I wanted.

Tutts and his assistant, Tony Burns, treated me well. After we got back from Bovey Castle, he pulled me into his office.

'I'm the manager, you're the first-team coach,' said Tutts. 'No one has a problem with you. Do the sessions like you used to. I decide what you do, not Colin Lee. Have you got that?'

My relationship with Colin wasn't a problem for much longer: he left the club at the end of January. At the same time, Tutts was confirmed as manager until the end of the season, with the promise of a three-year contract if we stayed up. He offered me the same deal. It was a fantastic offer, which I would have gladly accepted. I liked working for him and Burnsy. Now, we just needed to stay up.

Our biggest problem was scoring goals. After beating Derby on 2 January, we scored once in our next five league games. We spent £125,000 on a Dutch striker, Berry Powel. He came from Den Bosch in the Dutch second division but he was nowhere near Championship level. He wasn't Tutts' choice, or mine, so it must have been a boardroom decision. He scored three minutes into his debut at Cardiff, but never scored again. He went back to Holland in the summer.

Before he left, I told Colin that Arturo Lupoli, Arsenal's young Italian striker, might be available on loan. Lupoli was scoring tons for Arsenal reserves but wasn't ready for their first team. At first, Colin didn't take any notice. But, as the deadline approached, he changed his mind.

'Call your mate Arsene,' he told me. 'See if you can get Lupoli.'

I had met Arsene Wenger a couple of years earlier, while visiting England for my Pro Licence. Arsenal's media man, Andy Exley, arranged a fifteen-minute chat with him at their training ground, London Colney.

'Pleased to meet you, Mr Wenger,' I said. 'I am Stephen Constantine, the Indian national team manager.'

'I know all about you,' he said. 'If you'd done in Europe what you've done in Asia, you would be coaching in the Champions League by now.'

We ended up talking for 45 minutes. When our conversation ended, he asked where I was going.

'Back to Brighton,' I replied.

'Stay and watch training if you have time,' he said. I didn't need to be asked twice.

I stood on the touchline with Arsene and watched Thierry Henry, Patrick Vieira and Robert Pires fizz it round.

'Are you not tempted to join in?' I asked.

'Look at it!' he replied, as the passes got quicker and quicker. 'It's not possible.'

When I called Arsene about Lupoli he remembered me straight away.

'I have three questions,' I said. 'One: would we be able to take Lupoli on loan?'

'It's London, so we can see him often,' he said, thinking out loud. 'If he's interested – why not?'

'My second question – can I get two tickets for the Real Madrid game in March?'

'Call me closer to the time,' he replied.

'Finally,' I asked, 'can I be your assistant?'

We both laughed.

'You know the policy, Stephen,' he said. 'I only take former Arsenal players.'

'But Mr Wenger,' I replied, 'I have played many times for Arsenal in my dreams.'

We both laughed again. Unfortunately, Millwall couldn't get the Lupoli deal done before the deadline. Instead, we tried to sign the French striker, Vincent Pericard, on loan from Portsmouth. He wanted to come, but the board couldn't wrap it up, so he went to our Championship rivals, Plymouth Argyle. Two weeks later he scored a hat-trick in a 3–1 win at home to Coventry. With no one in his class, we slipped further from safety.

In February we played Sheffield Wednesday at home. They were near the bottom, so it was a huge game. In the second half, Tony Craig took a corner that swung into the net. The fans roared, the ref gave the goal, and the players sprinted across to celebrate with Tony. The problem was, the ref didn't give the goal: he was actually signalling for a free kick. As I screamed at the players to get back, Wednesday ran down the other end and scored. It summed up Millwall's season. Total chaos.

The players lost their confidence. Every defeat made things worse. Simple things – passing, crossing, marking – became hard. In March the club appointed Ray Wilkins as a consultant. He was good to me – he extended my contract until the end of June, for one – but he couldn't turn things round.

After the fantastic run over Christmas, we didn't win again until March, when Marvin Williams got a last-minute winner against Luton. On 17 April we lost 2–0 to Southampton – who played a young Gareth Bale – and were relegated. Tutts resigned, with Burnsy and Alan McLeary taking over for the final two games of the season. My race, though, was already run.

Two days before the Southampton game we played Plymouth at home. I was leading the warm-up when Mark Phillips cleared the ball into my hand and broke my finger. I drove to hospital on the way home. The doctor tried to realign the bone, but – after half an hour – realised I needed surgery.

I missed the end of the season and, a few weeks later, got my P45 in the post, confirming the end of my employment. There was no letter or call from the club. I thought the manager, or someone else at the club, might have called to say thank you. But that's football.

EVEN FOR AN ENGLISHMAN – AND A LONDONER – MY SEASON AT
Millwall was a culture shock. Apart from my spell at Bournemouth and Chichester,
I'd lived abroad for more than twenty years. In India, people respect the title, rather
than the person holding it. So if you're the national team manager, that's it – you're
respected. Sure, if you're useless, you lose it. But you start in credit.

In England, it's the other way round. Without a reputation, you start with nothing. You have to earn respect.

In India, people called me 'sir'. When I arrived at Millwall, it was: 'Who the fuck
are you?' Before the Burnley game in November, I came into the dressing room and
saw a picture of a skeleton. When I looked closer, it had my head Photoshopped on.
The players found it hilarious – I think Don Hutchison was behind it – and I didn't
mind. It was banter. But it would never happen in India.

At Millwall, even the kit man, Roy Putt, tried to test me. He'd put out everyone's
kit except mine. When I asked where it was, he'd say, 'In the tumble dryer. Get it
yourself.' Other times, my socks would be missing, or my shorts. It went on for
weeks until I put him in a headlock on the bus to Norwich in October.

'What's your problem, you old bastard!' I asked, being semi-serious.

'Steve, I'm only fucking about with you,' he said, half laughing, half choking.

After that, Roy was as good as gold. I think he wanted to see what I was made of.
When I went back to Cyprus, I even brought him back him some cigarettes.

The players – bar none – were fine with me. People like Dave Livermore, Mark
Phillips, Ben May and Paul Robinson were fantastic professionals. But not everyone
had their intensity. In the first half of the season, some players let their opinion of
Colin affect their training. They moaned and took the piss, rather than work their
socks off. After Colin left, Jody Morris spoke to me in the car park.

'Have you not left yet?' he asked.

'Why would I have left?' I replied.

'Your Colin Lee's boy, aren't you?' he said.

'Jody, I met Colin five months ago,' I said. 'I didn't know him before then.' Jody
looked surprised.

'Well, I guess we owe you an apology,' he said. 'We thought you were his boy.'

Overall, Millwall was a fantastic experience. There's a framed Millwall shirt in my
office, signed by all the players, and I still look out for their results. I'm grateful to
Colin for the opportunity, and to the fans for their support. They were superb, even
when the team wasn't. If we'd been as good as them, we'd have stayed up. One day,
I'd love to go back to the Den as manager.

I drove the Passat from Bromley to Brighton one last time. I was unemployed,
with three kids – Isabel had just arrived – living at my wife's parents' house. I am an
optimist at heart. Over the next six months I needed to be.

7
FROM MILLWALL TO MALAWI
MALAWI, 2007–08

IN OUR FINAL YEAR IN INDIA, LUCY AND I DECIDED WE NEEDED A base. We couldn't keep staying at her mother's in Brighton. We knew football would take me around the world, but the girls needed somewhere to call home. As I know, it's no good changing schools every five minutes.

We looked for somewhere on the south coast, but the houses were too expensive. We needed room for three kids but we couldn't afford it. Instead, we thought about Cyprus. Property was cheaper, and the girls could go to the Grammar School in Limassol, run by my old friends Nick and Deme.

After one of my trips to England for my Pro Licence course, I went to Cyprus to look for a house. We had one rule: we wouldn't build it ourselves. Unless you're on top of the builders, they shaft you left, right and centre. I saw twelve houses in three days but didn't love any of them. While I was there, I met an old colleague from the Grammar School, who invited me to his place. It was fantastic.

'How did you find this?' I asked.

'We built it ourselves,' he replied.

I spoke to his builder, who showed me three bits of land. One was on a hill above Limassol, with amazing views of the city and the sky-blue Mediterranean. There was nothing else around.

'I'll have it,' I said.

I went back to India with a topographic map. A splash of yellow marked our new home.

'There's your house,' I told Lucy. She went mad.

'You never listen,' she cried. 'I thought we were going to find something already built?'

When the shock wore off a few months later, we went to Cyprus to find the plot. When she saw it, she loved it. It's still our base and, although we've got more neighbours now, we can still see the sea. It's a beautiful place to live, and Nick and his family live within walking distance, which is a bonus.

The house was ready in the summer of 2006, after I finished with Millwall. The problem was paying the mortgage. I thought a year in the Championship – alongside five years of coaching national teams – gave me a good chance of a Football League job. I was wrong.

The Brighton job came up; it went to former Brighton player Dean Wilkins. The Bournemouth job came up; it went to former Bournemouth player Kevin Bond. The QPR job came up; it went to former QPR player John Gregory. The Norwich job came up; it went to former Norwich player – and my friend from Bournemouth – Peter Grant. I was banging on the door but no one was listening.

If someone had said, 'Leave Millwall in April, you'll have a new job in September,' I would have been fine. But if there's no end in sight, all you can think is: When? When will I get a job? When will I get a chance? Unless you've been unemployed, it's hard to imagine. But it's stressful. You doubt yourself. You become desperate. You consider jobs that, two months earlier, you wouldn't dream of touching.

I applied for jobs in Cyprus but got nowhere. I did some part-time work at the Grammar School in Limassol, and wondered if I should ask for a full-time role. The low point was when I applied to Walton & Hersham.

They were a part-time side near London, playing in the Isthmian Premier League, the seventh tier in English football. The former Millwall chairman, Theo Paphitis, was an investor, so I thought he'd put a word in. I spoke to his right-hand man, Kypros Kyprianou, but he said Theo wasn't involved day-to-day. Even so, I sent them my CV. This was nailed on, surely.

Clearly, I didn't want to work in the Isthmian Premier League. But Walton & Hersham were on the ladder, even if they were bottom rung. If I did well, I could move to a full-time team in the Conference. From there, you're one step away from the Football League. It was a start.

I thought they'd bite my hand off. Which non-league team wouldn't want an ex-national team coach with a Pro Licence? I waited days – weeks, maybe – but heard nothing. Eventually, they called back. They said I was overqualified. Instead, they appointed Bobby Paterson, a former Gillingham coach. Looking back, it was for the best: leaving our new house in Cyprus for a part-time job in England would have tested even Lucy's patience. But I would have taken it. That's how desperate I was.

After leaving Millwall, I spoke to Jane Bateman, the head of international relations at the FA, who I knew from my time in Nepal and India. She told me that Malawi were looking for a manager. I preferred to stay in England, but I asked her to pass on my CV.

The previous manager – a German called Burkhard Ziese, who managed national sides all over Asia and Africa – was sacked in September after falling out with the Malawi FA. At his final training session, according to the BBC, he was 'manhandled' by angry fans and suffered minor injuries. As I said, I preferred to stay in England.

At the end of the year I received a phone call. It was Walter Nyamilandu, the president of the Football Association of Malawi.

'We've heard lots of good things about you,' he said in his baritone voice. 'Please come to Blantyre for an interview.'

Perhaps Malawi would see something that Walton & Hersham didn't. I told Walter I'd see him in February.

The FAM narrowed it down to two people: me, and a Brazilian called Carlos Alberto da Luz. He had an impressive CV. He worked with the Brazilian national team in the 1990s, coached their under-23s, and had managed countries around the world, from Oman to Panama. I flew from Cyprus to Cairo, then down to Malawi. Although Lilongwe is the capital, the FAM offices were in Blantyre, the commercial capital in the south of the country. It was my first trip to southern Africa.

After I arrived, the FAM told us the interview was in two parts: a normal interview, then a practical session with their under-23s. Luckily, I'd brought my kit. Mr da Luz wasn't so fortunate. He did his session in his suit. 'I came here for an interview, not a training session,' he said, pissed off.

For the interview, I gave a PowerPoint presentation. I still have the slides. They weren't mind-blowing, but they were a cue; a way to organise my thoughts. The first said: 'Why I am the coach to lead you forward'; the last was called: 'The winning mentality'. Other slides had my CV, or my philosophy. One bullet point said: 'Disciplined, hard, but fair.' As it turned out, I'd need to be.

I ran my training session like I was still in India: warm-up, five versus two, attacking drill, defensive drill. It was sharp. The association liked it. Afterwards their technical director spoke to me.

'Very impressive,' he said. 'I think you've got the job.'

'How do you know?' I asked.

'I know,' he said.

I left Blantyre on the same flight as Mr da Luz. He was a gentleman, and we had a good chat. 'If I don't get it, I wish you well,' he said. As soon as I landed in Cyprus, my phone went. It was Walter Nyamilandu, offering me the job. I was delighted to accept.

'Lucy,' I said, as I walked through the door in Limassol, 'we are back in business.'

'Steve,' she replied, 'we are not moving to Malawi.'

We had gone to Nepal with one daughter, and left with two. We went to India with two, and came back with three. The thought of a fourth, perhaps, was too much.

ALTHOUGH WE MOVED TO CYPRUS IN SUMMER 2006, WE STILL hadn't unpacked by New Year. Our container took weeks to arrive from England, and then spent ages in customs. For a long time, we had no furniture. When the container did arrive, there were 160 boxes. We were still opening them when I flew to Blantyre for the interview. Just as the house became home, I moved to Malawi.

It's hard moving 5,000 miles from your family. Some nights – some days, actually – it's painful. But compared to what Lucy does, it's a piece of cake. While I chased my dream, she unpacked boxes. There was no family in Cyprus. No support. All Lucy had was three daughters and a husband in a different hemisphere. I can't imagine how she coped. What she does for me and the girls is awesome. Without her, there would be no career, and no book. I would have nothing.

As Lucy said, moving the family to Malawi was not an option. The girls needed a base. And besides – as we knew from India – I wouldn't be there much. National managers aren't normally home for tea. So I either left the girls behind, or I commuted from Cyprus, flying in for training camps and matches.

Plenty of Europeans do it. In October 2007, I went to Ivory Coast for a course and watched a top-division game in Abidjan. I sat next to Uli Stielike, the former West Germany midfielder. He has coached all over the world – from South Korea to Qatar – and, at the time, managed Ivory Coast.

'Do you come here often?' I asked.

'Not really,' he replied. 'It's the African Cup of Nations draw tomorrow – that's the only reason I'm in Abidjan. All of my squad play in Europe. Why would I live here?'

It's a decent argument. But for me, if you're the national manager, you should live in that nation, at least part of the time. OK, if you're the Ivory Coast boss, you need to watch European matches. Having a place in London, say, makes sense. But unless you're watching the local league, how do you find talent? How do you uncover the diamond that other coaches missed? I like to be across the under-23s, the under-21s – even the under-17s.

Also, living in the country sends a message. Africans are sick of Europeans taking their money and fleeing north. I wanted to be Malawian. I wanted to walk their streets, eat their food, and watch their television. When I take a job, I act like I'll be there forever. I commit, or I don't go.

Leaving the family was hard, but in truth, turning down Malawi didn't cross my mind. Firstly, we needed the money. The contract was around $6,000 a month for two years plus accommodation in Blantyre. Secondly, the challenge excited me. Malawi were ranked 103rd in the world but they had a chance of making the African Cup of Nations in 2008. In the same year, they entered World Cup qualifying. With Malawi – unlike India – I had a slim chance of reaching the biggest stage of all.

In March, soon after I arrived, I took charge of my first game. The under-23s, who I also coached, had the second leg of an Olympic qualifier against Zambia. We drew 1–1 after losing the first leg 3–2. At full time, I kicked the drinks over. 'We were technically and tactically naive,' I told the press.

Straight away, I could tell the players hadn't been coached properly. At times, the team shape was nonexistent. It's changing now, because of the increase in African academies and fully qualified coaches. But ten years ago, players across the continent weren't taught the basics. They were skilful, they were strong, and their technique on bad pitches was beautiful. But their positioning was bad. The wingers didn't track back. Their decision-making let them down.

My first senior games were in the COSAFA Cup, an annual tournament for teams in southern Africa. The matches weren't on the FIFA calendar – meaning European clubs don't release their players – so the FAM picked thirty African-based players for the camp. The players were fine: fit, skilful and keen to learn. But off the field, the organisation was woeful. Half the time, I was shaking my head.

We didn't have enough match balls. There wasn't enough training kit. And the players' accommodation – they slept in twin rooms at the training centre – was spartan.

The beds were hard, the floors were bare, and the mosquito nets had big holes in them. Not only that, but they weren't treated with repellent. I knew Malawi was poor, but I expected the national team to have standards. For African sides, it's especially important. If the guys are treated badly, the European-based players will stop flying home for games. There's enough FIFA money for the basics.

I soon realised the FAM was dysfunctional. Walter was great, but the general secretary, Yasin Osman, was not. He didn't like me from day one. He fancied himself as a coach – he was national team manager between 2004 and 2005 – and he resented my appointment. He wouldn't help me, so I had to help myself. I spoke to FIFA, who sent more match balls. I got Adidas to send more kit. And in the evenings, I went to functions for ex-pats and wealthy locals to look for sponsors.

Most people weren't interested, as they didn't trust the FAM. But my years selling flowers on Flatbush Avenue meant I wasn't shy. When people realised I was trying to help the players, they pitched in. An Indian businessman gave us thirty treated mosquito nets, plus some carpets and other furnishings. Slowly, the accommodation looked like a hotel, rather than a backpackers' hostel.

There were three COSAFA Cup groups, played in knockout format. Our group was in Swaziland in May, with the first game against South Africa, coached by the Brazilian World Cup-winning manager, Carlos Alberto Parreira. It was an honour to face him.

The match was played in the Somhlolo national stadium in Lobamba. An athletics track encircled the pitch and, on the far side, fans stood on a grass bank. The crowd was just 4,000. For Carlos, it must have seemed a long way from the Rose Bowl in 1994.

We played OK, drew 0–0, then lost 5–4 on penalties, despite having two chances to win. In the third-place playoff – held a day later – we lost 1–0 to the hosts, thanks to an 85th-minute goal. South Africa won the tournament, beating Zambia on penalties in the final in Bloemfontein in October.

If we'd won, my time in Malawi might have been different. We could have reached the finals, got some confidence, and started a run. Instead, we missed two penalties, got knocked out, and flew home cursing our luck. That's what happens, I guess, when you appoint an English manager.

MALAWI IS A POOR COUNTRY. IT WON INDEPENDENCE FROM Britain in the 1960s but still relies on aid. In 2007 (according to The CIA World Factbook) the GDP per capita was $600. I earned ten times that in a month.

That doesn't mean you should work for free – it's their money, and, if they chose to bring in a top-qualified coach, that's up to them. If I didn't take the money, someone else would. But it increases the responsibility. My wages were mind-blowing to most Malawians.

By African standards, Blantyre is a well-developed city. I lived in a cul-de-sac of six houses and the FAM gave me a car. When I drove to training, or the FAM offices, I saw nothing that shocked me. There were no slums. No street boys. But the rest of Malawi wasn't so lucky. When I drove to nearby towns, I saw boys selling food on sticks. When I asked what it was, they said they were rats from the bush. They are fatter and tastier than town rats, apparently. I never found out.

While I looked for sponsors in Blantyre, I met a woman called Mary Woodworth. She was born and raised in Malawi but studied in Preston. She married an Englishman, Keith, and in 2000, they set up an orphanage. It was called FOMO – Friends of Mulanje Orphans – and was based in Mary's village, forty miles from Blantyre. She asked if I would visit the children. I told her I'd bring the whole squad.

Mary's charity looked after thousands of kids. Their parents had died – often from AIDS – and FOMO helped them eat, learn, and fulfil their potential. My daughters were thousands of miles away, safe and well-fed. In Mulanje, I saw hundreds of girls their age with nothing. It was hugely moving. The players – who, by Malawian standards, were well-off – were affected too. I sponsored a boy's tuition for two years, and some of the players did the same. A couple of the lads even adopted children.

Our visit was shown on national television – we were filmed playing football with the kids – and, by coincidence, a British crew were there too. Granada TV were shooting a documentary about FOMO presented by Viv Anderson, England's first black international. We got on well, but it was a strange place to meet someone I'd seen lift the European Cup on TV almost thirty years earlier. The programme won a Royal Television Society award in the north-west, and the charity is still going strong.

Back in Blantyre, we had two games in a week. First was a friendly against Senegal, who had reached the World Cup quarter-finals five years earlier. I wanted to train at the national stadium, so I asked Yasin, the general secretary, to get the grass cut. When we turned up, it was three inches long. It was typical of him, I'm afraid. He was one of the least co-operative people I ever worked with.

We lost 3–2 to Senegal, which was no disgrace. Diomansy Kamara – who signed for Fulham for £6m that summer – started the game for the visitors, as did Demba Ba and Abdoulaye Faye. It was a decent warm-up for the real challenge six days later: Morocco at home in the African Cup of Nations qualifiers.

Morocco were ranked 35th in the world. The other team in our group, Zimbabwe, were 90th (they'd plummeted since I beat them with India in the Afro-Asian Games in 2003). Before I took over Malawi, they lost 2–0 in Rabat, but beat Zimbabwe 1–0 in Blantyre. The group looked like this:

	P	W	D	L	Points
Morocco	3	2	1	0	7
Malawi	2	1	0	1	3
Zimbabwe	3	0	1	2	1

If we beat Morocco on 16 June, we had a big chance of coming top of the group and making the finals. Although I hadn't won a game, I was confident – especially as our European-based players were back. Essau Kanyenda, a forward, played for Lokomotiv Moscow (on loan at Rostov). Clement Kafwafwa, a big defender, flew home from Denmark. With them, we had a chance.

As we settled into the dressing room, we heard a commotion. I went outside and saw the Moroccans standing by their dressing room. When I asked what was wrong, they pointed at a pool of water by the door. They thought it was black magic: crossing it was bad luck, so it had to be cleared before they went in. I never thought I'd see the continent's best players frightened by a puddle.

Inside the stadium, the atmosphere was fantastic. The ground was full to its 30,000 capacity. Some fans had climbed into trees that loomed over the roofless stands. Before kickoff, two of our players started singing in the dressing room and the other twenty joined in. It was a deep, joyful sound. I didn't join in – they sang in the local language, Chichewa – but I loved it. The energy was contagious.

I walked to the dugout but I could have floated. Like the players, the fans were singing. Every note was another drop of adrenalin. When the game starts, I don't hear the fans – it's background noise. But beforehand, I soak up every second. I stood still and looked round. I dreamed of this as a kid. Hell, I dreamed of this as an adult. That moment, in that stadium in Malawi, was heaven.

We started well. The players were pumped up. But after ten minutes, the ground fell silent. Morocco took the lead through Bouchaib El Moubarki. The big centre-half Talal El Karkouri – who spent three years in the Premier League with Charlton – was fantastic for the visitors. It finished 1–0. We were out.

In isolation, not qualifying wasn't a disaster. Malawi had only reached the African Cup of Nations once, in 1984, and we were the outsiders in our group. But, after losing to Morocco, I'd gone four games without a win. The criticism was growing. After the next game, it got worse.

Malawi's independence day is 6 July. To celebrate, they organised a friendly against Namibia in Blantyre. So far, so good. Except, before the game, they held military drills on the pitch, which didn't finish until ten minutes before kickoff. I couldn't believe my eyes: instead of running the warm-up, I watched soldiers shoot bullets into the air.

At one point, hundreds of people pretending to be demonstrators ran on the pitch, so the police – riot shields in one hand, batons in the other – could show how they dealt with trouble. In the stands, the president watched on, approvingly. A friend of mine, Stelios Vradelis, was visiting from Greece. 'What the fuck is this?' he asked. 'You're supposed to be having an international!'

When the show of force was finished, I asked my assistant, Kinnah Phiri, to run the warm-up at double speed. Kinnah was a good guy. He was a fantastic player in the 1970s and 80s and was caretaker-manager of Malawi before I arrived. We got on well. But instead of doing the session, he strolled to the side of the pitch and chatted to his mate.

I did the warm-up myself, picking up shell casings as I went. We lost the friendly 2–1. As I left the dugout, the casings jangled in my pocket.

IN SEPTEMBER, MY TOUR OF ROGUE STATES CONTINUED. THREE years after North Korea, our final qualifier – a dead rubber – took me to Zimbabwe. The trip started badly and went downhill from there.

At Harare airport, the immigration officers are elevated, meaning you're looking up at them. Or – to put it another way – they're looking down at you. I walked to the desk, smiled, and presented my burgundy British passport. Without looking at me, the officer slid it to one side and ignored me. After thirty seconds, I slid the passport back. Finally, the officer opened it, and turned to the visa page.

'Z.F.A.,' he said, pointing at my passport. 'What is this?'

'We're the Malawi football team,' I said, getting annoyed. 'We didn't know the name of our hotel, so we put Z.F.A. – the Zimbabwe Football Association. They're organising our accommodation.'

He stared at me again. 'You white people,' he said, eventually. 'You think you're special.'

'Well, my mother thinks I'm special,' I said.

I shouldn't have been flippant, but I was pissed off. Funnily enough, so was the officer. He called security and I was taken to a side-room. The players – who were still waiting at passport control – were getting agitated. I closed my eyes and saw the next day's headline: 'MALAWI COACH BANNED FROM ZIMBABWE AFTER AIRPORT ROW.'

An official from the Malawian embassy – who was waiting in arrivals – was summoned. He explained that I was the national team manager. 'He didn't mean to offend,' he said.

I apologised to the officer. In fairness, he apologised to me. We shook hands, and a diplomatic incident was averted. I was free to enter Africa's foremost failed state.

In 2007, Zimbabwe was imploding. There was hyper-inflation. Mass unemployment. Food shortages. We saw huge queues at petrol stations and hundreds of people at bus stops. When a bus did arrive, it was too full, so people climbed on the roof.

On the way to training, our coach stopped in traffic outside a supermarket. Its doors were open, so I looked inside. There was nothing on the shelves. I'd watched Zimbabwe on the news, but to see it first-hand was disturbing. It was like watching a country die.

Our hotel – a Holiday Inn propped up by foreign money – was nice, but it wasn't immune to Zimbabwe's illness. On the first day, I asked the chef if the players could have eggs for breakfast.

'There are no eggs,' he said. 'It's not the season.'

I started to laugh, but caught myself when I saw the chef's face. He was sad; embarrassed, even. As India manager, I made us leave the hotel in Jamshedpur when they gave us dhal for lunch. When we flew to Japan, I bollocked the staff for not giving us tables. But here, I couldn't say a word. It was beyond the chef's control. I told him not to worry. I wished I could have done more.

Although I lost my first five games, they were by one goal, or penalties. We hadn't done badly. But the Zimbabwe game was pathetic. Our captain Peter Mponda – top guy, top player – was suspended, as was Clement Kafwafwa. Zimbabwe went 1–0 up, Essau Kanyenda equalised, but we folded in the second half and lost 3–1. Group 12 of the 2008 Cup of Nations qualifiers ended like this:

	P	W	D	L	Points
Morocco	4	3	1	0	10
Zimbabwe	4	1	1	2	4
Malawi	4	1	0	3	3

After the game, I heard that two of our South African-based players – Fisher Kondowe and Joseph Kamwendo – had sneaked out to a club in Harare the night before. I was furious. On one hand, a guy like Kanyenda flies from Russia to play in a dead rubber. On the other, Kondowe and Kamwendo care so little they go out hours before a match? Kamwendo even drank beer on the way home. He was brazen. When we landed, I cornered him in the car park, but my words bounced off him.

I told Walter to suspend them both. He said they'd hold an inquiry. By now, I was sick of it. Sick of the indiscipline. Sick of Yasin Osman. Sick of the state of Malawian football, which was chaotic from top to bottom. I liked Walter but – as well as being president of FAM – he worked ten-hour days as sales manager at a sugar company. He couldn't do it all. I handed in my resignation.

The next day, Walter came to my house.

'The problem,' I told him, 'is that no one cares as much as you. We don't have facilities. We don't have equipment. There is no structure. No youth development. No coach education. No scouting. I've been here six months, but when I try to improve things, it doesn't get done. It's a mess.'

He asked me to reconsider. He said things would change. When I calmed down,

Me at my first school, St Luke's Primary in Mill Hill.

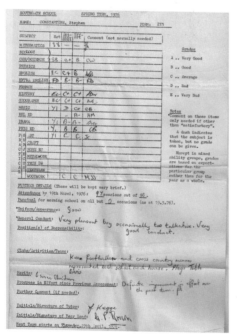

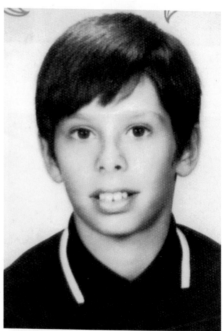

*An early school report: only
ever thinking about football…*

Me in my early years.

Southgate School football team, 1977. I'm standing at the back, first on the right.

Me in my playing days at the New York Pancyprian-Freedoms.

Me and my friend Andy Nicolaou in New York: the Gold Dust twins.

Selling flowers at Flatbush Avenue station in Brooklyn during my time in New York.

With Kevin Campbell and Ian Wright.

Celebrating becoming champions of the Cyprus Youth Cup, 1997, sealed with a 2-1 win against Paralimni.

Limassol Grammar School.

Perks of the job: the Himalayan Mountains in Nepal.

Leading a team talk with Nepal at the Bangabandhu tournament in Bangladesh.

With my Nepal squad at the opening of the SAFF Championship, held in Nepal in 1997.

On our way to be decorated by the King of Nepal.

A guard chops a goat's head off – a ritual in Nepal – after I score a goal in a game with the Nepalese royal family.

Presentation: receiving the Probal Gorkha Dakshin Baahu from His Majesty King Gyanendra Bir Bikram Shah.

With Brazilian legend Zico at a pre-game interview, India v Japan, Kolkata, 2004. Credit: AIFF Media department.

With soldiers of the Indian army in Assam, delivering a coaching course for local coaches. Credit: AIFF Media department.

Abhishek Yadav lifts me off my feet after the final whistle in the LG Cup. Credit: AIFF Media department.

Taking a warm up before a Millwall game.

Delivering a FIFA course in Ghana, 2016.

With Ian Rush.

At a camel auction in Sudan.

Watching on as assistant manager with Apollon Smyrni in Greece.

Watching closely as I put the Indian national team members through their paces.

Having a chat with Carlos Queiroz before our game, India v Iran. Credit: AIFF Media department.

Meeting young football fans in Mumbai. Credit: AIFF Media department.

SAFF Cup Final: watching on as we beat Afghanistan 2-1 in extra time.
Credit: AIFF Media department.

Celebrating our SAFF triumph with Bikash Jairu.
Credit: AIFF Media department.

Lifting the SAFF trophy with the Indian squad. Credit: AIFF Media department.

My coaching team in India.

With my wife and three daughters at the Taj Mahal, India.

Visiting school kids in Rwanda.

I realised I couldn't let him down. He gave me a chance when no one else would. I also knew that – from the outside – resigning wouldn't look good. Quitting after six months puts a question mark on your CV. I said I'd stay, but wouldn't pick Kondowe or Kamwendo again. We shook hands. The chapter wasn't over.

AWAY GAMES WITH MALAWI WERE HARD. THE FAM COULDN'T afford charter flights, and first-class tickets were out of the question too. We flew economy on whichever flights we could find. If there weren't enough seats, we took separate planes. Direct flights were rare. Usually, we went via Johannesburg.

If that wasn't enough, African teams were often unwelcoming. In November 2007, we flew to Swaziland – via South Africa – for a friendly in Manzini. We knew there was a nice hotel twenty minutes from the ground but, after we landed, they took us to one ninety minutes away. We couldn't have a three-hour round trip for training, so I asked our Swazi liaison officer to call their general secretary.

'We are not staying here,' I told the general secretary. 'If you don't move us, we will not turn up for the match. And that's a promise.'

He mentioned another hotel, which we'd been warned about.

'We're not staying there either,' I said. 'It's a brothel.'

We were moved to a better hotel, but the Swazis kept taking the piss. When we went to training, they laid on a minibus rather than a coach. Clement Kafwafwa – 6ft 4in – barely had room to breathe.

'This is why players don't come back from Europe,' he told me, shaking his head.

It harms the whole of African football. Any short-term boost is outweighed by long-term damage. The coaches get pissed off, and European-based players stop coming home. You can't blame them. Clement flew 24 hours from Denmark to Swaziland. He – and the rest of us – deserved more respect.

Swaziland was a big match. It was only a friendly but, when you've lost six in a row, they matter more. As promised, I dropped Kondowe and Kamwendo, and we looked better for it. We won 3–0. After six months – and seven games – I had a win. I didn't care who it was against.

At international level, it takes time for a coach to make a difference. A club manager sees his players every day, but a national manager needs a year to do a month's worth of training. It's harder to instil good habits. Six defeats in a row looks bad, but I never doubted myself. I knew it would be ten or twelve games before Malawi played my way.

In March, we flew to the other side of Africa for a friendly against Namibia. If that sounds glamorous, it wasn't. There was a six-hour wait in Johannesburg airport, so I asked our manager if there was money for food. 'Not much,' he replied. 'But enough for a burger.'

I looked at the menu, saw a cheeseburger with jalapenos, and ordered thirty. After ten minutes, the burgers arrived and the guys tucked in. Suddenly they started shouting.

'Ehhhh, coach!'

'What is this?'

'Too hot, coach, too hot!'

The players had underestimated the jalapenos. As they gulped down their drinks, sweat poured off their faces. One coach put a napkin on his head, which dissolved within two minutes. As he leaned back, it stuck to his face like papier mâché. He looked a sight. It was a ridiculous scene.

Malawi had lost five of their previous six matches against Namibia, drawing the other one, so we weren't favourites. But we played well, winning 3–1. They even subbed off their keeper. In midfield, Robert Ng'ambi was superb and our big striker, Russell Mwafulirwa, was excellent. He moved from South Africa to IFK Norrköping in Sweden three months later.

After the game, I was buzzing. I remember speaking to Ng'ambi and Mponda: 'It's starting to happen,' I told them. But off the pitch, things were going nowhere. Every day, I was fighting one-man battles. That month, I did an interview with an Indian website. It summed up how I felt.

> Q: How has your Malawi sojourn been so far?
> A: It has been a very difficult time.
>
> Q: Is talent in Malawi similar to other African nations?
> A: There is definitely talent, but there is no real youth development.
>
> Q: Do you think football in Malawi is on the rise?
> A: No. There are huge problems across the board. The players lack good facilities and proper coaching. The administration is also a major concern.

There was no point biting my tongue. I was there to fix things. Pretending it was hunky-dory wouldn't do any good.

I had another problem, too: the Malawian press. Some reporters were fine, but others were out to get me. Losing my first six matches didn't help, but there were personal reasons, too. I was Walter's man. If they didn't like Walter, they didn't like me. I got hammered week in, week out.

Once, I was coaching a young goalkeeper. His feet weren't right, so I pushed him in the shoulder.

'Don't stand there like that,' I said. 'Stand there with your hands out in front.'

It was totally normal. You see goalkeeping coaches do it fifty times a day. But the next day, a newspaper said I 'struck' the player. It was crazy. They even went to the keeper's house and offered to pay his father if he criticised me. He told them to piss off.

In December 2007, the Malawi under-20s went to Mpumalanga in South Africa for their COSAFA Championships. In the first game we were losing to Madagascar. I didn't coach the team, but I watched from the stands so, at half-time, I was asked to speak to the players. They weren't playing well so I let rip. I used some industrial language, but only to gee them up. I told them they should remember who they were playing for. No one minded. They improved in the second half.

The next day, a journalist – who, it turns out, was hiding behind the door in the dressing room – said I 'verbally abused the players'. It was an outrage, they said. They called for me to resign. Even the sports minister was critical. But why was a journalist hiding in the dressing room in the first place?

I don't mind criticism, but I can't accept made-up stories. One reporter even told Walter I'd turned up drunk to training.

'I've been out with him, he doesn't drink,' said Walter, before kicking the reporter out of his office. I tried laughing things off, but I didn't know where it would end. It felt lawless.

To make things worse, Yasin was still a pain in the backside. I used to fine our players for indiscipline. It wasn't major – $20 for being late, or $10 for the wrong kit, things like that. It came out of their allowances but Yasin didn't like it. In March, before the friendly in Namibia, he called me in a rage.

'How much have you collected in fines?' he demanded.

'About six hundred dollars since I've been here,' I replied. 'The players will decide how to spend it.'

'That money belongs to the FAM!' he said, almost screaming. 'You must hand it over!'

I hung up and spoke to the captain Peter Mponda. We decided to buy a wide-screen television for the training base, as Yasin's son had installed satellite TV. I went into Blantyre, bought a 52-incher, and went to see Walter. He asked about the fines, so I took him into the corridor and showed him my purchase.

'There's your fine money,' I said.

In fairness, he didn't mind. He told me to get it installed but, a few days later, we learned Yasin's son hadn't connected the satellite TV. The dish on the wall was useless. The last time I saw the TV was in Walter's garage: we couldn't leave it at the training centre in case it got nicked.

I'd been in Malawi for more than a year, and I was worn down. Since my 'resignation' after the Zimbabwe game, the results had improved, but everything else was the same. The FAM was still mismanaged. Yasin was still Yasin. And – to cap it off – the press were making up stories. I didn't know what they'd accuse me of next. I told Walter I was resigning. This time, I meant it.

I didn't announce my resignation. We had two African Nations Championship qualifiers coming up and I didn't want the distraction. The championship – which was new that year, and separate to the Cup of Nations – was for domestic players only. I thought it was a fantastic idea, as it gives young guys a chance. I suggested doing the same in Asia during my second spell in India.

The first leg against Mozambique was in the capital, Lilongwe. That was unusual, as most games were in Blantyre. Before the warm-up, I did something I don't usually do: I walked across the pitch on my own. I wanted the public's opinion. I wanted to know if the press vendetta had worked.

In all honesty, I thought I was going to get some serious abuse. But the fans were fantastic. They cheered and shouted my name. Afterwards, I spoke to Walter.

'I thought the fans didn't want me,' I said.

'They know what you've done,' he said. 'They know how hard you've worked. We have never lost badly. They can see improvement in the players.'

We beat Mozambique 2–1 but lost the second leg 1–0, going out on away goals. I formally resigned and flew from Maputo to Cyprus.

At the end of April I went back to Blantyre as – according to my deal – I had to work a two-month notice period. We agreed a settlement and I left in May. I had been Malawi manager for fourteen months.

The FAM appointed my assistant, Kinnah Phiri, as my replacement. The first thing he did was recall the Harare Two, Kondowe and Kamwendo. I couldn't blame him: Kamwendo, especially, was a good player. Under Kinnah, Malawi reached the finals of the African Cup of Nations in Angola in 2010.

I was pleased for them. I enjoyed watching guys like Peter Mponda, Russell Mwafulirwa and Essau Kanyenda on the biggest stage. I also felt I'd played my part. When I arrived, Malawi was a mess. I did what I could, from match balls to mosquito nets, and results were improving. Not many managers win their final two games – both away from home – 3–0 and 3–1.

Looking back, Malawi was an amazing experience. I worked with top-quality players. I travelled across Africa. I even won a couple of games. But – at the time – it was bloody difficult.

To be successful, I needed help from a well-organised FA. I never had that. Instead, I spent fourteen months fighting one-man battles. As I left Blantyre for the final time, I was back in the job market. There was no position, or place, I wouldn't consider. As I flew north, a thought entered my head.

I wonder how Walton & Hersham are getting on...

8
COACHING THE COACHES
FIFA, 2001–

IN 2000, MOHAMED BIN HAMMAM – A FIFA EXECUTIVE MEMBER, who became president of the Asian Football Confederation in 2002 – came to Nepal to open ANFA's new headquarters in Kathmandu. FIFA paid for the centre and, as part of the opening ceremony, I ran a session for Nepal under-16s on the new pitch. I met Mr Bin Hammam, who seemed like a nice guy, and thought no more about it.

Three months later, another FIFA official, Juerg Nepfer, came to Nepal. Juerg was the head of FIFA's development programme, so I did another session on the new pitch. That evening, I was invited to dinner in Kathmandu with Juerg and the bigwigs from the association. In truth, I didn't fancy it. I only went after Lucy persuaded me. As usual, she was right.

I went to dinner and sat with Juerg. We got on well: he's Swiss, has worked for FIFA since 1979, and has helped raise standards across the world. After speaking about my career, he asked: 'Have you ever thought about being a FIFA instructor?' My response was simple: 'What's a FIFA instructor?'

Juerg explained that FIFA has around fifty highly qualified people who are sent across the world to train coaches. They are not FIFA employees, but are paid for their time (around $200 a day at the moment) and have their expenses met. Some coaches do one course a year; others do more.

It sounded wonderful.

I needed endorsement from the English FA so Robin Russell, who was head of coach education, sent FIFA a letter. I also needed permission from ANFA, so I went to see the president, Ganesh Thapa. This is a formality, I thought.

Ganesh said no.

'We don't want to lose you,' he told me. I explained I'd be away for ten days, once a year.

'But other associations will see your work,' he said. 'You won't come back.'

I was pissed off. Being a FIFA instructor would take me around the world. It would do wonders for my CV, and open doors I never dreamed of. It was too important for Ganesh to ruin.

I went to see the ANFA vice president, Tashi Ghale. He listened, signed a letter on headed paper, and faxed it to Switzerland. I was in.

IN 2001 I FLEW TO ZURICH FOR MY INDUCTION. THERE WERE around 100 people there, including grassroots and women's coaches.

I looked round and saw some huge names: Erich Rutemöller from Germany, Jean-Michel Benezet from France, Jean-Marie Conz from Switzerland... the list went on. I got to play on the same pitch as Teofilo Cubillas, who scored for Peru in the 1978 World Cup with the outside of his boot against Scotland. At times, I honestly thought I was in the wrong place.

Over three or four days, we learned how to deliver a FIFA session. The detail was eye-opening. We also learned how to conduct ourselves: while running courses, we were FIFA ambassadors, which meant being respectful, and staying out of politics. In effect, we became FIFA spokesmen. The induction brought home what a huge honour it was. I couldn't wait to begin.

As it turned out, Ganesh Thapa needn't have worried: my first course wasn't until after I left Nepal. In October 2001, I put on my FIFA blazer and flew to Iran. It was a month after the 9/11 attacks.

The world felt tense. America and Britain were invading Afghanistan. The Ryder Cup, due to take place in late September, was postponed, and the New Zealand cricket team cancelled a tour of Pakistan. After getting my visa from the Iranian embassy in London, the British government phoned. They didn't want someone flying to Iran for the sake of a football course. They advised me not to go.

'Thanks for your concern,' I said. 'But I'm not cancelling.'

Lucy, too, was unhappy. She practically begged me to stay at home.

'It's my first course,' I told her. 'If I say no, they will never ask me again.'

BBC Radio 5 Live heard about the trip and, in a live interview, asked why I was going.

'First, this is probably the safest time to fly,' I replied. 'Every airport has increased its security. Second, my trip is nothing to do with religion or politics. It's about football, and nothing else.'

In truth – despite my wife's and government's concern – not going didn't cross my mind. Working for FIFA was too important.

In Tehran, eight or nine people met me at the airport. They brought flowers and were delighted to see me. The course went perfectly and halfway through – 16 October – the coaches bought me a birthday cake and sang to me in Farsi. It was a fantastic moment. I wish the Foreign Office could have seen it: that week, we did more for Anglo–Iranian relationships than any embassy.

The Iranians were the nicest people you could imagine. We judge countries by their leaders, or by headlines in the news, but it's a misleading picture. I was playing football in Tehran thinking: Everyone should have the chance to do this. I'm glad the British government called – it's nice to know they care – but I'm also glad I ignored them. Sadly, not every trip was as smooth.

In 2006 I went to Sudan. I arrived at one-thirty in the morning and – unlike in Iran – there was no one to meet me. It was too late to call the Sudanese FA, or FIFA in Zurich, so I waited. And waited. Eventually, someone turned up and drove me to my hotel. At least, he said it was my hotel.

My guide took me into a room. It had a concrete floor, a bed from the 1950s, no toilet and no TV.

'My friend, there must be some mistake,' I said. 'I am not staying here.'

He took my bag, went outside, and drove me to a second building. It looked slightly better. The staircase was outside the building: we walked up three flights, found my room, and switched on the light. The toilet was outside, the TV was ancient, and the ceiling fan was about to fall down.

'My friend,' I began, calmly, 'I have flown a long way. It is four a.m. I am very tired. I am not staying here for ten days. Please take me to the airport so I can go home. I will call the FA to explain.'

The guide listened, considered his options, and went back to the car. Fifteen minutes later we were outside the Hilton in Khartoum.

'Mr Constantine,' said a porter while taking my bag. 'Welcome to the Hilton. We have been expecting you.'

My guide – it seemed – wanted to put me somewhere cheap, cancel the Hilton and pocket the refund. Thankfully, not everyone in Sudan was like him. The rest of my trip was great.

Working for FIFA is a huge honour. To travel the world, passing on knowledge, is a dream come true. It's also a great way to see new countries: when you're on the FIFA list, you can go anywhere. I have run courses in almost twenty countries across Europe, Africa, Asia and the Caribbean.

I have been to Mauritius and caught marlin. I have seen Bob Marley's house in Jamaica. I have collected firewood in Bhutan (the hotel had no central heating) and was nearly electrocuted in South Sudan (a wire fell into a puddle on the floor). And, on a trip in 2008, I was deported from Iran.

I was told I didn't need a visa in advance: if I showed my FIFA letter it would be issued on arrival. I flew to Tehran, presented my letter to passport control, and received a blank stare in return. I wasn't allowed in.

It was 3 a.m. so I asked to stay in a secure room until FIFA or the Iranian FA woke up. They refused. I was escorted to departures and put on the first plane back to Europe. I had been in Iran for less than two hours. Officially, I hadn't been there at all.

At Hamburg airport, I called FIFA. They said that, if I went back, everything would be fine. I flew back to Tehran, showed them my letter, and was let in without a second glance. The course went well – the Iranians, again, were great – and I was glad I'd persevered. Until, that was, I tried to fly home.

I went to the check-in desk at Tehran airport and showed them my ticket.

'Sir,' said the worker, lowering his voice. 'I'm afraid your return ticket has been used.'

'Really?' I replied. 'When?'

'Ten days ago,' he said. 'Tehran to Hamburg.'

I tried to buy a new ticket, but they wouldn't accept my card. I had visions of being trapped in Tehran for weeks, wandering through the terminal in my FIFA tie and blazer. Luckily, I knew the assistant manager of Iran – my FIFA colleague Erich Rutemöller – was on the same flight.

I called Erich. He is a top-class person, so he came back from security and tried to buy my ticket home. His first card didn't work. When his second card also failed, I got nervous. Finally, he tried a company card from the German FA, who he also worked for. It went through. I left Iran indebted – in more ways than one – to the Deutscher Fussball Bund.

I'm well known for going anywhere. If FIFA ask, and I have time, I say yes. I'm not bothered by beaches and five-star hotels. In fact, I prefer less-visited places, which perhaps explains why – in a six-month spell in 2016 – I did courses in Mongolia, Bhutan and the holiday hotspot of North Korea.

It was thirteen years since I'd been to Pyongyang with India, and I was keen to see what – if anything – had changed. I flew into the country on a half-full Chinese flight from Beijing. When we landed, the airport was busier than in 2003, but the paranoia was the same. My laptop and two phones were checked and they asked if I was carrying any books. I wasn't – I prefer audiobooks – but I saw people have theirs confiscated. Anything that referred to North Korea or its leaders was banned.

The FA took me from the airport to my accommodation. Hotel Koryo had 44 floors, 500 rooms, and perhaps 20 guests. Staff outnumbered customers. The hotel was too warm – a sickly, suffocating heat – but my room was fine. The television had twelve channels: three in Korean, six in Chinese, plus Al Jazeera, Russia Today, and a Russian-language service. North Korean guests only had three channels.

The internet was $5 for half an hour. Twitter and LinkedIn were blocked, but I checked my email, and – to my surprise – was able to watch Raiders games on the NFL site (I am a big fan of American football, and the Oakland Raiders in particular: when I moved to the States in the 1980s, they were the 'No One Likes Us and We Don't Care' team, which suited my personality). You could also buy SIM cards with access to WhatsApp and Viber, but they were $150. I watched a lot of Al Jazeera instead.

Although North Koreans get foreign news, it is government-approved. We are used to instant information. Over there, things move slowly. During my trip, Donald Trump was elected as US president. The whole world was talking about it, but my guides didn't have a clue. I broke the news to them. One day, I told my translator that a friend of mine, Dan Harris, coached in South Korea.

'The enemy,' I joked.

'South Korea is not our enemy,' came the state-sponsored response. 'We are one Korea. It's the Americans who divided the country.'

Decades of dictatorship mean there's an obedient culture – more so than in other Asian countries. When I run courses, I like the coaches to ask questions, but North Koreans aren't like that. They wait for instructions. They listen and follow.

'Guys,' I said on the first day, 'I am not going to listen to myself speak for five days.' It took them two or three days to open up. When they did, the questions were very good.

I ran two five-day courses: one for elite club coaches and one for youth coaches. The players doing the drills came from an under-17 team. After one session, one of the translators spoke to me. She was excellent: her parents were government officials, so she knew about the outside world.

'You remind me of someone,' she said.

'Go on,' I replied, thinking Bruce Willis, or perhaps Arsene Wenger.

'Mary Poppins,' she said. I laughed.

'I've been called a lot of things, but never Mary Poppins,' I replied.

'It's the connection between you and the players,' she said. 'The boys follow you everywhere.'

On my day off, my translator took me on a tour of Pyongyang: famous buildings, the zoo, the national stadium (the biggest in the world with a capacity of 114,000). Photos were allowed but, before taking a picture of Kim Jong-il and Kim Il-Sung's portraits, I was warned not to disrespect them.

Compared to 2003, the city was busier – there were more cars, for one thing – but it wasn't exactly Las Vegas. United Nations sanctions, imposed after North Korean nuclear tests, were also having an effect. Foreign money had dried up. FIFA weren't allowed to send equipment or pre-pay for my hotel. I took a wad of euros and was reimbursed later.

On two nights, I had dinner with another national team coach. Jørn Andersen – a blond-haired Norwegian who played in the Bundesliga in the 1980s and 90s – was North Korea's first foreign manager since the 1990s.

Jørn was a nice guy: he had lived in Hotel Koryo for eight months, but he seemed happy enough. I asked why he didn't get an apartment. He said he wanted the service, and it wasn't like Pyongyang had many buzzing neighbourhoods. While I was there, he took his team to Hong Kong and qualified for the finals of the East Asian Cup. He was probably just glad to be out of the hotel.

On my last night, I was taken to dinner on a boat. It sailed up and down the Taedong River but, apart from us four, there were only two diners. A girl band provided the entertainment. There were eight or nine of them and they were fantastic. One was on saxophone, one on guitar, one on accordion, one on drums, with four or five singing in Korean. They could have been on Broadway. Instead, they were in the world's most secretive country, going up and down the same river, night after night.

AFTER LEAVING MALAWI IN MAY 2008 I WENT STRAIGHT TO Vietnam to run a ten-day course. While I was there, the Woking chairman David Taylor called me. They had sacked their manager – the former Scottish international Frank Gray – and I applied for the job. They were a full-time Conference team, just west of London, with a decent budget. To me, they were a Football League club in waiting.

Taylor and I chatted on Skype. After twenty minutes, he said, 'I've heard enough. We want to speak to you in person. Get yourself to England for an interview.'

I did the course in Vietnam, flew back to England, and headed to Woking. I could tell Taylor was keen. He called me three times before I reached London, and again as I travelled from Heathrow to Brighton. He even told me what questions they'd ask in the interview. Finally, it seemed, I was getting a manager's job in England. It was fifth tier, but it was a start.

The interview was at Taylor's house near Woking. There were three people on the board – Taylor, the owner Chris Ingram, and the director of football Colin Lippiatt – but after ten minutes something wasn't right. An interview is like any conversation: it flows or it doesn't.

'How do you evaluate the players?' they asked.

'Everything they do is an evaluation of sorts,' I said. 'The game is the big test. We keep a record of their performance, and occasionally post it on the noticeboard. Sometimes we put their physical test results there, too. It lets them know we are always evaluating. It keeps them on their toes.'

'What if they're in last place?'

'We might have a word to check everything is OK,' I replied.

'Who evaluates you?'

'You.'

'Not the players?'

'Absolutely not. There has to be a chain of command. The players can't control the manager.'

The interview lasted two hours. Every minute that passed, I felt less confident. I can't remember the salary, but I wasn't fussy. There was a £500,000 budget for players' wages. Taylor told me he'd call on Monday. On Saturday, I was outside Churchill Square in Brighton when a friend called.

'Have you heard the news?' he asked. 'They've given the Woking job to Kim Grant.'

I didn't even know he'd applied. I later read there'd been 39 applicants and 12 interviews: apparently I made the shortlist with Grant, the former Tottenham defender Justin Edinburgh, and the former Lewes manager Steve King. A short time later, Taylor called.

'I may have made the biggest mistake of my football career,' he began. My heart sank. 'But we've made a unanimous decision. We're going for Kim Grant.'

I thanked him and hung up. I was shattered.

I knew Kim. He was a striker at Charlton in the 1990s, won caps for Ghana, and had a number of spells abroad. In 2005/06 he trained with us at Millwall. I suddenly remembered a conversation we had while playing keep-away.

'You know, Steve, I will get a manager's job before you,' he said. 'You've got the qualifications – but I've been a player.'

He was proved right. Not knowing I'd applied, he even used me as a reference.

A few days later, Taylor called again. One of the applicants had broken the news of Kim's appointment on a Woking forum, before the club announced it. The chairman thought it was me.

'You're not doing yourself any favours,' said Taylor.

'I didn't even know you had a forum,' I replied.

'I know you're disappointed,' he said.

'You have no idea how disappointed I am,' I replied.

I asked why I didn't get the job. Apparently, they spoke to Colin Lee, who wasn't complimentary. That didn't surprise me.

I wished Woking well, but I wasn't optimistic. Kim was young and hadn't managed before. Even in the fifth tier, it's hard to hit the ground running. After seven games, Woking were second bottom with two points. Grant was sacked and Taylor offered to resign, saying he got it wrong.

Grant's assistant, Phil Gilchrist, was appointed manager in September. He had a good playing career – reaching the Premier League with Leicester – but had never managed. He was sacked in April and Woking were relegated. I was sorry to see them in a mess, but I wasn't surprised.

IT WAS SUMMER 2008 AND I WAS UNEMPLOYED AGAIN. I DID more FIFA courses – Iran in August (when I was deported) and Swaziland in September – but I needed something full time. I had Lucy and three girls to support. I couldn't afford to be unemployed for long.

It was a horrible time. From the moment I woke up, to the moment I went to bed, I thought about money. If I went shopping, I didn't buy anything without thinking: What's my bank balance like? Do I need this? At times, I told Lucy to put things back in the supermarket. It was a nightmare.

Every day you're out of work, the pressure increases. I tried to act normally but sometimes I snapped. My family suffered. At times, I was not someone you wanted to be around. On paper, I was a highly qualified football coach with more than twenty years' experience. But my CV guaranteed me nothing. If no one will employ you, what comes next?

I put my life into the house. I was worried we'd lose it. I had to borrow a couple of grand from a couple of friends to stay afloat. I even thought of doing something else: building work or painting and decorating, perhaps. You can't sit on your backside while borrowing money.

Football, though, was still my best chance of well-paid work. The industry is seductive. An agent says Country X fancies you. A friend says Club Y is nailed on. You're unemployed, but you're sure something's around the corner. The question, of course, is when. When will it happen? How long can I afford to wait? It's not knowing that gets you. You're willing the phone to ring.

At one point, I almost moved to India. Pune FC were an ambitious club in the I-League second division. They were owned by the Ashok Piramal Group – a huge business run by three fanatic Liverpool supporters, Harsh, Rajeev and Nandan – and had signed some of my old national team squad, including Shanmugam Venkatesh. The players recommended me, so I got a call from the club.

It was an exciting prospect. The I-League – which replaced the National Football League – was barely a year old. People thought India might, finally, have a proper professional league. Pune wanted to reach the top division and become the biggest club in the country. I was asked to manage the first team and develop the whole set-up. It was a rare opportunity: the chance to build, rather than rebuild. We agreed a salary and I waited for the contract.

Two weeks later – with no contract signed – they called again. Instead of paying $10,000 a month in my first year, they wanted to pay $6,000 for one, $8,000 in the second, then $10,000 in the third. I agreed but, a couple of weeks later, they reduced the third-year salary to $8,000.

Again, I agreed, but I didn't like their tactics. When they changed their terms a third time, I walked away. Things were getting desperate, but you have to stick to your guns.

By this point, I was low. There was no pressure from my friends, but I couldn't keep borrowing money. Every day that passed, the panic grew. I had to do something – but what? All I knew was building teams. I had gone months without work. I couldn't see an end.

And then, in December 2008, the Sudanese FA called me. Or, to be precise, the Sudanese FA's travel agent called me. The national team needed a coach and the agent had seen my website, which I set up in Nepal in 1999. I told him I was keen – I enjoyed my FIFA course in Sudan, once I found the right hotel – so the travel agent spoke to the FA president, Dr Kamal Shaddad.

I knew Dr Shaddad from the course in 2006. He was old – late sixties perhaps, or even seventies – but charismatic. We got on well, and since then, I had proved myself with my fourteen-month spell in Malawi. African countries prefer appointing people who've worked in the continent before. They are harder to shock. When the travel agent suggested my name, Dr Shaddad said: 'This is the one we want.'

He later said there were 34 applications from all over the world. Finally, I was number one.

9
DESERT LANDSCAPES
SUDAN, 2009

THE FIRST THING THAT HIT ME IN SUDAN WASN'T THE HEAT. IT was the cold.

After agreeing a two-year deal on $10,000 a month I flew to Khartoum to sign the contract. I walked into Dr Shaddad's office and froze. The good doctor was sitting behind a huge, wooden desk with two massive cooling towers either side. I shivered. It must have been three degrees, at most.

'It's very cold,' I said, rubbing my arms.

'Stephenson,' he replied, laughing (he often called me Stephenson). 'How do you think I preserve myself?'

Dr Shaddad was a character. He had wild, frizzy hair like the boxing promoter Don King. He drove a 1980s Mercedes because 'I don't trust the newer models'. And he was keen on me.

'You are not leaving until you sign,' he told me.

Sudan were a decent side – the previous year, they played in the African Cup of Nations finals – but Dr Shaddad warned me they were in decline.

'It will be a difficult job,' he said. 'The team is old. You will need to rebuild. You will face resistance from many sides, but I am with you.'

His warning couldn't dampen my enthusiasm. I had waited months for a chance. Now, I had one. For the fourth time, I was a national team manager. It was a wonderful feeling.

MY FIRST JOB IN KHARTOUM WAS TO FIND A FLAT. I ASKED THE estate agent for a penthouse, as I didn't want noisy neighbours upstairs.

'You don't want a penthouse,' the estate agent said.

'Trust me – I do,' I replied, stubborn as ever.

Eventually, we found one overlooking Khartoum airport. I moved in and, by 3 p.m., realised why I didn't want a penthouse: it was boiling. Sunshine scorched the roof while heat rose from below. Even with air-conditioning, it was hot. I made a note to ask Dr Shaddad for one of his cooling towers.

After finding my flat I went to the British embassy to register. I was in reception, filling in a form, when I was invited to a meeting room.

'Congratulations on your appointment,' the official said. 'But there's something you should know.'

He looked concerned. I felt concerned.

'I tell you this in the strictest confidence,' he continued, lowering his voice. 'In three days, the International Criminal Court will issue an arrest warrant for the President of Sudan, Omar al-Bashir. When the warrant is announced, we expect protests against the court. We advise Western citizens to stay off the streets. The ICC is seen as a Western body. We fear Europeans will be targeted.'

I had expected tea and biscuits. I was getting state secrets.

'But my first game is in a week's time,' I replied. 'We are playing Uganda in a friendly at home.'

'The stadium could be volatile,' the official replied. 'We advise you not to attend.'

'And coach the team by phone?' I asked.

'It's your decision,' he said. 'We can only advise.'

The ICC issued the arrest warrant for Mr al-Bashir on 4 March, three days before our friendly. He was accused of war crimes, and crimes against humanity, during the conflict in Darfur in western Sudan which began in 2003. The president was popular in Khartoum so, as expected, thousands of people protested on the streets. One of his aides said the warrant was 'part of the new mechanism of neo-colonialism'. The president himself was more direct. 'The warrant,' he said, 'is not worth the ink it is written with.'

The city was tense, but missing the game wasn't an option. I was the national team manager. If I missed my first match, what message would it send? I went to the stadium without a second thought. Bobby Williamson – the former Kilmarnock and Hibernian manager – was the Uganda boss. He's a tough bugger. If they turn on the Brits, I thought, at least there are two of us.

I needn't have worried. The ground was only half full, but the support was good. I didn't feel threatened at all. My bigger concern was the team. Uganda won 2–0 and we were poor. Like Malawi, Sudan had talented players, but they didn't play like a team. They had been trained but not coached.

Anyone can run a training session. That's just an exercise class with footballs. A coaching session – now that's the thing. A good coach spots mistakes and tries to fix them. When the ball reached our striker, for example, no one supported him. Ideally, one player is there for the lay-off, while another runs in behind, in case the striker can play a through-ball. Against Uganda, we didn't do that.

The next game was three weeks later: Mali at home in a World Cup qualifier. It was the first match in a six-game group. I barely saw the players before the Uganda friendly but we had a proper training camp for the Mali match. I was determined to make my mark. It didn't take long.

On the first day of camp, we held a team meeting. Halfway through, one of our defenders, Mohamed Ali Safari, walked out. I assumed he'd gone to the toilet but he never came back. After the meeting, I told my assistant to bring him back. I asked Safari where he'd been.

'I went to pray,' he said. Safari – like the rest of the squad – was a devout Muslim.

'But there are forty people in this room,' I replied. 'They are all Muslim. No one else went.'

'I don't care about anyone else,' Safari replied.

'Well, I don't care about you,' I said. 'Take your bag and go.'

Safari – who appeared nine times for Sudan in 2008 – never played for me. In truth, I was glad of the opportunity to put the hammer down and say, 'It ain't happening with me.'

Half the Sudan players were coasting. They took their places for granted. They walked round on their mobile phones like superstars. There was no intensity: if I turned my back, effort dropped by 50 per cent.

I thought back to my first national team ten years earlier. In terms of ability, you couldn't put Sudan next to Nepal. But in terms of effort, Nepal were miles ahead. Their amazing work ethic meant they punched above their weight. The laid-back Sudanese punched below.

On the second day of camp, I was sitting in the lobby of the hotel when two men approached me. One was Faisal Agab, a Sudanese forward. The other was an official from his club, Al-Merrikh.

'I have brought Faisal to the camp,' said the official.

'But the camp started yesterday,' I replied.

'He is here now,' the official said.

'The camp started yesterday,' I repeated. 'He didn't turn up, he didn't let us know, therefore he is not in the camp. I don't need him.'

Agab was seen as Sudan's best player. He was worshipped at Al-Merrikh, one of the biggest clubs in Sudan. He was almost like David Beckham: a celebrity as well as a footballer. In my opinion, he had nice feet but his legs were going. Even if they weren't, I couldn't stand the indiscipline. I sent him home and never picked him again.

The Mali game was played at the Red Castle stadium in Omdurman, a city on the other side of the Nile to Khartoum. The ground was full to its 43,000 capacity. The lights were on. The atmosphere was electric. The sound of a thousand drums hung in the humid air.

I tried to stay calm but adrenalin coursed through me. It's hard to describe the feeling: a mixture of excitement and nerves, with a dash of pride thrown in. Three months earlier, I was unemployed in Cyprus, waiting for the phone to ring. Now, I was centre stage in a World Cup qualifier.

After nineteen minutes, the Red Castle fell silent: the former West Ham and Tottenham striker, Freddie Kanoute, scored for Mali. But it wasn't quiet for long. Four minutes later, Mudather El Tahir flicked the ball over a defender and volleyed in from eighteen yards. The stadium shook. The game finished 1–1; the fans went home happy. Despite Mr al-Bashir's arrest warrant, I was safe in Sudan for now.

SUDANESE FOOTBALL IS DOMINATED BY TWO OMDURMAN CLUBS: Al-Hilal and Al-Merrikh. It's like Celtic and Rangers, but worse. They have won the league every year since 1992 (Al-Hilal 15, Al-Merrikh 9). In 2009, they lost one league game between them, with their nearest rival, Al-Khartoum, 24 points behind. That year, their combined goal difference was +100. In a 24-game season.

The rivalry in Omdurman is fiercer than Glasgow. The fans hate each other. Before the Mali game, we held open training sessions at each club's stadium. The first was at Al-Merrikh's ground, the Red Castle. It was a nice evening so I thought a few hundred fans might turn up. We got at least 10,000.

I was putting my boots on, pleased at the passion for the game, when my captain spoke to me. Haitham Mustafa, an Al-Hilal player, looked worried.

'Coach,' he said, 'we're going to have a problem.'

I walked on the pitch and was struck by the noise. Grown men were on their feet, shaking their fists, yelling in Arabic. Every Al-Hilal player was abused. We did the session but the players hated it. No one was comfortable. Our next open session, at Al-Hilal's ground, was the same. As we left the ground, fans threw stones at the bus. It was madness. There and then, I banned open sessions.

Later that year, I went to an Al-Merrikh game. A group of supporters asked to speak to me.

'Captain,' he began (Sudanese people often call the coach 'captain'), 'why do you close the doors on the training sessions?'

'Because the Al-Hilal fans abuse the Al-Merrikh players,' I replied, 'and the Al-Merrikh fans abuse the Al-Hilal players.'

'That's because their players are sons of dogs,' the supporter replied. At least he was honest.

'The players don't like open sessions,' I said. 'They are scared to come out of the changing rooms. If we restart them, do you promise not to abuse the Al-Hilal players?'

The supporter looked at me and smiled.

'La,' he said, which means no in Arabic.

'Then the doors stay closed,' I replied.

The Omdurman clubs didn't just dominate the Sudanese league: they also dominated the national team. Al-Hilal and Al-Merrikh were wealthy and could afford the country's best players. They paid well by African standards, which meant few Sudanese players went abroad.

Omdurman was a comfort zone. In the 2008 African Cup of Nations squad, all 23 players came from Al-Hilal (12) or Al-Merrikh (11). At the time, Sudan was the biggest country in Africa (it's now the third biggest after the secession of South Sudan). I couldn't believe the best players were all in one city.

One day, I looked at the Premier League fixtures and saw Al-Nil Al-Hasahesa were at home. I checked the map and realised Hasahesa was only around 100 miles south-east of Khartoum. I picked up my sunglasses and told my driver we were going on a day trip. He didn't look best pleased.

Three hours in – and with no sign of Hasahesa – Dr Shaddad called my mobile.

'Where are you, Stephenson?' he asked.

'Sir, I don't know where we are – there is sand in front, sand behind, and sand either side,' I replied. 'But we are on the way to Hasahesa.'

'Stephen,' he said, sounding serious. 'Pass the phone to the driver.'

From the passenger seat, I could hear Dr Shaddad yelling at the driver in Arabic. After a five-minute bollocking, the driver passed the phone back. He looked worried.

'You are in bandit country,' Dr Shaddad told me. 'The road is very dangerous. You could be kidnapped. You must turn around.'

'But we are almost at the game,' I replied. 'There's no point turning around now.'

Dr Shaddad paused. 'If you must,' he said, sounding pissed off.

Twenty minutes later, two jeeps appeared in the distance. Heat shimmered off the road. The sun beat down on the white sand. As the jeeps got closer, we saw they had guns.

The vehicles pulled alongside us. Suddenly, relief spread across my driver's face: Dr Shaddad had sent armed guards to protect us. One jeep drove behind, one in front, and we reached the stadium with no problems. It was my first taste of VIP security since Lucy arrived in Kathmandu ten years earlier.

It was pandemonium outside the stadium. I eventually found the directors' area, but I couldn't see the game: too many people were standing up. I asked to be moved – thinking I'd get a better seat – but instead I was taken to the touchline and put next to the fourth official.

There was a chair but no cover. With no cap, my bald head cooked in the desert sun. After twenty minutes, I went back to the directors' box and found my driver.

'I have seen enough,' I said. 'We're going back to Khartoum.'

I picked two Hasahesa players for the national team and never returned. From then on, I scouted players when they came to Khartoum or Omdurman. It was easier all round.

IN MAY AND JUNE, WE HAD THREE MATCHES IN THREE WEEKS: a friendly in Tunisia, before World Cup qualifiers away to Benin and at home to Ghana. They were huge games. The group winners went to the World Cup – Ghana were massive favourites – but the second and third-placed teams qualified for the African Cup of Nations in 2010. Our 1–1 draw against Mali was a decent start.

Since moving to Sudan, my profile had increased. In March, Russell Kempson from The Times in London interviewed me – 'The discipline here was shocking, the players used to come and go as they pleased,' I told him – and the Wall Street Journal interviewed me in Tunisia. 'In Sudan, a soccer coach faces his toughest test,' read the headline.

Despite my experience in Malawi, I am happy speaking to reporters. At the start of my career it was the Non-League Paper or Grimsby Telegraph who called me – I have the cuttings to prove it – so I guess the Wall Street Journal, with respect to those papers, was a step up. The article by Jeff Opdyke, which was published before the Ghana game, called me 'soccer's St Jude – the patron saint of lost causes'. It was a nice line, but Sudan were not a lost cause. Not yet, anyway.

We lost the friendly 4–0 to Tunisia – they played in the 2006 World Cup and were a good side – before heading to Libya for a training camp. It seemed like a neat, well-developed place, although Colonel Gaddafi's face was everywhere. We had dinner at the Sudanese ambassador's house then flew 1,800 miles south to Benin. The match was played in Cotonou on the Atlantic coast, a city less than 500 miles from the equator. That, and the 26,000 fans, meant the atmosphere was hot.

Razak Omotoyossi scored for Benin in the 22nd minute, but the best player – by far – was his teammate Stephane Sessegnon. He was fast, direct and skilful. When he dribbled, he took two or three players out of the game. Afterwards, I phoned Arsenal's chief scout Steve Rowley, who I knew from my time at Millwall. At the time, Sessegnon was at PSG.

'Don't worry,' Rowley told me. 'Arsene knows all about him.'

Sessegnon moved to England in 2011, spending five years with Sunderland and West Brom, but he was good enough for the Gunners. If Sudan had Sessegnon, we would have won. But despite creating chances, we couldn't equalise. Benin won 1–0. We had one point from two games.

To make matters worse, the players' hotel rooms were robbed during the match. They lost cash, phones and watches (I was OK – my stuff was locked in a suitcase). Although they were reimbursed – the hotel owner wired thousands of dollars to Sudan a few weeks later – it was a long trip home. Since leaving for Tunisia, we'd been away for two weeks. We'd flown 8,000 miles. We came back with two defeats, no goals and a police statement.

Two weeks later we played our third qualifier, against Ghana at the Red Castle. Their captain, Michael Essien, had scored in the Champions League semi-final for Chelsea a month earlier. Their centre-half, John Mensah, was at Lyon. Their keeper, Richard Kingson, was in the Premier League with Wigan. One of our guys, Hassan Karongo, played his football in Hasahesa.

Matthew Amoah – who played for NAC Breda in Holland – scored for Ghana after six minutes. I feared the worst but we didn't give in. Haitham Mustafa hit the bar. We had chances from corners. Then, in the second half, Amoah scored again. We lost 2–0 and were bottom after three games. From there, reaching the African Cup of Nations – let alone the World Cup – looked very hard.

AS THE WALL STREET JOURNAL POINTED OUT, SUDAN WAS 'RIVEN by civil war'. In the south, which was still part of Sudan, there was peace – of sorts – after years of conflict. But in Darfur the UN said 300,000 people had died, mainly from disease. Another 2.7 million had fled their homes. People asked how it felt working in a war-torn country. Was there a moral question mark over my job?

Honestly, I didn't think so. People want to eat, educate their children, and – in some cases – watch football. How does boycotting Sudan help an ordinary family in Khartoum? Do they, like everyone else, not deserve the best possible team? Do they not deserve a 90-minute escape?

I accept it's not black and white. I accept that people disagree. But football is a wonderful game, which unites people around the world, wherever they come from. It doesn't belong to presidents. It belongs to the people, regardless of race, colour or creed. That's who I work for.

In Khartoum, it was easy to forget Sudan's problems. The city was hundreds of miles from both Darfur and the south. No one – including the players – talked about the war. In fact, for the capital of Africa's biggest country, Khartoum was quiet. Occasionally, newspapers and magazines said the city could become 'Africa's Dubai'. But there was no chance of that. It was too strict.

You never forgot it was an Islamic city. Women covered up, there were no bars, and you rarely heard music. If you wanted to go out, you went to a restaurant or – if you were invited – a drinks reception at a Western embassy. Sometimes, the staff held parties at their homes. Although I don't drink – I was too focused on football as a teenager, then too stubborn to start – I went to one or two.

The police turned a blind eye to Westerners drinking at home. But if they thought locals were boozing, they took action. I was at one rooftop party, hosted by an Italian, when officers kicked the door in. They rushed upstairs, confiscated the booze, and shut down the party.

For Westerners, Khartoum was a different world. My goalkeeping coach in Sudan, Rogerio Ramos, was Brazilian. I met him during my first spell in India – he played for Vasco de Gama in Goa – and he was hard-working, respectful and talented. Sudan couldn't afford a full-time keeper coach, but I brought him to the first two camps. Another foreigner – an Australian, James Karageorgiou – came as sports science coach. I knew him from London. He was another fantastic worker.

At the first camp, James was very taken with the hotel's fruit salad. He must have had three or four bowls, but at training the next day, he looked green. It was 6.30 a.m. and it was already hot.

'You all right mate?' I asked James.

'No worries,' he said, before being violently sick all over the Astroturf. The lads were in stitches. So was I.

'Told you to go easy on the fruit salad,' I said, laughing.

Although we battered him, James had to go to hospital for two days. When we visited the ward, the locals tutted at Ramos, and security gave him filthy looks. Why? He was wearing shorts and T-shirt. Even in 30-degree heat, it wasn't conservative enough. Like I said: Khartoum was a different world.

After the 2–0 defeat to Ghana, there was almost three months before our next game. Faced with long, lonely evenings in my penthouse, I fell into my favourite bad habit: playing Football Manager.

I was introduced to Football Manager – or Championship Manager, as it was then – in Nepal. A neighbour who worked for the British Army installed it on my computer. I told him I wasn't interested – and really, I wasn't – but one day I clicked on the icon. And that, I'm afraid, was it.

I took over as Brighton manager. Twelve hours later I was still playing. If I won matches, I was elated; if I lost, I was furious. Being a real-life football manager didn't make a difference. Like millions of others, I was living my dream. At my computer, I was – at last – working in England.

Oh, I know. It's sad. But if you've played the game, you'll know. One night in Kathmandu, Lucy went to bed at 11 p.m. I told her I'd be there in ten minutes. The next thing I know, the cock was crowing and the sun was rising over the Himalayas. I'd been playing Championship Manager all night.

In the same week, Brighton sacked me. I applied for dozens of jobs but no one would have me (the irony…). I went to bed pissed off, muttering to myself.

'Where have you been?' asked Lucy.

'I've been sacked,' I muttered. She sat upright.

'Sacked? But I didn't hear the phone ring? You haven't played a game? What are we going to do?'

'Not Nepal,' I replied. 'The game. Championship Manager. Brighton sacked me.'

I can't repeat her response.

In 2002, before I moved to India, I went to see the makers of Championship Manager in their studio in London. Paul and Oliver Collyer were brothers from Shropshire who invented the game as teenagers in the 1980s; Miles Jacobson was a Watford fan who joined the team in the 1990s. I asked if I could be a consultant. As a Championship Manager addict, and real-life coach, I was perfect. Sadly, they had signed the former Liverpool and Ireland player, Ray Houghton, in the same role.

Although I wasn't on the team, I kept playing the game. I always started in the lower leagues, fulfilling my dream of taking a club through the divisions. I first appeared in the game in 2001. It was a huge moment – like an actor seeing his face on a billboard – but I wasn't happy with my stats. I had 8 out of 20 for man-management.

'If you'd seen the crap I dealt with in Asia,' I joked to Miles, 'it would have been much higher.'

I had better stats in the next game.

I'm not the only real-life coach, or player, who loves the game. At Millwall, the boys would pore over their profiles – 'Only 14 for speed?' – and it's well known that managers use the database to find players. Personally, Champ Man was a huge help when I worked in the Championship. I was familiar with the players – their names, positions and previous clubs – despite having been in Asia for six years.

In Khartoum I played Football Manager Live. Unlike previous games, you built your own team and played against other people online. I always called my team Atlas FC, because I liked the global connotation. Also, I knew how it felt to carry the weight of the world on my shoulders.

I was good at the game – my team was in the top division – but no one knew my real identity. Most of my opponents, I guess, were teenagers or students. When they weren't playing, they were doing essays, or nine-to-five jobs. I was a real-life coach trying to reach the World Cup.

In 2011, Miles and his team stopped Football Manager Live. It was a killer. A group of us spent two years trying to create a replacement called Ultimate Manager Live, but the coding was too expensive.

I now play an American football game – Madden NFL – on the PlayStation. I'm in an online league called NFLUK run by Bob_Champion. There are 32 of us from around the world, and it's very competitive. We have real drafts, real scouting, and use true-to-life playbooks. It sounds sad, but it's an escape. Some coaches play golf to relax, or go to the pub. I get the PlayStation out.

BACK IN THE REAL WORLD, THE CRITICISM WAS INCREASING. IF you drop big-name players and win, you're brave. If you lose, you're foolish. Even Dr Shaddad – my biggest supporter – told the Wall Street Journal I was 'a little exaggerating on discipline'. But that's my style. I have standards. I don't respect egos. When I piss people off, I paint a target on my back. I know that, but I won't change.

In August I went to an African Champions League game in Omdurman. Al Merrikh – home of Agab and Safari – were playing Zesco United from Zambia in the group stage. I went to the VIP area and sat with the Sudanese bigwigs. I was not welcome. If looks could kill, I would be dead.

At half-time Al-Merrikh were 3–1 down. Their big-name players were awful and, to be honest, I was delighted. I felt vindicated. Their fans were pissed off too: at one point, the game was stopped when missiles were thrown on the pitch. Al-Merrikh lost 3–2 and I left the ground with a smile on my face. Outside, a supporter jumped on my car. For a second, I panicked.

'Coach, you are right to drop the older players,' he said, to my relief. 'Let me kiss you.'

I'm fine, I thought. But thanks for your support.

In Sudan, I wasn't popular. But I wasn't worried. Criticism does not equal pressure. If I do the right thing – and dropping Agab and Safari was the right thing

– then critics don't bother me. If I work hard and make good decisions, I could lose ten games in a row and not doubt myself. It is, I guess, 'mental strength'. The best players have it. So do the best managers.

It sounds stubborn, but you have to be. If you're coaching a national team, you have to trust yourself. That doesn't mean you don't learn. Every day, I ask myself: 'What could I do better?' But you can't change your method when you lose a game. If you're scared of the sack, you take the easy option, not the right option. If I meet my own standards, I'm happy. If I'm sacked, so be it.

I have a video on my PC, filmed at the team hotel in the week before the Ghana game. We were training well but I wanted to squeeze in another session. We didn't have time to reach our pitch, so I took thirty chairs from a function room into the hotel grounds. We put the chairs out and used them for core exercises and explosive drills. Even with no pitch, and no cones, I will get the work done. Like I said: I have standards. Unfortunately, not everyone in Sudan shared them.

The FA were slow to help. Things weren't done quickly. In some cases, they weren't done at all. I wanted to put foundations in place. But when I asked for something, it was always IBM.

'Can we arrange a coach education session?' I'd ask.

'Inshallah,' they'd reply. God willing. The next day, I'd ask again.

'Bukra.' It will happen tomorrow. And then, when tomorrow came:

'Malesh.' Sorry. Never mind. Maybe next time.

It didn't help that Dr Shaddad was under pressure. He was serving a second term as president and wanted to run for a third. But, like any politician, he had enemies. In 2010 – after I left – the government barred Dr Shaddad from the presidential election. FIFA made them re-run it.

Before the Ghana game, we tried to train on a pitch in Khartoum. When we arrived, a club side was using it. The double-booking was deliberate: someone was playing games. I called Dr Shaddad and, half an hour later, the floodlights were switched off.

It was too dark to play, so the other team left. Once they did, the lights came back on, and we trained as normal. But I wasn't comfortable. My team was a pawn in a politicians' game.

The fourth game of our World Cup qualifying campaign was away to Ghana in September. On the day we flew, we trained in the morning, then met at the hotel at 6 p.m. The players arrived in their tracksuits but the captain, Haitham Mustafa, came in normal clothes. He was sniffing.

'I can't come,' he said. 'I'm not well.'

'You'll get better,' I said. 'We'll keep you separate from the other players. We need you out there. You're the captain.'

'Sorry, coach,' he replied. We couldn't change his mind, so he stayed at home. Two days later, he played in a friendly for Al-Hilal.

Haitham was a good guy – and a superb player – but he let me down. Yes, he was ill, but he was able to fly. The fact he played the friendly proved that. If I was captain of my country, I would walk to Ghana, even if I wasn't playing. But in Sudan they had a saying: 'God, then club, then country.' I guess Al-Hilal put him under pressure. Either way, I didn't pick him again.

There was another big problem. The game was in the middle of Ramadan, where Muslims fast during daylight hours. Playing Ghana was hard enough. Doing it without food or water was impossible. Before we flew, I asked the players if they would suspend their fast. In my understanding, the Koran gives Muslims exemptions from fasting if they are pregnant, ill, old, or travelling outside their country. The players said they would consider my request.

I am not religious but – it goes without saying – I respect people's faith. At training camps, we planned sessions around prayers. On the Ghana trip, I fasted with the players. Let me tell you, it was tough. By mid-afternoon, you're weak. Physically you don't want to move, but mentally it's worse. Your brain slows down. It's hard to think straight. To beat Ghana, the players would have to break their fast.

Two days before the match, we held a meeting. I asked, again, if they would eat and drink before the game. They said no. The game was due to kick off at 5 p.m. – around an hour before sunset – so, as a last resort, we asked Ghana to delay the kick-off until 7 p.m. I wasn't optimistic. Although they had Muslim players, we had more, and they could qualify for the World Cup if they won.

They said no. We had no chance.

On a warm West African evening, in front of 38,000 fans in Accra, Inter Milan's Sulley Muntari took the lead for Ghana after fourteen minutes. But we didn't fold. Despite having had no food or water for twelve hours, the boys were terrific. I was proud of them.

At half-time, we were still in the game. I begged them to drink, but not a drop passed their lips. Ten minutes into the second half, the fast ended, so the players sprinted to the sideline to gulp water. But if anything, it made them worse. They needed to sip, not gulp. The water sat in their empty stomachs. Michael Essien scored a second and we lost 2–0. We had one point from four games.

I spoke to Essien in the tunnel before the game. He was at Chelsea, and knew I was English, so we said hello. That night, as I brooded in my hotel room, a Ghanaian official called my mobile.

'Michael and the boys want you to celebrate with them,' he said.

'Excuse me?' I replied.

'We have qualified for the World Cup – we're partying!' he said.

'I'm fine,' I said.

'But Michael wants you to come,' he repeated.

'Really, I'm fine,' I replied, and hung up.

'Michael and the boys' had obviously never seen me after a defeat. I am not good company. I think about every decision. I rail against every mistake, whether by me, my players or the referee. At that point, I hated the Ghana team. I hate any team that beats me.

The last thing I wanted – literally the last thing – was to 'celebrate' in a nightclub with their hangers-on until 5 a.m. While they partied, I tried to sleep, before heading back to Khartoum the next day. The twelve-hour flight felt much longer.

THE NEXT GAME WAS A MONTH LATER IN MALI. GHANA HAD 12 points; Mali 5; Benin 4; and Sudan 1. To reach the Cup of Nations we needed one win, at least. On the plus side, Ramadan was over. On the down side, it was another trip to West Africa, with players squeezed into economy for hours on end.

After 41 minutes our new captain – Alaeldin Yousif Hado – was sent off for two yellows. Freddie Kanoute scored for Mali in the 89th minute, despite being a mile offside, before we got another red in injury time. We had lost again. The only positive was that our hotel rooms weren't robbed.

On the same day, Benin upset Ghana with a late winner. It meant we couldn't reach the Cup of Nations finals. We were bottom. We had failed. Unfortunately, there was still one game to go.

If my first qualifier with Sudan was a career highlight, my last was a lowlight. The bigwigs from Al-Merrikh wanted me and Dr Shaddad out. The game was at the Red Castle but it wasn't promoted. Only 600 fans turned up which, in effect, meant the ground was empty. We got ten times more for our training sessions. My shouts echoed round rows of empty seats. It was depressing.

Usually, Sudan games were like a carnival. A brass band played beforehand. Fans waved flags and blew whistles. The city game to life. But the Benin game was like a funeral. In the changing rooms, the younger players were crying. They didn't want to play. When we lined up for the national anthems, Benin's played but ours didn't. Again, someone was playing games. It was a message.

For the first time, the Red Castle felt a long way from home. Benin took the lead, we equalised with a penalty, but they scored a winner in the second half. We had one point from six.

	P	W	D	L	Points
Ghana	6	4	1	1	13
Benin	6	3	1	2	10
Mali	6	2	3	1	9
Sudan	6	0	1	5	1

Before the Benin game, I spoke to the New York Times. The reporter asked if I wanted to leave international football. My reply summed it up.

'There's nothing for me to do,' I replied. 'I don't have the players for as long as I'd like. I've been with national teams for seven years and I need to get back to the club scene.'

When you have games, managing a national team is fantastic. The whole country is behind you. Your team is centre stage. But when the curtains close, there's too much downtime. I was in Sudan for ten months and managed eight games. When I coached Millwall, I did eight games in a month.

Ask any manager: we live for the ninety minutes. It's our drug. When one match finishes we want another. But in Sudan I went weeks without a fix. When there weren't games, I tried to improve grassroots football, but the FA was riven. They didn't want to help and, if they did, there wasn't enough money. To most African countries, the manager is just a fly-by-night foreigner who looks after the first team then leaves through the revolving door. Sudan didn't know what to do with me.

I spent days in my penthouse on my own, with nothing but the hum of air-conditioning and Football Manager Live for company. I don't mind being alone but I missed my family. I flew back to Cyprus every couple of months and realised the girls – now aged twelve, nine and three – were growing up without me. It's the normal things you miss. Most dads take meal-times, or board games, or shopping trips, for granted. They became more special with every second I spent in Khartoum.

One night, Lucy phoned. She had a growth on her womb and needed an operation. If it was cancer, it didn't bear thinking about. Even if it was nothing, it was still major surgery. She would need eight weeks to recover, at least. She wouldn't be able to drive. I needed to come home.

I spoke to Dr Shaddad, who was great. He told me to take eight weeks off, unpaid, and come back in 2010. Despite the results, he knew I was rebuilding the team. But I didn't know whether eight weeks were enough. Also, Dr Shaddad's enemies were circling. If they got him, they got me. I wanted to leave. Reluctantly, he accepted my resignation. I flew home for Christmas and never went back.

My assistant, Mohamed Abdallah, became head coach. Mazda – as he was known – was a great guy. He took Sudan to the quarter-finals of the African Cup of Nations in 2012 (where they lost 3–0 to Zambia) and even picked four players that weren't from the Al-Firm.

Dr Shaddad is still going strong, but is no longer president. Although FIFA ordered the Sudanese FA to re-run the presidential election in 2010, he withdrew his nomination.

As for President Omar al-Bashir, he was re-elected in 2015 with 94 per cent of the vote. The ICC's warrant is still active. He has never been arrested.

10
IN THE CLUB
APEP, NEA SALAMINA,
ETHNIKOS ACHNA (CYPRUS), 2010–13

THANKFULLY, THE GROWTH IN LUCY'S WOMB WAS BENIGN, BUT I had to stay in Cyprus while she recovered. Although the $100,000 I earned in Sudan put me in the black, I needed a job.

Since I had last worked in Cyprus in 1999, my reputation had grown. I had coached four national teams, spent a year in England, and gained my UEFA Pro Licence. People knew about me. People respected me. I was no longer the outsider, turned away because I didn't have 'connections'.

In 2009/10, APEP – the club from the Troodos mountains who I managed before moving to Nepal – were in the top division. I knew one of their committee-men, Elefteris Eleftheriou. He worked at the hospital in Kyperounda and advised us about Lucy's operation. When I moved back from Sudan he told me APEP needed a manager, so I met the president, Panayiotis Neocleous. He was blunt.

'We are going down,' he told me. 'But we don't want to be embarrassed.'

APEP had played fifteen, won three, drawn three, and lost nine. Mr Neocleous offered me an eighteen-month contract on €5,000 a month, and said he wanted me to bring them back up. I signed the deal. Eighteen years after I moved from New York to Limassol, I was a manager in the Cypriot top flight.

Despite the president's pessimism, I didn't accept that we were down. We had twelve points and some decent players. Carlos Garcia was a strong Uruguayan centre-half. Francisco Guerrero, an Argentine forward known as Pancho, won the under-20 World Cup in 1995, scoring against Brazil in the final.

Most of the players were from overseas: we had more than a dozen nationalities, from Afghan to Hungarian. Despite that, language was never a problem. We normally spoke English, as most of the guys knew it. My part-time Spanish – picked up in New York nightclubs – came in handy, too.

My first game was against my old side, AEL. We lost 1–0 in front of 2,500 fans, but there were positive signs. The players said the previous coach, Nikos Andronikou, was too defensive, which is not my style. I wanted us to play with confidence; to attack when we could. Sadly – as I learned in my second game – fortune doesn't always favour the brave.

We were playing one of the biggest clubs in Cyprus, Omonia Nicosia. They have been champions twenty times. That season, they won the league by nine points, losing only two games. But it should have been three.

After two minutes, we took the lead when Garcia scored a header from a corner. After eighteen minutes, the big Uruguayan got another. Two minutes later, our Brazilian forward Gelson went clean through. He cut inside a defender, gave the keeper the eyes, then tucked it inside the near post.

The Omonia manager, a Greek called Takis Lemonis, turned round, closed his eyes, and rested his head on the dugout. Some fans rushed forward to abuse him. The rest jeered and whistled. In the corner, the APEP fans were going wild.

Lemonis couldn't believe what he was seeing, and neither could I. In my second game, we were spanking the champions-elect on their own ground. Even now, I get goose bumps thinking about it. And then something strange happened.

They pulled one back from a corner. Ten minutes later, our Danish defender Peter Gravesen – brother of the former Real Madrid midfielder Thomas – was sent off for a second yellow, when an Omonia player jumped over his outstretched leg. Soon after, Michalis Konstantinou – Cyprus's record scorer – ran past our defender at a corner. He fell to the floor, pointing at the spot. It was laughable, until the referee gave the penalty. From 3–0 up, it was now 3–2.

After an hour they equalised from a soft free kick. But with seven minutes left, it was still 3–3. We were holding on. Then a cross came in from the right. Garcia went to block it with his arms by his sides. From two yards away, the cross hit his elbow, which was tucked in. The ref gave Omonia their second penalty of the match. They scored. At full time I stood in the middle of the pitch, feeling sick.

On the way off, two Omonia players – Georgios Efrem, who came through the Arsenal academy, and Konstantinou – apologised to me. They were embarrassed.

The referee, Loizos Panayiotou, didn't referee another first-division game for four months. It was one of the worst performances I've seen.

In Cyprus, managers hold a joint press conference after the game. The away team goes first.

'The whole of Cyprus saw what happened,' I said. 'I don't need to comment any further.'

'It was a difficult game,' said Lemonis. 'But I made some tactical changes and we turned it round.'

Tactical changes. What bullshit. They won because of the referee's decisions. I stood up and walked off. A reporter asked where I was going.

'We all saw what happened,' I repeated, and left the room. To this day, people in Cyprus remember that game. They call it 'the slaughter'.

We drew our next game 3–3 against Paphos – they equalised in the last minute – before losing 1–0 away to Doxa. But, on 8 February, it seemed we had finally won. We were 1–0 up at home to Ethnikos. The fourth official signalled four minutes of added time. This was it, surely. Three points at last. A reward for the hard work. Then, in the 96th minute, the ref gave yet another soft free kick.

The ball was crossed from deep. We didn't clear it. They scored. As I stared at my shoes, trying not to scream, a committee member came to the dugout.

'Get them off the pitch,' he told me.

'What?' I replied in amazement. 'I can't do that. We have to finish the game.'

At that point, I looked across the pitch. The president, Mr Neocleous, walked out of the players' tunnel on to the middle of the pitch.

'You're coming off,' he bellowed at the players.

'You can't do that,' I pleaded. 'We'll get hammered for this. Let's take the point and move on.'

'You've only had this bullshit for a month, Steve,' he replied. 'We've suffered it all season.'

The players were in a difficult position. When the man who pays your wages gives you an order, it's hard to say no. And they didn't all need to walk. If five of them went, the game was abandoned. Eventually, the whole team followed the president off the pitch. I stood there, helpless.

Afterwards, the Cypriot FA threatened to suspend my licence for a year, meaning I wouldn't be able to work. In the end, the game was awarded to Ethnikos, we had six points deducted, the club were fined €32,000, and the players who walked off were suspended for a game. In effect, we were relegated.

Two weeks later – with half the squad banned, and me watching from the stands – we lost 3–0 away to Anorthosis.

After two months in the Cypriot top division, I was disillusioned. I thought there would be less politics than Sudan. If anything, there was more. All I wanted was a fair game of football. Was that too much to ask? But if I wanted to live with my family in Cyprus – and I did – I had to get used to it.

Our final match was in March – relegated teams don't contest the end-of-season play-offs – so I had plenty of time to plan our promotion campaign. An agent told me about a 28-year-old keeper, Derek Soutar, who was out of contract at Dundee in the Scottish First Division. I never sign a player unless I – or someone I trust – has seen them, so I flew to watch Soutar in a friendly against Celtic.

I stayed with Steven Tweed, a friend of mine, who was managing Montrose in the Scottish lower leagues. Steven played for Hibs, Stoke and Dundee, and also had spells in Greece, Germany and Japan. He is a clever boy, and I enjoyed his company. I watched Soutar against Celtic – he did well – and offered him a two-year contract. It was a good trip all round, until I tried to fly home.

The ash cloud from an Icelandic volcano meant Glasgow airport was closed. I took the train to London but, by then, all European airspace was shut down. I waited a week to get back to Cyprus. When I returned, I had a meeting with the president, Mr Neocleous.

'I've been pumping in money for years,' he told me. 'I've had enough. I'm walking away.'

Without the president's money, APEP were in trouble. When Soutar arrived in June, I was upfront.

'Get yourself a small house,' I told him. 'There will be days you don't get paid.'

I hoped Mr Neocleous would change his mind, but he didn't. He paid me three months' wages and I left in August. My contract lasted until June 2011, but it wasn't worth the fight. Soutar lasted until December. I don't know if he got paid, but I fear he didn't. Perhaps the ash cloud was an omen.

In September, Nikos Andreou called me. Nikos – who had been a close friend since we played for the Freedoms in New York together – lived in Cyprus and was godfather to my youngest daughter, Isabel. He played many times for a Cypriot team, Nea Salamina, and was still involved there.

Salamina were based in Larnaca after being exiled from Famagusta in 1974, following the Turkish invasion. They were a big club with a passionate, left-wing following, but were bottom of the second division. Nikos said they needed a coach. I was invited to see the committee.

I asked for €7,000 a month for three years, plus Nikos as my assistant and Rogerio Ramos as my goalkeeping coach. We agreed €5,000 a month for seventeen months, plus Nikos. There wasn't enough money for Ramos, which I accepted. But when the contract was drawn up, they changed seventeen months to seven.

'I will sign this,' I said. 'But when you renew, you will need to pay more.'

The team was a mess. The players were too casual. I told them to arrive thirty minutes early for training and I made the sessions extra-competitive. When you're bottom of the second division, something has to change. In return, I made sure the club paid on time. That did wonders for morale.

My first game was a 0–0 draw against Atromitos. In my second, we beat Omonia Aradippou 2–1 away with a late winner. After that, something clicked. We didn't lose in the league until March.

The unbeaten run was seventeen games, including five wins in a row after Christmas. When we did lose – 3–2 away to PAEEK – we won four on the bounce afterwards. The team was fantastic, and the fans were even better. They brought banners and flares. They chanted nonstop, home and away. We were flying.

Remember, I didn't win a game in Sudan. I won two in a year in Malawi. We were relegated at APEP and Millwall. I had forgotten the joy of winning matches. For years, I had been trying to turn teams around. Now I was on a roll. It was a long time coming, and I loved every second.

We played 4–4–2 and pressed teams, especially at home. Up front, Chris Dickson – the former Charlton striker – was fantastic. He was a lovely guy with bags of pace. In January I brought in four players, including the Estonian midfielder Martin Vunk, which increased competition for places. Training was sharp. No one was guaranteed a place. In April, I took the boys to RAF Akrotiri for team building and fitness work. Even military drills couldn't wipe the smiles off their faces.

We finished second in the league, which wasn't enough for automatic promotion. The top four teams went into a group, playing each other home and away, with the top three going up. But points carried over from the normal season – we were six points above fourth – so I wasn't worried. We stayed in second, losing once. We were up. I was elated. It was, I felt, a reward for years of shovelling shit.

When I arrived, we had four points from five games. Seven months later we were promoted, so I was in a good position to renegotiate my contract. We agreed a one-year deal on €7,000 a month, plus €10,000 if we stayed up, €10,000 for a top-six finish, and €10,000 for winning the cup. I also brought in Ramos as goalkeeper coach. As I predicted, not giving me a seventeen-month contract in September had cost the committee. But my contract was the easy bit: the hard bit was building a new squad.

I loved the promotion-winning team, but most of them weren't good enough for the top division. If we didn't sign players, we would come back down – no question about it. I finished bottom with APEP and couldn't face it again. We kept four or five, then went into the transfer market. I had €1m for players' salaries. Or, to put it another way, less than €50,000 each for a 24-man squad.

When you manage a football team, agents don't stop ringing. That summer, I got thirty or forty calls every day, plus emails, from every corner of the world. Others sent video clips, even though – for obvious reasons – I never sign a player based on a showreel. Clearly, a year at Nea Salamina on €50,000 wasn't the golden ticket. But the agents were desperate. Without a club, no one got paid.

Some managers hate agents. I don't. Salamina weren't rich – we couldn't pay huge transfer fees – so we relied on agents to offer us out-of-contract players. But before I dealt with anyone, I made one thing clear. Don't offer me money. Don't offer me a kick-back. If I like your player, I will take him. If I don't, I won't. I had that conversation a lot: that summer, we brought in nineteen players.

I heard about a 27-year-old Spanish midfielder called Diego Leon. Like many European players, he had chased his dream across the continent. He started at Real Madrid, never made the first team, then moved to Grasshoppers in Switzerland and Barnsley in the English lower leagues. We found him in the German third division with Wacker Burghausen. As I said, I like to see a player before signing him, so we invited him to our pre-season training camp in Greece.

He arrived at 3 a.m. We had a friendly that day, so I told him to watch and rest. But he was adamant: he wanted to play. I liked his attitude and within five minutes he played two beautiful passes, back-to-back. I brought him off and put a contract under his nose. He made 21 appearances that season.

Although we signed thirteen different nationalities, most were already in Greece or Cyprus. Imoro Lukman, a Ghanaian midfielder, came from APOP. Solomon Grimes, a Liberian defender, signed from Ethnikos Piraeus. Jimmy Modeste – a Cape Verde international – came from Paphos. We also got Carlos Garcia, the big Uruguayan who I knew from APEP. He was a born leader.

One of my best singings was Julian Gray, the former Arsenal and Birmingham City winger. Jules came to Cyprus to sign for another top-division team, Ermis, but the deal fell through. An agent said he was available, so I called him. At first he was unsure – he thought we'd struggle – but Chris Dickson persuaded him. I'm glad he did. Jules was super-professional with a touch of Premier League class.

Despite our signings, the press didn't fancy our chances. One paper said we had 'the worst roster in the division'. I pinned the headline in my office for motivation, but it didn't do much good. We won two out of ten in pre-season – including the tour of Greece – then lost our first league match 3–0 to AEL. In our second game, we drew 1–1 in the derby against Anorthosis, despite Jules giving us the lead in the 90th minute. It was an absolute screamer. It deserved to win the game.

Momentum is massive. When you lose, morale drops, and football is no different to any other job: you work better when you're confident. We needed a spring in our step. We needed a win. Thankfully, it came in our third game. We beat Ermis 1–0 to begin a four-match unbeaten run.

In November I spoke to Richard Keys and Andy Gray on TalkSport as part of their 'Brits Abroad' feature. They were keen to talk about Apoel, who reached the Champions League Round of 16 that season, losing on penalties to Lyon. Apoel's success – they finished above Zenit St Petersburg, Porto and Shakhtar Donetsk in their group – meant people were taking Cypriot football seriously.

'Everyone is standing up and taking notice of APOEL, who are doing ever so well,' said Gray.

'They're not taking notice of them as much as I am,' I replied. 'We've got them on Sunday.'

'Oh no …' said Gray.

But Andy needn't have worried. Diego Leon scored with the outside of his boot after eighteen minutes – what was he doing in the German third division? – and we won 1–0. Although we were underdogs, it wasn't smash and grab. We deserved it. We even had a second goal disallowed for offside. Beating one of the best sixteen teams in Europe was huge. There's a picture of the starting eleven in my office.

When the transfer window opened in January, Chris Dickson went to AEL for €100,000 (and helped them win the league) while our Belgian forward Dieter van Tornhout moved to Kilmarnock. We needed strikers, so I went into the transfer market.

Our Estonian midfielder, Martin Vunk, told me that Estonia's record goal-scorer, Andres Oper, was training with Bolton Wanderers after being released by AEK Larnaca. We snapped him up. Another forward, a Ghanaian called Samuel Yeboah, came in from Ashdod in Israel. But trouble was brewing. Our players weren't being paid on time.

I was straight with our new signings, telling them money might be a problem, but they decided to come anyway. Andres had nothing to lose – he was a free agent – while Sammy was looking to leave Israel. And we weren't the only club in trouble. Across the island, the financial crisis meant players weren't being paid.

In short, Cypriot football doesn't add up. That season, our average attendance was 1,650. That doesn't sound a lot, but it was the seventh highest in the division. Some clubs averaged less than 1,000. Some games got less than 100. The TV deal wasn't massive, and neither was the prize money. Clubs needed sponsors to fill the gap, but that year, football was an unaffordable luxury.

In February 2012, the global players' union FIFPro released a survey of 315 professionals in Cyprus. Only 23 per cent were paid on time. Of those who didn't get their wages, 74 per cent had to wait up to three months, 21 per cent up to six months, and 3 per cent up to a year. The union said one player – a Venezuelan called Cesar Alberto Castro Perez – was punched, slapped and threatened with a gun by hooded men when he tried to claim three months' unpaid wages from Olympiakos

Nicosia.

At Salamina, people shared cars to training because they couldn't afford petrol. The better-off players cooked for the poorer ones. People think footballers are millionaires, but most of our squad were getting €30,000 or €40,000 a year. Three months without wages was a crisis.

The club offered to pay my salary but I refused. How could I take money while the players weren't getting theirs? At one point, I went four months without my wages. Some squads in Cyprus went on strike in protest at not being paid. Others missed training. Our players spoke about striking, but it wouldn't do them any good. If they wanted to leave – and they did – we had to win games.

Our penultimate match of the regular season was away to Alki. If we won, we were guaranteed to finish in the top eight, which meant we were safe. If we drew or lost, we could finish in the bottom six, meaning relegation was a possibility. The week before, Alki – who were also mid-table – played a reserve team against Ethnikos, in order to save themselves for us. It was a huge game.

In the 94th minute it was 0–0. They got a corner. The ball was cleared to Sammy Yeboah – our signing from Israel – thirty yards inside his own half. He outpaced one defender, took on another, and sprinted towards their goal. As he reached the area, their keeper came out. Sammy slipped it past him. 1–0.

Our whole bench emptied. The subs sprinted to celebrate in the corner. It felt like winning a cup final. If we had finished in the bottom six, we were fucked. As a newly promoted team, the other sides would have conspired to send us down. But Sammy's goal meant we were safe.

At full time, I had a pop at the Alki players. 'If you played like that every week,' I told them, 'you would be in the Champions League.'

They didn't appreciate the sarcasm, and there was some pushing and shoving. I was fined €3,000.

We won our last game, too, and finished sixth in the normal season. After the play-offs – which had no bearing on relegation or the European places – we finished seventh. It was Salamina's highest position for six years. As players and people, the squad had my total respect.

Salamina wanted to renew my contract, but with only €600,000 for players' salaries. A London-based agency offered to provide South American players – and pay some of their wages – but the deal fell through. I asked the club if the reduced budget meant they'd pay on time.

'We will still have problems,' they replied.

I couldn't lie to their players. I couldn't watch them sign their contracts, knowing that, in two or three months, they might be worthless. There were some fantastic people at Salamina, but I was fed up. There were too many broken promises. A year after winning promotion, I turned down the new contract and left. I couldn't face another year of players knocking on my door, desperate for money.

A number of the squad moved. Carlos Garcia went to Racing Club in Uruguay. Diego Leon and Martin Vunk went to Greece, although Julian Gray stayed with Salamina for another season before returning to England. Eventually, most of the players got their money. I waited a year to get all of mine, including bonuses. Without a left-wing politician, it wouldn't have happened at all.

Kikis Kazamias served as minister for finance in Cyprus between 2011 and 2012. He was also Salamina through and through. When he realised I was owed thousands, he worked behind the scenes to get my wages. Sometimes, we would meet at a coffee shop, so he could hand over €1,000 or €2,000 in cash. Other times, we met at the bus stop. He was a massive help. Without him, I couldn't have paid the bills.

UNLIKE, SAY, JOSE MOURINHO OR WAYNE ROONEY, I DON'T 'have an agent'. No one represents me exclusively. I work with them on an ad-hoc basis: if they can help me, I will help them. Like any profession, there are good ones and bad ones. I've been lucky to know some good ones.

Alamgir and Faisal Kashmiri at Strata helped me get the Nepal and India jobs when I started out. They were fantastic. Stelios Vradelis – who saw the military parade in Malawi – was a journalist when he contacted me in Nepal. He wrote about me for a Greek magazine and we remained friends. He became an agent, and is now director of a firm called Altius Fortius Agentius. He speaks five or six languages, is super-intelligent, and knows the game. He has connections everywhere.

Fredrik Risp, the former Swedish international who played for me at Ethnikos Achna in Cyprus, has in-depth knowledge of Scandinavia and Turkey, where he also played. Unlike some, he won't offer you something you haven't asked for.

In the States, the former Swindon player Stefani Miglioranzi has good contacts in Mexico, Brazil and the rest of South America. I like the way he handles himself – he's very calm, concise and honest. His friend Graham Smith, who founded the First Wave agency, is another fantastic person. He knows US soccer like the back of his hand, as you'll read later.

Massoud Roushandel, who's also US-based, knows America and Costa Rica. Tony Antoniou is a great guy based in London, while Max Eppel, also in London, is a sports lawyer of the highest order. I'm pleased to call him my friend. There are others, too: if they can help me, I will deal with them.

In England, David and James Garley have been very supportive. They are a father-and-son team from Hertfordshire with a company called Achieve Management. In the summer of 2012, after I left Nea Salamina, they put me forward for the Gillingham job.

To be honest, I expected nothing. When you've applied for hundreds of jobs, you don't get your hopes up. But, to my surprise, Gillingham invited me for an interview. I packed my bags, wrote a PowerPoint presentation, and flew to England.

James was away so David drove 100 miles from Stevenage to Brighton to pick me up, then another 80 miles to Gillingham for the interview. That shows their commitment. After arriving at Priestfield, David introduced himself to the chairman, Paul Scally.

'Do you know how long you'll be?' David asked.

'Forty-five minutes,' Scally replied.

'I'll wait and have a cup of tea then,' David said.

I was taken to a suite in the stand, overlooking the pitch. Scally and Andy Hessenthaler were in the room (Hessenthaler had been sacked as manager, but remained as director of football). Scally talked about the club. Hessenthaler talked about his role. I looked at my watch.

'I don't wish to be rude,' I said, 'but if we've only got forty-five minutes, do you mind if I do my presentation?'

As always, I'd done my research. I knew Gillingham had four or five good players coming through, so I told Scally and Hessenthaler they should be in the first team, not stuck in the reserves. I said I'd use my contacts to bring in young, hungry players from Africa and Asia, who we could sell on. I talked about in-house coach education. I also asked Hessenthaler what they did to prevent injuries.

'The university checks them over before the season,' he replied.

'And what about during the season?' I asked.

'We warm up, we do the normal things,' he replied.

I said I'd appoint a sports scientist, who would monitor the players' output and work out when they were at risk. Two and a half hours flew by.

'We have a real problem with set plays,' said Scally, keen to pick my brains. 'We concede lots and don't score many. How would you fix that?'

'Allow me to show you,' I replied. The previous season with Salamina, we scored sixteen or seventeen goals from corners, free kicks and long throws, so I showed the clips.

'Bloody hell,' said Scally. 'This is great stuff.'

'It's not rocket science,' I replied. 'It's basic coaching.'

When the clips finished, Scally looked at me.

'You've given me a massive problem,' he said. 'Before you walked in the door, I couldn't see you as manager of this club. Now I've got some thinking to do.'

Andy and I left the room. 'You were the best candidate,' he said once the door was closed. 'I'm sure you'll be back.'

Andy showed me the gym, which was some weights and a few bikes.

'Will I have a budget to improve this?' I asked.

'I'm sure we can sort something,' he said. He then showed me the dressing rooms.

'We get changed here, drive to the training ground, then come back to get showered,' he said.

'We can't have this,' I said. 'The players need changing rooms, a gym and a canteen at the training ground, so they can work on and off the field.'

I was surprised by the facilities. Gillingham were one of the biggest clubs in the fourth tier. Their average attendance in 2011/12 was more than 5,000. They had an all-seater stadium with a 12,000 capacity, but their players were piling into a minibus like a pub team.

Even so, I wanted in. I liked Scally and Hessenthaler. Their club had bags of potential. Gillingham spent five seasons in the second tier from 2000 to 2005 and they could easily return. When David drove me home, I was full of optimism. I expected a second interview, at least. But I heard nothing. Ten days later, Martin Allen got the job. It was his eighth Football League appointment.

I'm not knocking him. He knows the lower leagues, which he proved by winning the title with Gillingham. Scally had more than sixty applications, and interviewed sixteen people, so Allen must have been impressive. But I don't think it was a level playing field. Scally's remark to me – 'I couldn't see you as manager of this club' – certainly suggests that. Either way, I'm sure Gillingham found my interview useful. Soon after Allen was appointed, they employed a sports scientist.

I WAS BACK ON THE JOB MARKET. I DID FIFA COURSES IN Lithuania and Vietnam and waited for the phone to ring. For once, I wasn't worried. After APEP and Nea Salamina I had a good reputation, and the chaos of Cypriot football meant there were always vacancies.

In one week in September, four clubs changed their manager. The former Scotland manager George Burley left Apollon after two games. There were rumours that Omonia Nicosia and Anorthosis Famagusta were interested in me, and people asked if I was going 'green or blue'. In the end, I went blue. But not Anorthosis blue.

I have spoken to the president of the Cyprus FA, Costakis Koutsokoumnis, three times about the national team job. Although nothing came of it, I know he rates me. In December, he recommended me to Ethnikos Achna, a first-division team from a village near Dhekelia.

They had a good run in Europe in 2006 – knocking three teams out of the

Intertoto Cup, before reaching the UEFA Cup proper – but were in trouble in 2012. They hadn't won a game all season. I agreed a short-term contract on €5,000 a month but warned them I wasn't a miracle worker.

On my first day, I walked into the dressing room and met Fredrik Risp. I had done my research, so I knew about his impressive career. 'You're one of the team captains,' I told him. With him at the back, we lost two and drew two, before winning three in a row in January: 1–0 away to Salamina, 2–1 at home to Ayia Napa, and 3–0 at home to Paphos. I was plotting our great escape when the phone rang. UEFA had flagged up the Paphos game. The police had begun a match-fixing inquiry.

I went to the stadium to be interviewed. 'We are fighting for our lives,' I told the police officers. 'We have done nothing wrong.'

They asked me if there was anything suspicious about the Paphos game.

'If anything happened, it wasn't on our side,' I replied.

My conscious was clear, but the police were right to be concerned. Cypriot football stank.

In February 2014 – by which time I was working in Greece – the head of the Cypriot referees' association had his car bombed. All first-division matches were postponed that weekend. Eight months later, a pipe bomb exploded outside the association's office in Nicosia. Three months after that, a 60-year-old woman, Maro Mouskos, was thrown from her bed when a bomb exploded at her house in Limassol. Her son, Thomas, was a referee. Thankfully, he wasn't at home.

In December 2014, a 34-year-old referee, Marios Panayi, spoke out. He said referees – with help from the FA – were fixing first-division games so certain teams were relegated or promoted. He handed over documents and recorded conversations.

'Referees can use any trick in the book,' he said. 'It can be a minor or major decision depending on the match and whether it is televised. Where there aren't cameras, they can do big things.'

Only 10 per cent of refs were clean, he added.

In 2015, the players' union ran a two-month pilot, where players could report suspected match-fixing. In the first division, 67 per cent said games were rigged. Almost a quarter said they had been approached to fix matches, either before the game or at half-time. In November 2016, a UEFA vice-president, Marios Lefkaritis, said there had been 75 suspected fixed matches in Cyprus since 2011.

'We're among the top three or four countries that have the most matches suspected of being fixed,' said Lefkaritis, who is also an honorary president of the Cyprus FA. 'It ceases to be a suspicion. It becomes extremely worrying when you have a file sent to you almost every week.'

During my career, I have been approached twice.

Once – and I won't name the club – I was asked to play our reserve side in a league match. My response was simple: 'Fuck you.'

Another time, I was asked not to attend a cup match, so it could be fixed. My response was the same. At other times, I heard stories like everyone else. But I never saw evidence of match-fixing, and I never heard the players talk about it.

The police took no further action after the Paphos game in 2013. But I had another problem: Ethnikos weren't paying my wages. I resigned and began legal action against the club. Ethnikos paid up after receiving a letter from my solicitor, but I was still €150 down on legal fees.

It was depressing. I had been in Cyprus three years, managing three top-division teams. Each time, I resigned over money. I loved living with Lucy and the girls but I was tired of Cypriot football. The financial crisis meant clubs couldn't pay the bills. The smell of match-fixing was growing. In my front room, by the television, is a big, blue globe. I gave it a spin. It was time to pack my bags again.

11
SPINNING THE GLOBE
APOLLON SMYRNIS (GREECE), 2013–14

AFTER LEAVING ETHNIKOS I GOT AN EMAIL FROM A YOUNG English agent, asking if I was interested in managing the Guinea-Bissau national team. I knew they had some good players, mainly based in Portugal, so I said yes. To be honest, I fancied anywhere that wasn't Cyprus.

The agent introduced me, via email, to a guy who worked for Guinea-Bissau in Europe. A fake agent from Bahrain once tried to charge me €500 to put me forward for a job, so I checked the Guinea-Bissau guys out. They were genuine. I told them to book me a flight when the federation were ready.

Weeks went by, so in May, I arranged to fly to Greece for an interview with a third-division club, Larissa (previous managers included Chris Coleman and my friend from North Korea, Jørn Andersen). Then, two days before the interview, the guys from Guinea-Bissau got in touch. They had booked me a flight to London, then on to Bissau. I cancelled the trip to Greece and flew to England instead.

I met the English agent in an expensive townhouse in a north London square. It seemed to be a base for Guinea-Bissau nationals in Britain – people were coming and going, including a young Southampton player, Alberto Seidi – so I stayed there the night before we flew to Africa.

I had agreed, in principle, a two-year deal on $10,000 a month, plus bonuses. I expected to sign the contract, have a look round, then come home to prepare for my fifth national team job. After the long flight to Bissau I met the federation president, Manuel Lopes Nascimento.

'There's a problem with the contract,' he said. 'It's only two years. We want you for three.'

'That's fine,' I replied. 'Increase the salary in my third year and it's a deal.'

He agreed. He then asked how much time I would spend in Bissau.

'As much time as possible,' I said. 'I'll also need to watch plenty of games in Portugal.'

'We have a deal,' he said. 'Now the government needs to sign off the contract. Stay the weekend and come back on Monday.'

It was Friday, so I spent the weekend looking round Bissau. It was nice enough. I saw the national stadium and met the general secretary, Alberto da Silva Dias, who was a fantastic guy. But with all due respect, I was ready to go home by Monday. As planned, I went to the federation to sign my contract. One problem: the president was 5,000 miles away at the FIFA congress in Mauritius.

The federation said he would be back by Wednesday. I wanted to leave, so I asked if we could sign the contract by fax. They said it would be easier to wait. I agreed, reluctantly, but was starting to get pissed off. To pass the time, I ran a coaching course at the national stadium – a thousand people came to watch – but mostly, I kicked round the hotel. One evening I spoke to the guy in the room next door. He was a colonel in the Senegalese army, who was part of a peacekeeping force in Bissau.

'Nothing is what it seems in Guinea-Bissau,' he told me. 'If they tell you it is night, it will be day.'

I told him I was about to sign a three-year contract to coach their national team.

'Get everything in writing,' he said. 'And trust no one.'

Now I was worried. It didn't help that, in order to get my visa, the federation had my passport. They also told me there were only two flights out a week.

By Wednesday, there was still no sign of Mr Nascimento. I asked the English agent to help but he was powerless. I felt trapped, like I was a hostage. The next morning, it got worse: I saw dozens of soldiers running round outside the hotel with guns. I knocked on the Senegalese colonel's door.

'Coach,' he said, sounding serious, 'get out as soon as you can.'

Guinea-Bissau was a volatile country. In 2009, soldiers shot dead the president in his palace. In 2012 there was a military coup. From my hotel, it seemed like another was brewing. I was thousands of miles from home and worried. Larissa were still keen – they called me to identify players – and a season in the Greek third division on €5,000 a month seemed a better bet than Bissau on twice that.

I was losing my mind. I phoned the federation to demand my passport. My tone was not diplomatic. Eventually – after more than a week in the country – they gave it back. I went straight to the airport and took the next flight north. The 'coup' never happened but the city didn't feel safe. Two months later, the agents asked me to go back. I took the Senegalese colonel's advice and said no.

COACHING A NATIONAL TEAM IS A HUGE HONOUR. REPRESENTING Nepal, India, Malawi, Sudan and Rwanda has been the biggest privilege of my life. Leading someone else's country – to wear their badge and face their flag – is humbling. I don't take the responsibility lightly. But there is something bigger.

I would give five years of my life to represent England. If you offered me one cap – five minutes in a friendly – you could take me early. No problem at all. I am a proud Englishman and, if anything, living abroad makes me prouder. I appreciate it more. Working in England isn't a picnic, but you don't have to worry about getting paid, getting malaria, or being caught in a military coup.

After I got back from Guinea-Bissau, Stuart Pearce left the England under-21 job. My ears pricked up. I was an outsider, but the FA – publicly, at least – was changing. Roy Hodgson, a former PE teacher, was England manager. Dan Ashworth was director of elite development, despite never playing professionally. The national training centre, St George's Park, opened in Staffordshire, and coaching qualifications were in vogue. The FA also stressed they wanted 'international coaching experience'. I met their criteria. I was cheaper than Pearce. Finally, I thought, I had a chance.

I spoke to my friend John Peacock – who coached England under-17s and worked in coach education – and sent my application to London. I asked for £250,000 a year which, I understood, was half of Pearce's salary. I knew I wasn't favourite, but I was worth an interview.

I had coached four national teams. I had spent twenty years doing FA courses, and was one of the most highly qualified coaches in the world. Interviewing me would show the FA took those qualifications seriously. Every self-made coach in England would gain hope. But 36 hours later I got an email.

'Sorry,' it said. 'We're going in a different direction.'

I asked for feedback. They didn't reply. There were dozens of applicants but I deserved more than that. If anything, I felt like I was wasting their time. In August, they appointed Gareth Southgate on a three-year deal, even though he didn't have international coaching experience. It was seven years after he got the Middlesbrough job, despite not being qualified.

I'm not knocking Gareth – he seems like a good guy – but it was frustrating. He coaches one Premier League team, takes them down, then gets the England under-21 job. Three years later, he's managing the senior team. His face seems to fit. Mine doesn't.

At the end of June I went to Jamaica to run two five-day courses for FIFA. As usual, there was a press conference to start. The compere was a local TV presenter. He talked about the president of the federation, Captain Horace Burrell, before turning his attention to the 'chief guest' – me. He read my CV word for word – which, as you know, takes some time – before turning to Captain Burrell.

'Mr President,' he finished, 'if I were in your shoes, I would give this man the job now.'

The audience laughed. I didn't know where to look. At the time, Jamaica didn't have a national team manager. Two weeks before I arrived, the former Hull City midfielder Theodore Whitmore resigned after losing 2–0 to Honduras in a World Cup qualifier. I stepped up to the microphone.

'I'd just like to thank my new agent ...' I began.

The next day I went on the compere's TV programme, Smile Jamaica, which was the biggest breakfast show on the island. They asked if I was interested in the national team job. Being in the country when they needed a coach was sheer co-incidence, but Jamaica were a top-fifty side. They had good players across North America and Europe. They reached the 1998 World Cup. Most importantly, there was a vacancy, and I was out of work. I told Smile Jamaica I was interested.

Two days before I left, the Jamaican FA spoke to me. I said I was keen, and we spoke about my salary and budget for backroom staff. We agreed a figure, and a week later an 'FA source' told the Jamaica Observer I was a 'front runner'. My hopes rose. I waited for the call. Unfortunately it never came: the former Cameroon and Thailand manager, Winfried Schafer, got the job. As it turned out, the FA chose wisely. Schafer reached the 2015 CONCACAF Gold Cup final, beating the US on the way.

Jamaica wasn't the only job I missed that week. Years earlier, I got a LinkedIn in-vitation from the former Manchester City and Manchester United midfielder Terry Cooke, who was playing for Colorado Rapids in the MLS. That's quite common in football: you see someone's name, you add them, and before long you're chatting.

Terry suggested looking for work in the States, so he introduced me to Graham Smith, an Englishman with a sports marketing company in California called First Wave. Graham is a fascinating guy: he was a goalkeeper in the 1960s and 70s with Colchester and Cambridge, among others, and was a director at Chelsea before moving to the States.

By 2013, Graham was technical director of a new club, Sacramento Republic, who were due to enter the United Soccer League (America's second tier) in 2014. He asked if I was interested in managing the team. When I told him I was, he sounded surprised. 'You're used to a higher level,' he said.

It's true: the Cypriot top division, and African World Cup qualifying, was a better standard than the USL. But Sacramento was a chance to build. All my career – from Nepal to Nea Salamina – I have dragged teams out of the shit. At Sacramento, there was no shit: just a blank canvas, ready for my ideas. That, and the prospect of moving the family to California, meant it was a dream job.

Graham interviewed me over Skype when I was in Jamaica. As always, I had done my homework. We spoke about the league, the standard of players, and the salaries they would expect. In the end, it was a choice between me and Preki, the Belgrade-born former American international who had played in the Premier League and played and managed in the MLS. They went for him.

I was gutted, but I couldn't blame them: when you're setting up a new team, a high-profile coach is helpful. And Preki wasn't just a name. Under him, Sacramento won the USL in their first season.

After two weeks in Jamaica, I was back in Cyprus without a job. When you're out of work, you watch football differently. The managerial merry-go-round turns in your head. Part of you thinks: 'I hope this team plays badly' or 'A defeat here and he's under pressure'.

I would never undermine a manager. I would never speak to the press, or – even worse – turn up in the directors' box for three matches in a row. There are plenty who do, and it makes me sick. But if you're out of work, you want certain teams to lose. It's human nature. My year in Sudan, and my three jobs in Cyprus, meant I was out of the woods financially. But I was a long way from being comfortable. As usual, things were tight.

I watched games, sent emails, and suffered. While waiting for the phone to ring, I did something useful. By 2013, I knew people everywhere, but at the start of my career, I was green. In Nepal, India and Africa, I had no idea. I would have loved to ask someone: 'What's this place like?' or 'Can you put a word in for me?' So, in September 2013, I set up the British Coaches Abroad Association.

I wanted it to be a network for people working overseas. I was sick of seeing the German, French, Spanish and Dutch federations put their coaches forward for jobs while the English FA did very little.

I created a LinkedIn page to connect Brits working abroad. We soon had more than 100 members, with no one paying a penny. I spoke to my friend Efrem Leigh – a recruitment specialist – who designed a website and added a jobs page. I bought the domain britishcoachesabroad.com, then roped in Owen Amos, a BBC journalist who I've known since 2011.

Owen agreed to look after the site and interview our members. Crucially, the fantastic website football365.com carried the articles as well. Before long, thousands of people were reading about our members every week.

Some of the stories were amazing. Our first interview was Paul Ashworth: one minute he's first-team coach for Barry Fry at Peterborough, the next he's managing Ventspils in Latvia. Jack Brazil, a guy studying at Coventry University, spent a summer coaching in the Mongolian Premier League. Simon McMenemy went from the Ryman League to the Philippines national team.

The tales were inspiring. Some of them were funny too, like this from my good friend Steve Darby:

> After leaving Bahrain, I got an offer from Tasmania. I thought I was off to Africa. The minute I arrived in Launceston, a feller threw me a ball and said: 'Juggle it down the steps of the plane'. I thought: 'If I could do that I wouldn't be here.'
>
> I was player coach, and in our first game, we travelled from Devonport to Hobart (around a three-hour drive). Halfway there, we stopped. The captain got out, opened the boot, and let a load of pigeons out. He was a pigeon fancier! I thought: 'What have I come to here.'

I know how it feels to be unrecognised, so we tried to publicise lesser-known coaches. I wanted to introduce our members to the wider world. But we also spoke to big names.

Perhaps the biggest was the England manager, Roy Hodgson. Roy spent most of his career abroad, so Owen asked the FA for an interview. In August 2014, Roy was meeting the Swiss press at the St Pancras Hotel in London – England were playing Switzerland – and Owen was given twenty minutes.

By coincidence, I was in England at the time, so I came to London to listen in. Roy is a nice guy – we had met before – so I asked him a question.

'As you may know, I am manager of Rwanda,' I began. 'Would you be interested in bringing England to Kigali for a friendly?'

It was a tongue-in-cheek question. I didn't expect him to agree. But I do think England should get out of their comfort zone.

A week in Rwanda would do more for the players' development than another friendly against Sweden, and it would do wonders for the country's reputation. If England went to Rwanda they would be treated like gods. A whole continent would think England was the finest, most generous country in the world. It would be PR gold. We would be 'arrogant England' no more.

Unfortunately, Roy didn't know where Rwanda was.

'I know about north Africa and South Africa,' he replied. 'But I don't know about much in between.'

And this is the England manager, I thought.

BY NOVEMBER 2013, I HAD BEEN UNEMPLOYED FOR ALMOST TEN months. My last game – the 3–0 win for Ethnikos over Paphos in January – ended in a grilling by police. My last interview – in Guinea-Bissau – ended in me fleeing the country. I was driving Lucy and the girls crazy at home. I needed a job.

Thankfully, I still had my FIFA work. In October I went to Bhutan and a month later I was in Cambodia. I was on the way back from Cambodia, in Dubai airport, when Lawrie Sanchez called.

I knew Lawrie from my FA courses, and I always found him good company. He understands the game and is intelligent outside football. Not many people have scored the winner in an FA Cup final, managed in the Premier League, and earned a degree in management sciences from Loughborough University.

'I'm in Greece speaking to a top-division team, Apollon Smyrnis,' said Lawrie. 'What do you know about them? Do they pay on time?'

I made some calls and phoned him back.

'They're a small club but the president is solid,' I said. 'They pay on time.'

'Right, get yourself over then,' he replied. 'I need an assistant manager.'

I was surprised. When I checked out Apollon Smyrnis, I had no idea Lawrie would offer me a job. For him, it made sense – he didn't speak Greek – but I wasn't sure. On one hand, after working for Colin Lee, I swore I'd never be an assistant again. On the other hand, I was ten months out of work. It was sacking season in Cyprus and Greece but I wasn't guaranteed a job. I told Lawrie I'd think about it. He called back the next day.

'If you get offered a manager's job, you can leave,' he said. 'The money is only €3,000 a month, but they pay for your apartment, car and petrol.'

I needed to get back in the game. I told him I'd take it.

'Great stuff,' he said. 'And by the way – can you bring some cones? I can't see any here.'

Apollon were a small club from Athens. That season, 2013/14, was their first in the Greek top division since 2000. After back-to-back promotions, they were struggling in the Super League, with only two wins from eleven by November. When the previous manager – a Greek called Babis Tennes – lasted only four weeks, the president, Stamatis Vellis, found Lawrie via an agency in London.

We trained on Panathinaikos's old training pitch. Although Lawrie is a good coach, I ran most of the sessions, as I spoke the language. Straight away, I enjoyed working with him. He was humble. There were no airs or graces. And he didn't talk shit. When I thought about his coaching career – the FA Cup semi-final with Wycombe, taking Northern Ireland almost 100 places up the FIFA rankings – I was amazed he wasn't working in England. He deserved more than a Greek club with no cones.

We lost our first game 1–0 at home to OFI. Our second game – also at home – was against the Greek giants, Panathinaikos. Almost 3,000 fans turned up, which was three times the OFI crowd. The lights were on. The stadium shook. Marcus Berg, the Swedish striker, scored for Panathinaikos after six minutes, but we equalised just after half-time. We held on for a 1–1 draw. It was a massive result.

At full time, a TV reporter approached me and Lawrie. I told Apollon I wouldn't translate for Lawrie in press conferences – I am a coach, not a translator – but I was happy doing quick post-match interviews. The reporter asked Lawrie how he felt. As I translated, Lawrie put his arm round me.

'We feel great,' he said. 'We have worked very hard. We are delighted with the point.'

The media picked up on Lawrie using 'we'. So did I. It showed he respected me. It showed he valued my work. For some managers, the assistant is the bloke who collects the bibs. In Greece, Lawrie and I were a proper partnership. It was a million miles away from Colin Lee and Millwall.

Our next league game was away to PAOK, a club in Thessaloniki in northern Greece. If you have a football 'bucket list', put PAOK on it. Every fan, player and coach should experience it. They are the most fanatic supporters in the world. And when I say 'fanatic', I mean abusive. My word, it was top-of-the-range stuff. From my hair to my homeland, they abused me for it. It was a good job Lawrie didn't speak Greek, because he got it too. But really, I loved it. It was pleasurably frightening.

When the match started, the stadium was set on fire. Half the ground had flares. The other half banged drums. When their players went down, the fans howled. If the ref didn't give the foul, they turned on him. It was the most intimidating atmosphere I've witnessed, but our players responded.

We played superbly and drew 0–0. That season, PAOK played twenty league games at home. They won eighteen and drew two, and were also unbeaten at home in the Europa League group stages. Hours later I could still hear the drums. When I closed my eyes, I saw the flares. I fell asleep a happy man.

We went on a good run, losing once in seven league games – a 5–0 thumping at home to Olympiakos before Christmas – but we needed new players. In January, Lawrie brought in Darren Ambrose on loan from Birmingham City. He was a good guy, with great vision and an eye for goal. At first, we didn't know where to play him. He wasn't quick enough to play wide, and he didn't kick people in centre-midfield, so we put him number 10. It was a good decision. He scored six in eleven games.

I also brought in two of Freddie Risp's Swedish boys: Tom Söderberg and Mikael Dahlberg. Tom, a defender, played ten league games for us, while Mikael, a forward, played seventeen times, so they were decent transfers. Our other English signing, the former Watford and QPR winger Lee Cook, was less successful. He was a terrific guy – and a good player – but we only picked him once in the league. It's hard to settle when you're not playing.

After the Christmas break we won 2–0 at Aris, another team based in Thessaloniki. Again, it was another feisty atmosphere – there is no running track between the fans and the players – and it got nasty before the end. As the fans kicked off, police fired tear gas into the terraces.

The gas hung in the air. Our eyes stung. At full time, we ran to the dressing room and were told not to leave. We couldn't board the bus for two hours. Thank goodness we had three points.

In our next game, we beat PAS Giannina 4–0 at home. It looked like we were staying up. The Great Escape was on. But after Giannina our results fell away. We won once in two months and slid towards the relegation zone. On 22 February we played at home to Panionios. Ambrose scored after sixteen minutes, before Andreas Lasnik equalised fifteen minutes later.

After 38 minutes, Panionios got the softest penalty of the season – which in Greece is saying something – and went 2–1 up. In the second half, Ambrose went down in the box and got nothing. We lost. For Mr Vellis, it was the final straw.

The president was convinced that Greek football, from the federation downwards, was corrupt. Match-fixing was rife, he said. Referees were bent. After the Panionios game, he phoned me.

'There are forces working against us,' he said. 'I am pulling Apollon out of the league.'

Mr Vellis wasn't bullshitting. He was a successful businessman – he made his money in shipping – but to him, football was a rigged market. He asked me to tell the players. When I did, the dressing room fell silent. I felt sick, but perhaps it wasn't a surprise. Like everyone, I'd heard the stories about Greece.

In 2011 – two years before I arrived – UEFA said 41 games during the 2009/10 Greek season were suspicious. A criminal investigation began, and the Greek prosecutor named more than eighty suspects, including owners, players, referees and a chief of police. One newspaper said up to 800 people may have been involved. The Olympiakos owner, Evangelos Marinakis, was charged but acquitted.

The scandal was known as Koriopolis – a play on Calciopoli, the Italian match-fixing affair – and two clubs, Olympiakos Volou and Kavala, were demoted. A government minister, Giorgios Nikitiadis, called it 'the darkest page in the history of Greek football'. But nothing changed.

In February 2012, there was an explosion at a bakery owned by referee Petros Konstantineas. A bomb had been placed in his oven. He says he refused to fix an

Olympiakos game a month earlier.

In November 2014 a member of the referees' committee, Christoforos Zografos, was attacked with wooden clubs in Athens. Two years later, the head of the committee, Giorgios Bikas, had his house set on fire. Thankfully, he was out.

Like Cypriot football, Greek football stank. We finished the season – Mr Vellis changed his mind after consulting the fans – but the atmosphere was heavy. When Lawrie wanted to spend a week in England, Mr Vellis asked me to take over if he didn't come back. Out of loyalty to Lawrie, I said no. He brought me to Greece, so we fought together – even if we had one arm tied behind our backs.

When your president thinks the league is fixed, you become suspicious. In March, one of our relegation rivals, Platanias, won 7–0 against a mid-table team, Kalloni. I'm sure they deserved it, but in their other 33 matches, they averaged less than a goal a game. It was a strange result.

A week later we had Panathinaikos away. Before the game, I injured my knee in training and needed surgery. Mr Vellis liked me, and insisted that I was on the bench, so I had my operation – which the club paid for – the day before the game. The surgeon, Andreas Karayiannis, was outstanding – I couldn't believe what he pulled out of my knee – and I went straight from hospital to the team hotel. My knee was wrapped in ice. I injected myself in the stomach every few hours.

I couldn't sit down so I stood by the bench, propped up with crutches, with ice on my swollen leg. We went 1–0 down, Darren Ambrose equalised in the 80th minute, but they scored twice in the last five minutes. By this point, we had one win in seven games. The pressure was building.

On 30 March, we played away to Panthrakikos. We had a goal disallowed after half an hour and Lawrie lost it. In suit, tie and sunglasses, he grabbed the TV reporter's microphone and shouted: 'You cannot allow this to happen on live TV!' This time, I didn't bother translating. We got a penalty in the 75th minute to win 3–2 so, in hindsight, it was funny. But it showed the stress he was under.

In our final home game, we scored an injury-time winner to beat Ergotelis 1-0. It meant that, going into the final day, we were a point clear of the drop zone. In 23 games, Lawrie and I won 28 points. It was mid-table form. Despite everything, we had built a decent team. I was proud of the players. There was one problem: our two rivals, Xanthi and Veria, had home games against teams with nothing to play for. We were away to Olympiakos.

Xanthi played Panathinaikos at home, who had the Greek Cup final against PAOK two weeks later. Panathinaikos had a man sent off after sixteen minutes and Xanthi won 3–1. That put them on 38 points.

With twelve minutes left, we were drawing 0–0 at Olympiakos and our other rival, Veria, were scoreless against Asteras Tripolis. As it stood, we had 37 points. We would finish third from bottom and enter the relegation play-off against a second-tier team. Veria – on 36 points – were down.

Then, after 78 minutes, Veria scored. They moved to 38 points. Ten minutes later, our 37 points dropped to 36 when Javier Saviola scored for Olympiakos. The full-time whistle went. We finished second-bottom and were relegated.

As the fans filed out, cheering another win for the Greek champions, I stood in the empty stadium, heartbroken. Lawrie deserved better. The players deserved better. But in football – and Greek football, especially – you don't always get what you deserve.

Lawrie resigned. He was popular with the fans – deservedly so – and wrote them a thank-you letter.

'Many factors contribute to a relegation season, and as we all know, some are outside our control,' he said, pointedly.

'I would like to put on record my thanks to Mr Vellis… although I did not agree with his decision to withdraw Apollon from the Super League, I do believe his values are correct. I strongly urge him to stay and change Greek football from the inside… football is a microcosm of a country and football needs people like Mr Vellis. I leave you (with a bow to Eric Cantona) with these words. In the magic kingdom that is Super League, even a magician can only have so many powers.'

Mr Vellis didn't want the players taking three months off, so after checking with Lawrie, I ran training for a month. It was another's month's salary, but I didn't want to stay longer. The smell was growing.

After I left Greece, Mr Vellis gave evidence to a district attorney, accusing owners and officials of match-fixing. He also said Olympiakos had offered Apollon a player on loan, which – he thought – was an attempt to control his team. In 2013/14, the champions sent four players to Ergotelis, three players to Platanias, and two to Aris. Three other Super League teams got one player each. At the time of writing, a criminal investigation into Greek football is active.

Amid the gloom, there was one bright spot. Towards the end of the season I went to watch Iraklis Psachna in the Greek second tier. They had a Malawian player, Tawonga Chimodzi, who I had picked for the national team six years earlier, aged eighteen. He made his debut in the COSAFA Cup against South Africa (the game we lost on penalties) and won five caps in total under me.

For him, reaching Europe was a dream come true. It was a reminder that football is a fantastic sport, which gives joy – and hope – to people around the world. After a season in the Greek Super League, I needed reminding.

12
NYAMIRAMBO DREAMS
RWANDA, 2014

IN MARCH, WHILE I WAS WORKING IN ATHENS, A CYPRIOT
agent asked if I was interested in the Rwanda national team job. When I left Sudan
in 2009, I was in no rush to return to Africa. I was bored of the back-stage politics,
but after four years in Cyprus and Greece, I realised European football was just as
murky. Also, the salary would be more than €3,000 a month. I told the agent I was
interested.

Apparently, 25 coaches applied. On 7 May, the Rwandan press said I was on a
shortlist of seven. I looked down the list. It was an interesting group.

Peter Butler, the Yorkshire-born former West Ham and West Brom midfielder,
was Botswana manager. Ratomir Dujkovic played for Yugoslavia in the 1970s, took
Rwanda to their first African Cup of Nations in 2004, and managed Ghana in the
2006 World Cup. Kim Poulsen, a Dane who never played professionally, had just
left the Tanzania national job.

Wojciech Lazarek was a Polish veteran who managed Sudan between 2002 and
2004. Paulo César Lopes de Gusmão had coached across Brazil and was working for
Al Arabi, a club side in Qatar. Desi Curry was the former technical director at the
Northern Irish FA. Interestingly, there were no Africans on the list. At the time, the

Rwandan coach was Eric Nshimiyimana, a former national team midfielder. His contract was running out but the FA wanted an outsider to replace him.

There is nothing wrong with looking far and wide. But in my opinion, African countries should trust their own coaches more. The associations don't think Africans are disciplined, or impartial, compared to Europeans. But let me tell you: there are plenty of bad white coaches, too.

Of course, Europe does have more qualified coaches than Africa, so – at times – appointing a European makes sense. Like everyone, Africa can benefit from outside help. I think I've improved all my African sides, for example. But there should be more opportunity for home-grown managers.

Look at someone like Stephen Keshi, the Nigerian coach who sadly died in 2016. He qualified for the 2006 World Cup with Togo, but was replaced by a German, Otto Pfister, before the finals. He then won the African Cup of Nations in 2013 with Nigeria before taking them to the knockout stages of the 2014 World Cup. Other Africans could have that success, but they need the chance.

The Rwandan FA – Ferwafa – reduced the shortlist to three (I don't know the other two). They phoned FIFA to ask about me. 'He's a maniac,' said FIFA, in a good way. 'If you want someone to run the whole thing, he's your man.' At the same time, Ferwafa emailed me about my terms.

We agreed $10,000 a month, plus flights, transportation and accommodation. Three days later, they sent a draft contract. It said $10,000 a month with two flights and no extras. I told them I wasn't interested. The money wasn't the problem – I survived on €3,000 in Greece – but I couldn't let them take the piss. We had agreed a deal, and I knew accommodation would cost at least $1,000 a month.

Ferwafa came back with $11,000 a month and no extras. I agreed, but said if I couldn't find accommodation for $1,000 a month, they would have to increase it. Ferwafa said fine and, on 15 May, announced that I was the next manager.

'We are impressed with Constantine,' the Ferwafa president Vincent Nzamwita told the BBC. 'He is ready to come and work.'

Nice words – but I still hadn't met him.

Rwanda were playing Libya on 18 May in the first leg of the first round of African Cup of Nations qualifiers. The match was in Tunisia – at the same ground where I lost 4–0 with Sudan in 2009 – so Ferwafa invited me over. I flew on 17 May: the day Arsenal played Hull in the FA Cup final.

I watched the first ninety minutes at home, then tore myself from the TV during extra time. In the taxi, I asked the driver to put the match on the radio. When Aaron Ramsey scored the winner, I yelled so loud he almost crashed. More than half a lifetime away from London hadn't dimmed the flame.

We reached the airport – just about – and, on the plane, I thought about my last trip to 'sign a contract' in Africa. In Guinea-Bissau, my passport was confiscated, I stayed a week too long, and a Senegalese colonel told me to flee the country. I buckled up and crossed my fingers.

I arrived in Rades and met the Ferwafa officials for the first time. Vincent Nzamwita was in his mid-forties. He was a nice person – very friendly – but I sensed he was a ducker and diver. He told me we'd sign the contract when we returned to Kigali. I wasn't officially in charge, so I watched the match from the stands. Rwanda drew 0–0 but Libya were the better side. The second leg would be hard.

(During the game, I met a German guy called Michael Fietzek. He had an amazing story: he married a Rwandan woman, ran a bakery in Kigali, and watched the national team home and away. We might be knocked out of the African Cup of Nations, I thought, but at least my croissants are sorted.)

We flew south to Kigali, and I was shown to my office in Ferwafa's Maison du Football (French is an official language in Rwanda, but English is more common). As I opened the door, I realised 'office' was stretching it. It was, in fact, an empty room with half the floor missing. My first job as Rwanda manager was to drag a desk from another room and pinch loose tiles from the corridor outside, so my floor wasn't bare. After 24 hours in Rwanda, I was already on my hands and knees.

The other problem was my contract. Despite holding a press conference on 21 May, I still hadn't signed one. The piece of paper I signed for the photographers was just that – a piece of paper. Publicly, I was national team manager. Legally, I was nothing. But we didn't have time to waste. The Libya second leg was on 31 May. My contract could wait.

Libya were 62nd in the FIFA rankings – we were 131st – but I thought their defence was weak. We had to put them under pressure from the first minute. We had to make them defend deep, then get balls in the box. All week, we worked on getting it wide and attacking the area.

The venue also suited my game plan. Rwanda had a modern, all-seater stadium in Kigali, but the Libya game was played in the Stade Regional Nyamirambo. It was smaller, older, and in a poorer part of the capital. For big games, I was told, it came alive. I couldn't wait.

It was a hot, sunny afternoon in Kigali. The ground was packed. There were wide, open spaces at both ends, but at the side, the fans could see the whites of the players' eyes. We started well. The Libyans didn't like the stadium or the out-of-date Astroturf. After 39 minutes, a cross went into the box. Our striker, Daddy Birori, got in front of their defender. He headed it downwards. Goal.

The fans roared and sprinted down the stands. One guy did a somersault. Birori ran to the corner and celebrated for a minute, at least. It felt like we'd kick-started a carnival. All around me, people were hugging and blowing horns. On the outside, I was calm. But inside, I was doing somersaults too.

It was 1–0 at half-time but we needed a second. If Libya equalised, they were through on away goals. In the 64th minute, the ball broke down our right-hand side. The cross came in. Birori found space between their two centre-halves. As the ball reached the six-yard box, he leaped forward, twisted his neck, and headed the ball downwards. It hit the net before their keeper could move.

The fans danced on the sun-kissed concrete steps. Horns were blown into the hot Kigali air. In the posh seats, Ferwafa officials slapped each other's backs. Nine minutes later, the win was confirmed.

Again, we crossed it from the right-hand side. Again, Birori found space between their two centre-halves. Again, the keeper didn't move. Three crosses, three headers, 3–0 to Rwanda. Thank you very much. The ground was a sea of joyous faces. It was a special moment.

At full time, their manager, Javier Clemente, shook my hand. 'I don't know what you did to those boys,' he said, putting his other hand on my face. 'But that was fantastic.'

Eighteen years earlier, I watched Clemente manage Spain against England in Euro 96, when Stuart Pearce scored in the penalty shootout. I had just been turned down for the APEP job in the Cypriot second division. For our paths to cross in Kigali, nearly two decades later, was unbelievable.

THE DAY AFTER WE BEAT LIBYA, I PHONED VINCENT TO SAY I was leaving. I didn't have a contract and I hadn't been paid. The problem was my accommodation. I couldn't find a serviced flat for under $1,000 a month. So, as I told Vincent before I arrived, I needed $12,000. He wouldn't budge.

'I have a return ticket for next week,' I told him. 'I can't stay here without a contract.'

'Don't move,' he said.

'Why do I have to lose my mind?' I asked when he arrived. 'Yesterday, we beat Javier Clemente. He earns much more than $12,000 a month. And you're fighting me over one or two grand?'

The contract was signed within three days. It should have been done weeks earlier. By Rwandan standards I wasn't even expensive. After I signed, the New Times newspaper said I was their fourth highest-paid coach of recent times. Apparently, the Ghanaian Sellas Tetteh (2010–11) and the Croatian Branko Tucak (2008–09) earned $20,000 a month, while the Serbian Milutin Sredojevic (2011–13) got $16,000 a month. As I said, Vincent was a nice guy. But he wasn't easy to work with.

I moved into a hotel apartment five minutes from the federation. It was a great place to live with a good ex-pat community. Kigali itself was a revelation. I have never seen a cleaner city. Seriously, the place was spotless. On the last Saturday of every month, everyone aged 18 to 65 is required by law to spend three hours tidying up. The knock-on effect is that no one drops litter in the first place.

The president, Paul Kagame, divides opinion. Born in Rwanda, he fled to Uganda with his family as a child. He joined a rebel army in Uganda, helping to overthrow the government, before joining a Rwanda refugee army. In 1990, it invaded Rwanda, leading to civil war. After the Rwandan genocide in 1994 – when 800,000 people, mostly Tutsis, were killed – Kagame, a Tutsi, led forces that took control of the country. He became vice president, then, in 2000, president.

To some, he is authoritarian, or worse. He is supported by Western governments, but criticised by human rights groups. While GDP increases, dissent is silenced. I don't judge. But I do know that, having lived in three African cities, Kigali was the best. It looked good. It felt safe. The investment was obvious. Kagame wants Rwanda to develop like Singapore, so it becomes a 'middle income country' by 2020. Having walked the spotless streets of Kigali, I wouldn't bet against him.

Ferwafa didn't share Mr Kagame's efficiency. The second round of qualifiers for the African Cup of Nations – a play-off in which the winner advances to the final group stage of qualifiers – was in the middle of July. It meant that, after beating Libya, we had almost two months off. We needed games, so I spoke to an agent, who organised a friendly against Indonesia in Jakarta.

There are no rules for organising friendlies. Usually, the host pays for accommodation and local expenses, and the visitors buy their own flights. Sometimes the host pays for everything, and bigger countries might also get an appearance fee. Because Indonesia needed games – they had the Asian Games in South Korea in September – they offered to pay for everything, including flights.

For Rwanda, it was a huge offer. But it wasn't enough for Vincent Nzamwita. When I told him, he demanded an appearance fee for Ferwafa – around $10,000 – and business-class flights for himself.

'A business-class flight is possible,' I said. 'But we won't get an appearance fee. We're Rwanda, not Nigeria.'

The Indonesian FA told their media the game would take place on 25 June. After Vincent's demands, it was cancelled.

With no game in June – the highlight of the month was a visit to the British High Commissioner's residence in Kigali, to celebrate the Queen's 88th birthday – I started planning for the next qualifier against Congo. At short notice, we arranged a home friendly against Gabon, which we won 1–0. We then flew across Africa to Pointe-Noire, Congo's second city, on the hot and humid Atlantic coast.

When I moved to Rwanda, I brought in Lee Johnson as technical director. FIFA want all countries to have them: while the coach runs the team, the TD looks after youth football, coach education, grassroots, the women's game, and other infrastructure. I remained in charge, but I couldn't do it all.

Lee, from Kent, was a bright, hungry coach in his early thirties. I met him at the NSCAA (National Soccer Coaches' Association of America) convention in Philadelphia in 2013. He spent six years working for the Chelsea academy, and worked in America. When I needed a TD, he ticked all the boxes.

I wanted to again bring in Rogerio Ramos, the big Brazilian, as goalkeeping coach, but Rwanda already employed a Ugandan called Ibrahim Mugisha. I also thought I was getting a sports scientist called Danny Deigan – an Australian I met through James Karageorgiou – but, at the last minute, Ferwafa said they couldn't afford him. So, for the trip to Congo, I roped in my good friend Nick de Long. He almost turned round at the Congolese border.

Nick was a highly qualified physical training instructor for the RAF in Cyprus. He was also a superb coach: in his spare time, he worked for Aris and AEL, and also managed the RAF's football team (he is now manager of the armed forces team). Most importantly, he was a fantastic person.

I had a Rwandan assistant – a great guy called Vincent Mashami – but we needed a sports scientist for the qualifier. As we arrived in Congo, we saw a line of doctors. If you didn't have proof of a yellow fever vaccination, the doctors would give you one there and then. Nick went white.

'They're not sticking a needle in me,' he said.

'It's just an injection,' I replied. 'If you don't get one, you don't go in.'

'Then fuck it,' he replied. 'I'm not going in.'

Sweat was pouring down his face. Nick isn't a wimp – he has served in Afghanistan – but fifteen years in the military had given him a fear of foreign needles.

Despite flying halfway round the world, he was ready to head straight back to Cyprus. In front of us, Vincent Nzamwita walked through. I had my jabs, so I followed him. Nick put his head down and followed me. Somehow, he made it past the doctors' needles. The colour returned to his cheeks.

'You won't look so clever if you get yellow fever,' I said, laughing. Thankfully, he survived.

The Congo game was played on Astroturf. I don't mind that, but, as usual, our opponents played silly buggers and gave us a grass training pitch. The rules are clear: you must be allowed to train on the surface at least twice if it's artificial. In the end, we got it, but we had to fight. It wasn't a good start.

The match was played in a small, sun-baked stadium. A huge scoreboard loomed at one end. There was no running track so fans lined the pitch, hemmed in by a ten-foot metal fence. On the far side, propped up by the corner flag, were three gold-framed portraits of their players. The Congo squad were royalty, and their loyal subjects were out in force.

Before kickoff, I saw the long-haired Congo manager Claude Le Roy by the pitch. Claude has been everywhere – from Cameroon to Cambridge United, via Shanghai and Syria – and is one of the few people to manage more national teams than me.

'Hello, Claude,' I said, my hand outstretched. He eyed me up.

'Who are you?' he replied.

'I'm the Rwanda coach,' I replied. His scouting obviously didn't include the opposition manager.

After chatting to Claude – we got on well, despite the slow start – I went inside while the players warmed up. The cool, quiet changing rooms are a good place to think. I did the team talk and geed up the players. I thought they were ready, but mentally they stayed in the changing room.

Congo were a good side – their captain, Delvin N'Dinga, played for Olympiakos in Greece – and they almost scored after twenty seconds. As the ball cleared the bar, a huge roar came from the terraces. The fences shook. The drums banged. A thousand Congo flags – red, yellow and green – waved in the warm, heavy air. They were up for it; we hadn't started. It was going to be a long afternoon.

After 66 minutes they scored a peach from outside the box. A party started in Pointe-Noire. The fans bounced in the stands. One guy set off a flare. Twelve minutes later, energised by the atmosphere, they scored again. For some reason, the police opened a gate in the fence near our dugout. Two Congolese fans, freed from the cage, ran towards our dugout. Our Ugandan goalkeeping coach Ibby – a big guy with a booming laugh – grabbed one, took him to the floor, and leathered him.

As usual, I stood on the edge of the technical area, trying to coach, while the melee took place behind me. Claude was also in the technical area. I looked up and caught his eye. At that point, I had managed five national teams, and he had managed eight. A goalkeeping coach fighting a fan was a new one for both of us. Thankfully, the police saved the intruder from further damage.

We lost the match 2–0. The Senegalese referee was poor, so at full time I went on to the pitch.

'I have to say, that was absolutely horrendous,' I told him.

'Fuck off,' he replied.

'Pardon?'

'Fuck off.'

'Did you just tell me to—'

'FUCK OFF!' he shouted, and that's where our cultured conversation ended. I found the match commissioner and told him what happened.

'Don't worry, don't worry,' the commissioner said, before walking off. I didn't hear anything more about it.

There were two weeks until the second leg so after the Congo game, we flew an hour north for another friendly against Gabon (their ranking meant they were already in the group stage of qualifying). It was a difficult trip. One night, the hotel in Libreville ran out of food. Another night, it ran out of staff: we waited an hour for dinner, getting hungrier by the minute, until a chef turned up.

Gabon said the game would be held in the main stadium, as the country's president wanted to watch. The stadium had an artificial surface, so we travelled an hour every day to train on plastic, even though a grass pitch was nearby. But at the last minute the venue was changed. When we arrived at the stadium, it was – you guessed it – a grass pitch. The president didn't show up.

It wasn't the most glamorous match in history. The stadium had one stand, which held perhaps 1,000 people. On the other three sides, the only feature was a tall, concrete wall. It was like playing in a prison yard.

Despite making seven changes from the Congo game, we played well. In the second half, Meddie Kagere ran on to a short back-pass and scored the only goal. At the far end, two guys updated the home-made scoreboard, which was nailed to the whitewashed wall. Gabon 0, Rwanda 1.

It was only a friendly, but it was my third win in four. Within two months, I'd won more matches than in Malawi and Sudan combined. I liked the Rwandan team. They were hard-working. They wanted to improve. The second leg against Congo was a huge test but, despite being 2–0 down, I was confident. Crucially, the game was being held at the Stade Regional Nyamirambo. After Libya, anything was possible in the Kigali cauldron. Let the carnival begin.

It was a sunny August afternoon and the atmosphere was hot. The stadium held 22,000 but it looked twice as full. The fans roared us on. When we attacked, there was a crescendo of noise, but we couldn't score. At half-time, the players came into the dressing room. We took a deep breath.

'A chance will come,' I told the players. 'One goal and Congo will panic.'

We were showing them too much respect. I told the boys to push higher up the pitch and press them in their own half. We couldn't give them an inch. After 51 minutes the stadium exploded. Our young right-back, Michel Ndahinduka, put us 1–0 up. As expected, Congo started to panic.

Seven minutes later, Meddie Kagere got a second. The noise was deafening. People were jumping out of the trees that surrounded the pitch. We were heading to extra time.

With five minutes to go, my assistant Vincent Mashami spoke to me.

'Get the penalty-takers on now,' he said.

'Why?' I replied. 'We've got thirty minutes of extra time.'

'No we don't,' he said. 'It's straight to penalties.'

'No one bloody told me!' I yelled.

In the last minute, I brought on a striker, Jimmy Mbaraga, and a young defender, James Tubane. For some coaches, bringing people on as penalty-takers is counter-productive, as it increases the pressure. But these boys had the technique. James went first; he scored. Jimmy went second. He also scored.

We had practised penalties in the week, but you can't replicate the pressure. Meddie Kagere missed our third. Thankfully our keeper, Jean-Luc Ndayishimiye, saved three. He was only playing because our normal keeper, Jean-Claude Ndoli, was injured in Congo. If teenager Patrick Sibomana scored our sixth, we were through. He stepped up. He scored. It sounded like we'd won the Cup of Nations.

The fans invaded the pitch. After shaking hands with Claude le Roy and the Congo staff, I joined them. The players picked me up and carried me round the pitch. As they threw me round like a rag-doll, all I could hear was the fans' singing. The Stade Regional Nyamirambo felt like heaven. I have dealt with lots of crap in my career, but moments like that made it worthwhile.

When I came down to earth, the president of Ferwafa, Vincent Nzamwita, gave me a hug.

'You have no idea what you've done for this country,' he told me, just as the King of Nepal had done fourteen years earlier.

'Thank you for the opportunity,' I replied. It was a special moment.

After the game, the squad squeezed on to our minibus. It seemed like the whole city knew the score. Hundreds of cars beeped their horns. Fans waved flags from their windows. Inside, the players sang a deep, traditional song. I didn't know a word but the beat was awesome. I sat there, an Englishman far from home, with a huge grin on my face. In every sense, I didn't want the journey to end. I tried to take pictures but the bus was rocking. In any case, a photo wouldn't capture the feeling.

Beating Congo meant we qualified for the group stages of the Cup of Nations qualifiers. The draw had already been made: we would play Nigeria, South Africa and Sudan, home and away. I was like a kid on Christmas Eve. I couldn't wait to play Nigeria. I couldn't wait to revisit the Red Castle in Sudan. Hell, I couldn't wait to play South Africa. They were huge games, but I thought we could qualify. Since I took over, we had won four out of five. At home, we hadn't even conceded a goal.

The group stage began in September so, after the Congo game, I flew to England. The girls were in Brighton, escaping the summer heat of Cyprus. It was wonderful to see them. While I was there, I got a call from Ferwafa. I couldn't believe what they told me.

Rwanda could be disqualified from the Cup of Nations.

Congo had complained that our striker, Daddy Birori, had two identities. For Rwanda, they said, he was Daddy Birori. But for his club side – AS Vita in DR Congo – he played under a different name, Etekiama Agiti Tady, with a different date of birth, and a different passport. Later, I read the Confederation of African Football's website with horror.

'Rwanda disqualified,' said the headline. 'Congo qualify.'

The story read:

> On the basis of documents provided by the federations of Rwanda, Congo and DR Congo, and hearing the player's testimony on August 11 at CAF headquarters in Cairo, CAF established that the two identities only referred to a single person.
> While the Rwandan Football Federation maintained that to their knowledge the player Daddy Birori had one identity, investigations revealed that he was summoned as Etekiama Agiti Tady by Ferwafa to join the national team of Rwanda.

I phoned the president, Vincent Nzamwita. 'We will appeal,' he said, sounding calm. 'You don't need to worry.'

Congo weren't the first to complain to CAF about Birori. Libya appealed after the first round, but Ferwafa argued that, while Birori had a DR Congo passport, he also had a Rwandan one. There was no ban on dual-nationality players. He had played for Rwanda since 2009, so Libya's complaint was dismissed. Before the Congo game, I had even asked Vincent if I was OK to pick the hat-trick hero.

'No problem,' he said.

In fairness to Vincent, it was strange that Congo's complaint succeeded, while Libya's didn't. As I pointed out on Twitter, the ruling – whether right or wrong – was inconsistent. The inconsistency was never explained. There is a lot of politics, and horse-trading, in CAF.

Our appeal was heard in Egypt on 27 August, with the result announced on 30 August. The decision was upheld.

'It was established that Daddy Birori, playing with Rwanda, was the same that played in the Champions League with AS Vita using the name Etekiama Agiti Tady,' the CAF statement said. 'Based on the documents on record, it was evident that the Rwandan federation was aware of this double identity but proceeded to feature the player for the national team.'

Ferwafa threatened to go to the Court of Arbitration for Sport, but they didn't. We were out. After qualifying on the pitch in Kigali, we were knocked out in a conference room in Cairo. I was heartbroken. The irony was, after starting the first leg against Congo – which we lost – Birori didn't play in the second leg. He was injured. In September, he was banned from football for two years.

I WAS TEMPTED TO WALK AWAY, BUT THERE WAS A CONSOLATION prize on the horizon.

The African Nations Championship – the tournament for domestic-based players, known as CHAN – was being held in Rwanda in January and February 2016. We qualified automatically and had a chance of winning. Most of our players were in Rwanda – Daddy Birori, of course, was an exception – and the stadiums would be full. But in the meantime, we needed games. After the Birori furore, our calendar was empty.

I couldn't sit on my backside in Kigali for months on end. I went into the mountains to see the gorillas, which was awesome. I travelled round the beautiful Rwandan countryside. I also went two or three times to the Kigali Genocide Memorial, a museum about the mass killings in 1994. The remains of more than 250,000 people are interred there. It's hard to leave without shedding a tear.

But – as important as those experiences were – I was a coach, not a tourist. It was fifteen months until the CHAN. World Cup qualifying didn't start for a year. Without games, we would go backwards. I was desperate to play but Vincent Nzamwita was – shall we say – more relaxed.

'Why do you want to work so much?' he asked.

'I didn't come here to admire the beauty,' I replied.

'You get paid, don't you?' he asked.

'But we have so much work to prepare for the CHAN,' I replied. 'The team needs games. I need games.'

I looked for fixtures, but trouble was brewing. The players and staff were due bonuses for beating Congo. The players got $3,000 each; I got $4,000. In total, twenty players and five staff were owed money. Vincent was not one of them, but when Ferwafa sent the bill to the government, his name was on the list. The letter was leaked in October and Vincent backtracked.

'It was a mistake for my name to be on that list,' he told the press. 'Mistakes can be made anywhere in administration.'

The government paid the bonuses directly, despite Ferwafa asking for the money in its account.

I always got my wages, but not always on time. One month, they were three weeks late. I was due to fly home so I went to see the general secretary, Olivier

Mulindahabi.

Olivier took me to the bank, withdrew some money, and changed it at Western Union. He then sent me back to Europe with $8,000 in cash. It was the most money I'd seen since Peter de Savary tipped ten grand on to the dressing room floor at Millwall. I stuck an extra padlock on my hand luggage.

The players' wages were also delayed. They were due $200 for a training camp and $500 for a friendly, going up to $400 and $700 for a Cup of Nations qualifier. But three months after the Congo and Gabon games, they didn't have their money. In November, we played our first game since August, a friendly away to Morocco's CHAN team. The players could have gone on strike – it's not uncommon in Africa – but they played on.

'We met Vincent Nzamwita,' our captain, Ismael Nshutiyamagar, told the press. 'He promised that we shall receive our wages after the friendly.'

The Morocco game also highlighted how hard African trips can be. We left Kigali at 3.30 p.m. on a Wednesday, flying to Entebbe in Uganda. From there, we left the continent entirely for Doha, where we had a three-hour wait before flying to Casablanca.

We arrived at 8 a.m. on Thursday, then spent two hours waiting for the Moroccans to process our papers. By the time we arrived at the Ramada Hotel in Fes, four hours away, we had been travelling for twenty hours. I cancelled our training session and told the boys to sleep. You could see, perhaps, why Ferwafa weren't so keen on friendlies.

With one eye on the CHAN, we picked a young, domestic-based team and drew 0–0. Morocco passed the ball better than us, but we kept our shape. As promised, the players got their money after the game, but they shouldn't have had to wait. Footballers deserve their wages like everybody else.

Despite the Morocco match, I was getting restless. I couldn't wait three months between games. I watched league matches every week, but if there was no squad to pick, it was pointless. I helped Lee Johnson run workshops around the country but, day-to-day, there wasn't much to do. I will always be grateful to Vincent and Ferwafa for appointing me, but – in my opinion – they didn't share my drive.

Our results meant I was being noticed. Rwanda's FIFA ranking went from 131 in May to 68 in December, their highest-ever position. Improving a team by more than sixty places in seven months was massive for my reputation. After years in the shadows, I was now in the spotlight.

In late November my former India captain, Baichung Bhutia, called me. He was advising the AIFF after retiring from the national team. Their manager – a Dutchman called Wim Koevermans – had just resigned. Ever since our first meeting in Jamshedpur, when he apologised after arriving late, Baichung and I got on. He asked if I was interested in managing India for the second time.

I wasn't desperate to leave Rwanda. I liked the players and Kigali was great. But after being kicked out of the Cup of Nations, the lack of games was a huge problem. We also needed to rebuild the squad. After the Birori affair, Ferwafa banned naturalised players, so we lost five or six men.

In December, we drew 0–0 at home to Burundi in a friendly, meaning we'd gone 180 minutes without a goal. We were so desperate for strikers I picked one – Danny Usengimana – from the second division. Rwanda had potential but India, with their resources, will always have more. Also, the start of the Indian Super League meant football was bigger than ever.

I told Baichung I was interested and the AIFF put me on a four-man shortlist. Ashley Westwood, the former Crewe, Bradford and Sheffield Wednesday defender, had just coached Bengaluru to the I-League title. Trevor Morgan, an ex-Football League striker, managed East Bengal in the same league. Ricki Herbert, who took New Zealand to the 2010 World Cup – and then went unbeaten, drawing all three games in the group stage – was coaching NorthEast United in the ISL.

They were tough competition. I spoke to the AIFF vice president, Subrata Dutta, and the general secretary, Kushal Das. In December, the AIFF reduced the shortlist to two – myself and Ricki Herbert. Baichung, who was on the panel, said national team experience was a key factor.

By now, the Rwandan media – who read the Indian press online – knew I could leave. I was in a difficult position. I couldn't burn my bridges in case I wasn't offered the job. But I couldn't lie.

'I know there is interest from India,' I said, diplomatically. 'To what degree they are interested I don't know. There is no offer so I don't have anything to think about other than my current job.'

In one paper, a cartoon showed me – bald head, glasses, suit, briefcase – staring at a sackful of Indian rupees. The package was $20,000 a month and I can't say money wasn't an issue. But I was more excited by the challenge. I wanted to harness India's potential. I wanted to spark the fire. When Indian football clicks, a football coach will become a national hero. I wanted to be that coach.

In early January, the AIFF offered me the job. It was a fantastic feeling. To be chosen over someone like Ricki Herbert was a huge compliment. In my career, I have spent months out of work, waiting for the phone to ring. I have spent hundreds of hours applying for jobs, only to be ignored. I have borrowed money to survive. Now, at last, I was in demand.

I was sad to leave Rwanda. The people were wonderful and the players were even better. The comebacks at the Nyamirambo were once-in-a-lifetime, and we did it twice in six weeks. I will never forget the joy on the fans' faces, or the noise when we scored, or the drive through Kigali in the minibus. Without the Birori affair, I truly believe we would have reached the Cup of Nations finals. After being reprieved, Congo qualified ahead of Nigeria and reached the last eight. It could have been us.

A 29-year-old Northern Irishman, Johnny McKinstry, replaced me as Rwanda manager. We interviewed him on britishcoachesabroad.com in 2014 – he became Sierra Leone manager after working for the Craig Bellamy Foundation for three years – and he seemed like a talented, driven coach. He only lasted fifteen months in Kigali but I'm sure he'll bounce back.

After I left, Vincent Nzamwita and the general secretary, Olivier Mulindahabi, were charged with corruption over Ferwafa's plans to build a four-star hotel using $3m of FIFA money. Olivier was given a six-month jail sentence, but Vincent was cleared. He remains the president of Ferwafa.

13
FIGHTING THE SUPERSTARS
INDIA, PART ONE, 2015

IT WAS TEN YEARS SINCE I'D LEFT INDIA, AND PLENTY HAD changed. The population rose by 200 million between 2005 and 2015 and it showed. The country was busier. There were more people on the streets. More cars on the road. More buildings reaching the sky.

The AIFF opened new headquarters in New Delhi in 2007 so I moved to Gurgaon, a yuppie city on the edge of the capital. I was given an apartment in a modern, wealthy development. Down the road is the Ambience Mall, a huge shopping centre which also opened in 2007. It's packed with Western names like McDonald's and Starbucks. For better or worse, it's a symbol of modern India.

Indian football had also changed. The Indian Super League had the world's attention. The competition began in 2014 and is separate to the I-League, which remains the 'official' top division, and runs earlier in the year. The ISL has no promotion or relegation. The season runs from October to December with eight franchises playing fourteen games, followed by an American-style playoff.

The franchisees are super-rich and pay fortunes to sign well-known foreigners. Alessandro del Piero, David Trezeguet and Roberto Carlos have all been marquee players. The fans followed the money, and the average ISL attendance reached

27,000 in 2015. Big, bold and dazzled by wealth, the ISL is also a symbol of modern India.

One thing that hadn't changed was the Indian national team. They were still underachieving. When I left India in 2005, they were ranked 135 in the world. When I returned in 2015, they were 171st. While the country moved forwards, the football team slipped back.

Their World Cup qualifying campaigns in 2010 and 2014 amounted to four games: two draws and two defeats. By winning the 2008 AFC Challenge Cup – the tournament for emerging nations – they qualified for the 2011 Asian Cup, but, once there, didn't win a game. They didn't even win the most recent SAFF Championship, losing to Afghanistan in the final in 2013. Full of potential but failing to perform, the national football team was a third, less positive, symbol of modern India.

When a country of 1.3 billion people is 171st in the world, things have to change. Before I took the job, I spoke to the general secretary, Kushal Das. He joined the AIFF from the International Cricket Council in 2010 and didn't know me.

'You have a reputation,' he said.

'I will get things done,' I told him. 'I will fight people if I have to. But that's why you want me.'

In fairness, Kushal and the president, Praful Patel, were fantastic. They backed me. I wanted staff who I could trust; who I knew would hit the ground running. I asked for Rogerio Ramos as goalkeeper coach. I got him. I asked for Danny Deigan as sports scientist. I got him. I asked for Lee Johnson as the under-19 coach. I got him. If you want to improve, you must invest. Yes, it takes time, talent and hard work. But it also takes money. Having the best backroom staff is essential.

One of my best buys was a GPS system for $60,000. When I began coaching, I had a stopwatch and a whistle. If you'd told me that, in 2016, a satellite would know how far, fast and hard my players ran in training, I would have laughed. The players wear trackers and the data is loaded on to Danny's computer. We look at distance covered, number of sprints, accelerations and decelerations, time in the red zone – above the player's maximum heart rate – plus other stats.

My teams play hard so they train hard. If someone is slacking, I want to know. At international level, players average between 2,000 and 3,000 metres of high-speed running a match, roughly 30 sprints, and around 140 accelerations and decelerations, depending on the player's position. We aim to do three to four times that amount in a week's training. That way, the players are ready for the match.

Players are human. If they know they are being watched – in this case, by an eye in the sky – they work harder. If they work harder, they play better. You can't let the data take over. A coach still needs his eyes – we call it the eye-o-meter – but the stats are a massive help.

When I re-joined India, I realised we needed to discover more talent. The AIFF had an 'elite academy' in Goa, which picked players from the finals of two schoolboy tournaments in Delhi, the Subroto Cup and the Coca-Cola Cup. And that was our scouting. For the seventh biggest country in the world, it wasn't good enough.

India is hosting the under-17 World Cup in October 2017, but we didn't have the best players in the country. How could we, when the players came from just two schoolboy tournaments? I wanted to find players across India, at junior and senior level. There was huge untapped potential.

With the blessing of Kushal Das, I appointed Abhishek Yadav – who scored the winner in the LG Cup final in 2002 – as our unpaid director of scouting. Abhishek is super-smart and runs football schools across the country. We then picked 25 scouts – fifteen former players and ten from the Sports Authority of India – and held a workshop in Goa. Over four days, we taught them how to pick a player.

We gave them twenty criteria, from technical to tactical, and told them to give players marks out of 200. Over 140, we want them. Under 125, we don't. If they're in between, they're worth a second look.

I flew in Derek Bragg from England to run the workshop. Derek is an old friend who has been chief scout at Derby County, Stoke City and Sunderland, among others. He didn't cost the AIFF a penny: Derek didn't ask for money, and Abhishek found a sponsor for his flights.

Derek's message was clear. The scouts shouldn't pick players 'who they like'. They are the eyes of the coach, so they should pick players who meet the criteria. Within a year, we found 29 players for the elite academy in Goa.

I might not benefit from the scouts' work. When those players reach the senior team, I could be long gone. But short-term thinking is why India was 171st in the world. As I said earlier, when I take a job, I act like I'll be there forever. Indian football should be a machine that works whoever the head coach is. Putting those systems in place takes time. But it's the only way to get long-term success.

FOR INDIA, THE ROAD TO THE 2018 WORLD CUP BEGAN IN MARCH 2015. Our ranking meant we entered the first round of qualifying alongside the likes of Bhutan and Brunei. We were drawn against Nepal with the first leg at home, so I asked for the match to be played in Guwahati in the north-east. They love their football, and we needed as much support as possible. Nepal were only nine places below us.

In 2014, the average age of the India squad was 29. We had to bring it down. I wanted a young squad playing fast, aggressive football. With help from my assistant

Shanmugam Venkatesh, who played for me in my first spell, I picked a 26-man squad. Uncapped players included Eugeneson Lyngdoh, a former engineering student who played centre-midfield, and Jackichand Singh, a lightning-quick winger from the north-east.

We also brought in Jeje Lalpekhlua, a chunky striker who hadn't played for two years, and a keeper, Gurpreet Singh, whose only appearance was as sub in 2011. Gurpreet was our only foreign-based player. In 2014, he moved from East Bengal to Stabaek in Norway, which is a culture shock by anyone's standards. He wouldn't start but I wanted Ramos to look at him.

The camp started a week before the first leg. The I-League, which runs from January to May, is quicker than the ISL, but that's not saying much. The players weren't fit enough. We did two sessions a day using GPS, pinpointing what we needed to work on.

In my first press conference in Delhi, a journalist asked 'how the captain was'. He meant Sunil Chhetri, the skipper under the previous manager.

'We don't have a captain,' I said. 'Every player starts with a clean slate.'

I had nothing against Sunil, who is one of India's greatest-ever players. A hard-working striker with superb technique, he earned a three-year contract with QPR in 2009 but failed to get a work permit. He also had a brief spell with Kansas City Wizards in 2010. But I couldn't make him captain before I knew him. The skipper reflects the manager's personality, and I knew nothing about Sunil.

Nepal was a huge match. If we won, we reached the group stage, with another eight games guaranteed. We would test ourselves against Asia's best. We would grow as a team. But if we lost, we got nothing. Our diary would be empty. Losing to Nepal would also eliminate us from the Asian Cup, missing another set of qualifiers. In my opinion, it was India's biggest game for ten years.

I picked our goalkeeper Subrata Pal as captain and Sunil reacted superbly. He opened the scoring after half-time – we won the ball high-up after harrying their defence – and got a second fifteen minutes later after a counter-attack. We should have scored four or five – Sunil had a penalty saved at 2–0 – but I was happy enough. It was India's first World Cup win since beating Singapore in February 2004. I was manager then, too.

The second leg was five days later in Kathmandu. It was my first visit since my life-changing spell as head coach, and the reception was fantastic. I was surprised how many people remembered me.

I stood in the Dasarath Rangasala stadium and looked round the wide, concrete terraces. When I closed my eyes I went back in time. My first international against Bhutan. Walking round the pitch in national dress. The 2–1 win against Maldives in the semi-final. My hug from Crown Prince Dipendra. The agony of Hari Khadka's shot hitting the underside of the bar in the final.

My time in Nepal put me on the map – even if I was a tiny speck – and I will always love the place. But this was business. We had to knock them out.

The sky was blue but a Himalayan wind whipped round the ground. The pitch was bobbly and bare in places. The stand opposite the dugout was empty – the old place was finally being renovated – but the other three sides were full.

The Nepali players came out like tigers and the fans roared every tackle. Subrata Pal was fantastic in goal, but our 2–0 advantage looked slim. If we conceded one, I feared we could collapse, like Libya and Congo did against Rwanda. We made it to half-time at 0–0.

'It has been eleven years since we played in the group stage of the World Cup qualifiers,' I told them. 'If you continue to play like this, we ain't going anywhere.'

The match finished goalless but we were lucky. The team didn't have enough leaders. I thought back to my first Indian team, with Baichung Bhutia, I.M. Vijayan, Jo Paul Ancheri and the rest. Technically, they weren't better than my new side, but they were more physical. We needed more of that.

We were drawn against Iran (ranked 41, the best team in Asia), Oman (101), Turkmenistan (173) and Guam (174) in the group stage. Only the winners – almost certainly Iran – would progress.

The first game was at home to Oman on 11 June. The I-League didn't finish until 31 May and by the time we got visas for Guam – which took two days in Delhi – we only had four days of training. Oman were together for two and a half weeks, and played two friendlies against Syria and Bahrain.

Two and a half weeks seems like a long time. But the longer you have, the better you can prepare. The players become fitter. The set pieces get sharper. Getting the players for two or three days is fine if they're ready. But if they're not playing in top leagues, that's not always the case.

In India, the boys weren't in great shape. Their clubs didn't work them hard enough. Also, they weren't used to my style of play. If they played in the ISL and the I-League – the leagues ran separately, so the best Indians played in both – I was their third manager of the season. For the players, it takes time to adapt.

Despite that, I was optimistic. The camp went well. The new players were hungry. I gave five players their debut (including subs), bringing the total to thirteen in three games. Oman – led by the former Rangers coach, Paul le Guen – were beatable. Then, after nineteen seconds, we went 1–0 down.

In that situation, people say, 'The game plan goes out of the window'. Actually, the opposite happens. If we chased the game, Oman would pick us off. Our patience paid off. Again, I had overlooked Sunil Chhetri for the captaincy – the centre-half Arnab Mondal got the nod – and again he responded.

After 26 minutes Sunil got the ball on the edge of the eighteen-yard box. Facing away from goal, he smacked a left-foot curler towards the top corner. Ali Al-Habsi – who played for many years in the Premier League with Bolton and Wigan – dived full length but couldn't get near it.

The 19,000 fans in Bangalore went mad. In fact, the only person who didn't celebrate was Sunil. It might have been a message for me. To be honest, I wasn't bothered. After dropping him as captain, I wanted a reaction. I got one.

Oman retook the lead with a penalty before half-time, but we should have equalised from a corner in the 67th minute. We had worked on a routine in training. When I saw Oman line up to defend the set piece, I turned round and told the bench: 'This is a goal.'

I was proved right but the South Korean linesman flagged our striker, Robin Singh, for offside. I still have the highlights on my computer. I still don't think it was offside: their defender got the last touch, apart from anything else. It was our last big chance. We lost 2–1, but the reaction was good.

'This side is different from previous ones,' Sunil told reporters. 'These guys are not scared.'

The press were also positive. 'Constantine's India showed a new, fearless side,' read one headline. But you don't get points for headlines. We needed something from our next game away to Guam.

Guam is a tiny US territory in the middle of the Pacific, halfway between Japan and Australia. In other words, it's a long-ass flight from India. We set off the morning after losing to Oman: Bangalore to Tokyo, then south to Guam.

We were as professional as possible. We arrived at 4 p.m., did a light session on the beach – you're always near a beach in Guam – then held a team meeting at 9 p.m., before eating. We didn't want them sleeping too early. If they did, they would be up half the night and out of sync for days.

On paper, Guam versus India is a mismatch; a speck versus a subcontinent. The island is 210 square miles and the population is less than 200,000. In 2005 they lost 15–0 to Hong Kong and 21–0 to North Korea. But their side had changed.

Under their English manager Gary White they were picking American-based players with Guam heritage. While we lost to Oman, they beat Turkmenistan 1–0 at home. Against us, six of their starting eleven played in the US. Their centre-half, A.J. DeLaGarza, was a three-time MLS winner with LA Galaxy. Only one player, the skipper Jason Cunliffe, was based in Guam. We couldn't take them lightly. In fact, given India's recent record, we couldn't take anyone lightly.

The game was played on plastic at Guam's national football centre. It was an unlikely venue for a World Cup qualifier. At one end was a training pitch; at the other, a car park. Palm trees and gazebos lined the field. Most of the 3,000 fans were packed into one stand, while a cameraman stood on the roof. In between the long plastic dugouts was a blue Portaloo. It was for the fans, not the coaches.

A tropical island on a sunny June afternoon is not the ideal place for football. The artificial turf shimmered in the heat. For some reason, Gary came out in a cardigan and cravat. I was hot just looking at him.

'Are you sure?' I asked, with a nod to his outfit.

'There's a price to pay for quality,' he responded, smiling.

For once, I ditched the suit and wore an AIFF polo shirt. Shortly after kickoff I was told to wear a bib – my shirt was clashing with Guam's kit – and I was soon bothered, as well as hot.

We passed the ball nicely but we were coasting. There was no intensity. No snap. I turned to Danny Deigan, our sports scientist, and asked what our warm-up was like. He pulled a face. Not great.

I hate that. If the players don't prepare properly, you have problems. Sure enough, Guam took the lead after 37 minutes. It was a header from a long throw, which infuriated me. We knew they had two long-throw specialists, so we had practised defending them in training. It didn't do any good. I made two substitutions at half-time but, given the chance, I would have made seven or eight.

After an hour, they went 2–0 up. Sunil scored a superb header in the 93rd minute but it meant nothing. For the second match in a row, we lost 2–1.

Losing to a team of Americans restarted the debate on picking foreign players. In theory, I would love to select two or three Indian-origin players from Europe or North America. They would improve the squad and set the bar higher for domestic players. It's not a long-term solution. If you pick too many, you harm Indian-born players, and the team loses its integrity. But it's a catalyst. A boost. Almost every other team does it, but in India, it's impossible.

The rules are simple: the Indian constitution does not allow dual citizenship. You either have an Indian passport or a foreign passport. You can't have both. If – for example – a British-Indian wanted to play for India, he would have to give up his UK passport, then meet the criteria for Indian citizenship, which can take years. Understandably, most people don't fancy it, even for an international cap. There are forms of dual-citizenship known as Overseas Citizen cards, or Person of Indian Origin cards, but the government has said holders are not eligible for sports teams.

If it were up to me, I would award temporary passports, which allow people to play for the national team. When the game is finished, they hand them over. If they're selected again, they get them back. It can be done: I had a Rwandan passport when I travelled with their national team.

In my first spell with India I phoned Michael Chopra, then a young striker at Newcastle United. Michael is English but has an Indian father, so I asked if he was interested in playing for us. It would have meant losing his UK passport, but it would have made him a superstar. If Baichung was big, Michael could have been bigger. He could have broken every Indian record, but his heart was set on England. I didn't blame him – he played for their youth teams – but he never won a full cap.

Thirteen years later, there were more Indian-origin players to choose from. Danny Batth, a centre-half for Wolves, and Ricardo Kishna, a winger at Ajax, would have helped us beat Guam. But while they were eligible for India under FIFA rules, they were barred by the government.

I spoke to Kushal Das and asked him to lobby the sports ministry. I even spoke to the British High Commission in Delhi, who had a bold idea: why not raise the issue with the Indian Prime Minister on stage at Wembley?

Narendra Modi was due to give a speech in November at England's national stadium. An official at the High Commission suggested flying me over, putting me on stage, and asking about Indian-origin players in public. 'It will be great for Anglo-Indian relations,' he said. But the AIFF was less keen.

'Thanks for your efforts,' said the president, Praful Patel. 'But it's not going to happen.'

The Guam game highlighted another problem: the looming shadow of the Indian Super League. The auction, where ten of the best Indian players went to the highest bidder, took place on 10 July, a month after the Guam game. But the players' medicals were two days after we got back.

Our players could earn huge sums in the ISL – Sunil went for almost $200,000, while Eugeneson got $150,000 – but not if they were injured. In my opinion, the medical had a huge effect on our performance. I'm not pointing fingers – Sunil and Eugeneson have been fantastic for me – but, overall, we were flat. It wasn't the last time the ISL would affect my team.

We played Nepal in a friendly in August, a young side drawing 0–0 in Pune, before losing 3–0 to Iran in Bangalore in our third qualifier. We were only 1–0 down at half-time. I told the players to believe, but six minutes later, two silly mistakes had put us 3–0 down.

It was a decent performance – 'We didn't expect them to play with so much determination,' said the Iran manager Carlos Queiroz – but it was another loss. In October, we had back-to-back away qualifiers: Turkmenistan on the 8th and Oman on the 13th. But the circus was rolling into town. The ISL started on 3 October.

At the ISL auction in July, I met a number of teams' managers, including David Platt, Roberto Carlos, Zico and Marco Materazzi. They were all supportive. I said I wanted the players from 26 September for the Oman and Turkmenistan games. No one objected, so I planned a ten-day training camp.

When September arrived, Kushal Das said I would get the players on 5 October, three days before the Turkmenistan game. It was unacceptable. You can't prepare for a World Cup qualifier with two training sessions, especially as the players were in pre-season. Like I said: if the guys were coming from the Premier League or La Liga, three days might be OK. But they weren't. They needed to work.

I told Kushal to pull rank, but he couldn't. The league was too powerful. In Indian football, it seemed, the ISL outranked the national team. We got the players on 5 October, like the ISL wanted, with some players not arriving until the evening. But even that wasn't enough for some.

I met Roberto Carlos, the former Brazil left-back, at the auction in July. He had just been named coach of the Delhi Dynamos. We chatted in the lobby and got on well. He said he'd heard good things about me, and asked to watch us train. A week before the Turkmenistan game, he called me.

'Can you do me a favour?' he asked, speaking via a translator.

'Like you did for me?' I replied, pissed off.

'What do you mean?' he asked.

'I wanted my camp to start on September 26th,' I said. 'You said that was fine. But thanks to you – and some of the other managers – I'm getting them on October 5th.'

'That's nothing to do with me. And by the way – I want my players for the Dynamos game on October 4th.'

Although the FIFA dates were 5–13 October, the players had to leave on the 4th, in order to make the camp.

'Not a chance,' I told Carlos. 'It is not happening.'

The phone call ended. Any rapport from the ISL auction was gone. Frankly, I couldn't care less. I don't care about buttering up big names. That week, Carlos moaned to the press.

'I did not like the way he spoke to me at all,' he said.

I had to laugh. He obviously wasn't used to people saying no.

I am not anti-ISL. It has done a fantastic job for Indian football by attracting fans – and sponsors – who never looked at the game before. The chairperson Nita Ambani deserves all the credit in the world. She thought big, which I love, and it has worked. Indian football was sleeping and she has woken it up. But you can't have a league that doesn't work in sync with the national team.

The FIFA calendar has five dates for international matches: late March, early June, early September, early October and early November. Across the world, leagues take a week or two off for internationals. But in 2015, the ISL scheduled twelve games in the first half of October. It was madness.

In my opinion, both leagues – the I-League and the ISL – should play at the same time. The top four from each division would go into an MLS-style playoff, with the winners the national champions.

To make it fair, the national coach would select the top forty Indian players, who would be divided equally between the clubs. Each team would be allowed three foreigners, with the season lasting seven or eight months. Crucially, the league would respect the FIFA calendar, to give the national team the best chance.

Sadly, this wasn't the case in 2015. We arrived in Ashgabat 48 hours before kick-off.

The Turkmen capital is a surreal place. The buildings are made from marble but the streets are empty. It has been described as a cross between Las Vegas and Pyongyang. I first went in 2003 for an Olympic qualifier with India under-23s. While sightseeing, I asked a soldier if I could photograph a gold-plated statue of then-president Saparmurat Niyazov. He said 'da'.

I stepped over a chain-link fence with my camera. Something, however, was lost in translation. As I approached the statue, the soldier thrust his bayonet an inch from my neck. I jumped back, heart racing, and took the photo from distance.

By 2015 Mr Niyazov was no more – he died nine years earlier – but a huge portrait of the new president, Gurbanguly Berdimuhamedow, loomed over the halfway line at the Kopetdag stadium. He was riding a bike.

In the eighth minute the president saw Turkmenistan carve open our back four to go 1–0 up. They gave us an equaliser after 28 minutes – their keeper tried to chip the ball over Jeje Lalpekhlua – but they scored another fantastic goal on the hour. From then on, they sat deep, and we ran out of ideas. For the third time in four World Cup matches we lost 2–1.

I was frustrated. If we'd had a ten-day camp – or even five days – we could have won. Turkmenistan weren't better than us. It sounds like I'm making excuses, but I've been doing this a while. I know the difference a week of training makes. As it turned out, our problems were about to get worse.

The game finished at 8 p.m. on Thursday. Our flight was due to leave Ashgabat at 5.30 p.m. on Friday, but bad weather meant the incoming flight didn't arrive. After hanging round the airport for hours, we tried to return to our hotel, but we had only single-entry visas. We weren't allowed to leave.

After hours of discussion between us, immigration and the Turkmenistan FA, we were allowed to stay in a hotel near the airport. But, by Saturday morning, the plane still hadn't arrived, so we spent all day waiting for news. By now, morale was low. There are only so many magazines you can read.

We eventually left at 9.30 p.m. – 29 hours later than expected – and, after changing in Dubai, arrived in Oman at 2 a.m. on Sunday. To top it off, we then waited another hour for the bus to the hotel. The whole journey, from Ashgabat to Muscat, was supposed to take five hours.

People see England's World Cup squad posing on the steps of a British Airways flight and think international footballers travel in luxury. In fact, they spend half their lives in airports, staring at departure boards that don't move. Waiting 29 hours for a flight in Ashgabat isn't glamorous.

The Oman game was on Tuesday, two days after we arrived. I had planned four sessions. Instead we had two. It's hard to imagine a worse trip. Before kickoff, I knew the boys were dead on their feet. It was five days since the Turkmenistan game and they hadn't recovered. How could they?

There was no one to blame, but we didn't stand a chance. We reached half-time at 0–0 but they scored from a set piece after 54 minutes and won 3–0. In all honesty, it could have been six. Gurpreet Singh – starting his third game in a row – was superb. I was down, so the last thing I needed was another fight with the ISL. But that is what I got.

Before Oman, the AIFF said the ISL wanted their players released as soon as the full-time whistle went, so they could fly home immediately. It was a bad idea: the players needed to rest after a long week. The sooner they got home, the sooner they would play, and I wanted them to recover. I told the AIFF we shouldn't release them. Soon after, I got an email from Pune City manager David Platt.

'After agreeing we could fly players back independently, there seems to be a change of decision,' he wrote. 'It would be very much appreciated if you could release the players.'

'At no point did I agree to the players travelling separately,' I wrote back. 'I am not releasing any players for any team.'

I had no problem with David Platt. His email was polite, and I know he – like me – wanted the best for his team. But I couldn't let the ISL run the national team. No club is bigger than India.

If we want to become a top-100 team, or qualify for the World Cup, we have to think big. Sadly, the AIFF weren't able to resist the ISL. I was overruled and the players left Oman in dribs and drabs in the early hours. They didn't even stay for the post-match meal. The 'India team' that arrived in Delhi consisted of seven members of staff and two players. It was embarrassing.

The optimism of Nepal, and the first Oman game, was gone. We had lost five out of five. We were bottom of the group. On the way back from Oman, I read the news on my laptop.

'AIFF set to sack Indian coach Stephen Constantine,' said the headline.

14
PATIENCE IS A VIRTUE
INDIA, PART TWO, 2015–

I AM NOT AFRAID OF THE SACK. IT IS NOT SOMETHING I CAN control, and so far it hasn't happened.

I loved my job, but if they sacked me, they sacked me. There was nothing I could do. I worked hard. I did things my way. If that wasn't good enough, so be it.

Other websites said I was 'under pressure'. Of course I was. I have been under pressure since the day I left home aged sixteen. I have been under pressure since becoming a football coach, despite my limited playing career. Believe me, losing to Oman didn't increase the pressure. Beating Oman wouldn't have decreased it. For me, the pressure is always there. I apply it myself. I like it.

As it turned out, the story about being sacked was bollocks. Four days after losing to Oman, Baichung – the AIFF's adviser, and chairman of the technical committee – spoke to the Times of India. 'Stephen will complete his contract,' he said. 'I can assure you that.'

Our next game was against Guam in November in Bangalore. The local I-League team, Bengaluru, have a group of fans known as the West Block Blues. They model themselves on European Ultras and bring banners to every game. European shirts are banned. Singing is mandatory. They even travel to away games, which is rare in

175

Indian football, for obvious reasons.

For the Guam game, I walked on to the pitch and looked at the West Block. A huge banner – 5,200 square feet, apparently – almost covered the top tier.

'The road is long,' it said. 'But the belief is everything. Stand up for Indian football.'

My heart filled with pride. In three lines, and fourteen words, they had captured my message. It gave me a massive boost. To see that after losing five in a row was fantastic. I can't thank them enough.

I made five changes from the Oman defeat, including a debut for Romeo Fernandes. I wanted to pick him for the Nepal game in March but, it turned out, he had just signed for Atletico Paranaense in the Brazilian top division (the AIFF has a partnership with Paranaense).

We left him out of the Nepal squad – we didn't want him flying halfway across the world two weeks after leaving India – but he returned in May, after playing only 21 minutes for the Brazilians. I didn't pick him for Oman or Turkmenistan because he wasn't match fit. But after starting for FC Goa in the ISL, I chose him on the right wing against Guam. It was, it turned out, the last time I picked him.

It was a dark, wet night in Banagalore; a world away from the beaches and palm trees of the Pacific. The rain delayed kickoff, but the opening goal was worth the wait. Our big striker Robin Singh had the ball on the left-hand side of the penalty area. He beat his man with a left-footed Cruyff turn then shot with his weaker right from eighteen yards. It was too quick for the keeper and went in off the bar. The West Block went mad, especially as Robin was a Bengaluru player.

On 41 minutes, our midfielder Sehnaj Singh was sent off for a late tackle, so I took Romeo off. To be honest, I would have subbed him anyway, he was so poor. Seeing him against Guam, I wasn't surprised he only got 21 minutes in Brazil. We defended well and held on for a 1–0 win, which was a fantastic effort. Finally, we had three points.

In some countries, international football is a step down from domestic football. Most England games, for example, are a walk in the park compared to the Premier League. But for Indian players, international games are a step up. We had the stats to prove it.

After the ISL season started, we gave our GPS bibs to FC Goa, with permission from their manager Zico. They wore them for a week's training, plus a game. When Danny got the data he couldn't believe it. The distance covered – in one game plus four sessions – was equal to one of our games.

It confirmed my fears about the ISL. It was a slow, one-paced league. To go from that, to defending with ten men in a World Cup game, was superb. The players fully deserved their win against Guam, and I was grateful too. There would have been more headlines if we'd lost.

In December we hosted the South Asian Football Federation Championship. I last experienced the tournament in Bangladesh in 2003, when we came third after beating Pakistan. It wasn't my priority.

India has to stop thinking regionally. In football terms, South Asia is a small pond, and we're the big fish. I don't wish to sound arrogant, because I love our neighbours, especially in Nepal. But we should set our sights on South Korea and Japan, not Sri Lanka and Bhutan. I told the press that – if it were up to me – I would pick an under-19 team. Sadly, the rules wouldn't allow it.

The other problem was the timing. I wanted the tournament in June, after the trip to Guam. The I-League would have finished, and the ISL pre-season wouldn't have started. Instead, it started on 23 December, three days after the ISL final, and during the I-League pre-season. Our training camp began on 10 December, when the ISL was in full swing. Twelve players turned up. More players arrived later, but it comes to something when a national team can't have a full-sized practice game.

I had spent months watching games across India – I took between twelve and fourteen flights a month – so I used the SAFF Championship to pick young players seen by me or Abishek's scouts. Koushik Sarkar was a university student who played in the Calcutta Premier League. I chose Jain Punchakadan and Arjun Tudu after watching them play for the Army XI. Daniel Lalramzuava and Lallianzuala Chhangte (known as Zola) came from the under-19 league. Although most of them didn't make the final squad, I wanted to see what was out there.

In most countries, picking players from state leagues, youth leagues or the armed forces would be madness. But in India, talent goes unseen. There is potential everywhere, but you need to know where to look – and what you're looking for.

For players like Koushik and Arjun, the call-up was a huge honour. But some players didn't even bother turning up. Romeo Fernandes – who I subbed off against Guam – and Mandar Rao Desai both played for FC Goa in the ISL final on 20 December. They were due at camp on 23 December, two days before our first game, but they never showed. Three other Goa players arrived but Fernandes and Desai didn't even bother phoning. The club claimed they were injured but I never got the report.

In March, the AIFF banned them from football for three months and fined them $600. Perhaps Romeo was pissed off after Guam. Either way, neither of them will be picked any time soon. Their complete lack of respect for the team, and the country, was – in short – a disgrace.

After the camp in Kochi, we drove four hours south to Trivandrum, a city on the southern tip of India, where the games would be played. Our hotel was chaos. Two other teams, Afghanistan and Nepal, were sharing the hotel and the rooms weren't ready. It took five hours to check in the team. Nepal ended up moving to different accommodation. And the hotel was just the start of it.

There were seven teams in the tournament but only two training pitches. Both were rock-hard with no lines. You wouldn't walk your dog on them. Again, it came back to standards. The Indian national team is not a Sunday league side. We deserved better, and so did the other sides.

Before our second game, I was so pissed off I took the squad to the match-day stadium. It was locked, so I climbed over a two-metre fence and told the boys to follow. I was halfway over the fence, in full AIFF training kit, when an official emerged from the stadium.

'You can't climb over there!' he said.

'Then call the police,' I said, dropping over the other side.

It was our best session of the tournament. We didn't even use the pitch: the stadium was used for cricket and the outfield was lush.

At a press conference before the first game, I slaughtered the organisers, who were a private company employed by the South Asian Football Federation.

'If you ask me what is wrong with the organisation, I say everything is wrong,' I explained.

Afterwards, the Nepal manager Patrick Aussems spoke to me. Patrick is Belgian, played for Standard Liege in the 1980s, and has coached around the world, including a spell with Al-Hilal in Sudan.

'Thank you for speaking out,' he said. 'When we complain, no one listens. But when the host nation complains, people realise things are bad.'

As a symbol of the chaos, the first game of the tournament was hard to beat. Sri Lanka played Nepal in front of 200 fans. The problem was, no one could tell which team was which. Nepal came out in red while Sri Lanka were in burgundy. I was in the stands thinking: What on earth is the match commissioner doing? Why has the ref allowed this? Nepal had to change into blue at half-time.

We played Sri Lanka in our first game – we wore blue – and won 2–0 in front of 6,000 fans. We then beat Patrick's Nepal side 4–1. I made five changes from the Sri Lanka team and saw two of my 'wildcards' get the headlines. Rowllin Borges, who scored the equaliser, didn't have an ISL club but was better than half those who did. He was a humble guy from a village in Goa whose hard work, on and off the pitch, was an example to everyone. If all the players were like him, we'd be OK.

The third and fourth goals were scored by 18-year-old Lallianzuala Chhangte, aka Zola. He was an exciting winger with a trick, who became India's third-youngest scorer of all time. The youngest was one of mine, too: Jerry Zirsanga was sixteen when he scored in our 3–2 win over Kuwait in 2004.

After winning our two group games, we played Maldives in the semi-final. By now, the mood had changed. A trophy was in sight. More than 30,000 fans watched the game, which was four times the Nepal attendance.

Sunil Chhetri – captaining the side – opened the scoring with a header, before Jeje Lalpekhlua put us 2–0 and 3–1 up. The small group of noisy, red-shirted Maldives fans were given hope when they pulled another one back with fifteen minutes left, but we held on. We were in the final.

Our opponents were our hotel buddies, Afghanistan. They were a good team. They walked through the group stage, beating Bangladesh 4–0, Bhutan 3–0 and Maldives 4–1, before whacking Sri Lanka 5–0 in the semis. They were another side taking advantage of their diaspora: of the eleven who started the final, only one played in Afghanistan. Six were from Germany. They were rising up the rankings, and the final was their last SAFF appearance, as they wanted to test themselves in Central Asia.

Afghanistan did a fantastic job representing their homeland. They were friendly, polite people. But as a team, they wound me up. Every time they left for training, they got in a huddle in the lobby and shouted 'Afghanistan!' at the top of their voices.

One morning, their coach – a German-Croatian called Petar Segrt, who has managed across the world, including the Georgian national team – spoke to me at the hotel.

'Let's make the players shake hands before breakfast,' he said.

'Knock yourself out,' I said, with a distinct lack of enthusiasm. My boys thought it was strange, but they played along.

On the day of the final, I saw two or three Afghan players lounging by the pool two hours before kickoff. I also heard they'd booked the hotel's restaurant to celebrate their win.

'This is what they think of you,' I said in my team talk. 'They are already celebrating.'

More than 40,000 fans filled the stadium. The atmosphere was fantastic. In September, I wasn't bothered by the SAFF Championship, but now I was desperate to win. The players deserved it. The fans deserved it. And I couldn't have the Afghans' party keeping me up all night.

In the 70th minute, Zubayr Amiri, a Germany-based midfielder, took the lead for Afghanistan. Petar Segrt appealed for calm but the players thought they'd won the tournament. The whole team, subs included, celebrated in the corner. The pocket of Afghan fans waved their red, green and black flags, while the rest of the ground fell silent. We had twenty minutes to equalise. We needed only one.

Holicharan Narzary, another new pick, crossed from the right. Sunil headed towards goal. The Afghan centre-half was sleeping and Jeje flicked it past the keeper.

The 40,000 fans went crazy. Everywhere I looked, green, white and orange flags were flying. The Afghans were suddenly quiet.

By the start of extra time I hadn't made a substitution. The players were so fit I didn't need to. After three games and a two-week camp (for some) they were finally up to speed. From the touchline, you can tell when a player is running on empty, but none were. Their hard work in Kochi was paying off. I made the first sub after 97 minutes, bringing Pronay Halder on for Eugeneson, who had just been booked. Five minutes later, Jeje played a long ball forward.

The ball landed on the Afghan centre-half. He headed it backwards, but Sunil nipped in front of the other defender. As the keeper rushed out, trying to clear up the mess, Sunil knocked it past him. The ball rolled towards the line. It felt like an eternity. Eventually it hit the net. The stadium erupted.

As the players celebrated, the noise reached new levels. For a second, I looked round the stadium and took a deep breath. No one thought 'It's only the SAFF Championship' any more.

Five minutes from the end, Afghanistan chipped a free kick into the box. The ball hit Arnab Mondal's arm, but it was accidental. No penalty. While the Afghans appealed, one of their players smacked the ball past Gurpreet. It hit the post and bounced out. Somehow, we cleared our lines.

In the chaos, Petar Segrt was sent off for complaining to the ref. Instead of going to the VIP area, he joined the Afghan fans, putting a scarf on for good measure. If anyone asks why football is the global game, show them highlights of the 2015 SAFF Championship final. It was a privilege to be there.

Eventually, the full-time whistle went. We had won. Like in Kigali, the players threw me round like a rag doll. To go from twelve players in a training camp to champions of South Asia was amazing, especially with such a young squad.

As the spotlights shone, and the artificial smoke billowed, I joined the boys on the podium to lift the trophy. I had spent too many nights in Cyprus, waiting for the phone to ring, to be blasé about winning a regional title. Back at the hotel, the Afghans' party was cancelled.

WE FINISHED OUR WORLD CUP CAMPAIGN IN MARCH, LOSING 4–0 in Iran and 2–1 at home to Turkmenistan. I could handle the Iran result, but Turkmenistan was different. In my second spell with India, we have given away two games. The first was in Guam. The second was at home to Turkmenistan.

For a start, the atmosphere was flat. The support in Trivandrum during the SAFF Championship was superb, so we went back to the state of Kerala, playing in Kochi.

But only 3,000 fans turned up.

In fairness, the players didn't lift the crowd. We were lethargic beyond belief. Normally, I don't say much during a game. If we've trained well, there's nothing much to add. But in Kochi, I found myself yelling the basics. Tuck in. Pull wide. Close him down. Honestly, it was schoolboy stuff.

We went 1–0 up in the first half but lost 2–1. As I watched the players, I thought: This cannot be a team I coach. Four hours after the game I held a staff meeting. The atmosphere was downbeat.

'You do realise,' said my physio Gigi George, 'that six of the starting eleven will play in the derby in four days' time?'

I kicked myself. The Calcutta derby between East Bengal and Mohun Bagan is the biggest match in India. The crowds are massive – 131,000 turned up in 1997 – and the stakes are huge. The clubs would have told the players to take it easy against Turkmenistan and some of them, subconsciously or not, would have listened. I should have realised. If I had, the team would have been very different.

In June, we played Laos in the Asian Cup qualifiers. If we won, we reached the group stages, with a guaranteed six games. If we lost, we got nothing. Laos were eleven places beneath us – they were 174th – and we were expected to win. Anything less and my job was at risk. The Turkmenistan game was fresh in people's minds.

The first leg was played in Laos's national stadium in Vientiane. The ground holds 25,000 but just 1,200 turned up. In the first half, our performance matched the atmosphere. We sat back. We were flat. Luckily, Laos weren't much better and in the 55th minute their keeper parried a cross. Jeje headed into an empty net from two yards. We flew back to India with a one-goal advantage.

As it turned out, that advantage didn't last long. Laos took the lead after sixteen minutes. Like the first leg, we started slow, which gave me a dilemma. Our nineteen-year-old winger, Udanta Singh, was having a shocker. The occasion got to him. Nothing was going right. His family were in the crowd – the game was in Guwahati in the north-east, the region he comes from – and he looked nervous.

I thought about taking him off after 25 minutes. I called over my assistant, Venky, who I bounce ideas off. We decided it was too early, but fifteen minutes later there was no improvement. I made my mind up. Udanta came off before half-time. It was embarrassing, but the team comes before everything. His feelings would recover. Our Asian Cup campaign might not.

Udanta's replacement, Jackichand Singh, was another north-east boy. He came from a poor family: his dad was a farmer and his mum ran a roadside tea stall. He learned the game with a borrowed ball and second-hand shoes a size too small. He only realised he was named after the Hong Kong film star when, aged fifteen, a journalist at a school football tournament made him call his mother to ask.

I picked him for my first camp against Nepal but also left him out a couple of times. Like a lot of Indian players, he hadn't been coached properly. That can be a massive problem – we worked on his position without the ball, as he always looked to bomb on – but it's also exciting. After he came on, he set up two goals in five minutes. From 1–0 down after forty minutes, we were 2–1 up at half-time.

The scoreline didn't change my team talk. We weren't playing well and I let the players know. If Laos scored another, it was game on. Thankfully, we got a third just after half-time when our young defender, Sandesh Jhingan, headed in a Eugeneson free kick. Game over.

We ended up winning 6–1, with Jackichand getting three assists. I spoke to Udanta and he was fine. He is a fantastic player with a big future. The competition with Jackichand will be good for India.

The result – India's biggest win since beating Cambodia 6–0 in 2007 – was fantastic for morale. A performance like that shows people you're on the right track. I knew that, behind the scenes, I was improving India. The team was younger and fitter. The set-up was more professional. But only results convince people.

The win also showed the depth of our squad. Six players, including Robin Singh, Rowllin Borges and Pronay Halder, were injured, but we still scored six. Our left-back against Laos, Keegan Pereira, was the 27th player to make his debut in my second spell. Fulganco Cardozo, who came on and scored the sixth, was the 28th. Not all of those 28 will have international careers. But, for the first time in years, we had a pool of players fighting for places.

After Laos we had no games scheduled. The group stage of the Asian Cup qualifiers wasn't until March 2017, so we planned something big: a summer tour of America.

Graham Smith, the technical director of Sacramento Republic, had introduced me to an Englishman of Indian origin called Ranbir Shergill. He is a great guy. In 2006 he formed a semi-pro club in California called Ventura County Fusion, which now hosts Premier League and MLS clubs every pre-season. He's also a FIFA match agent, which means he can organise friendlies between clubs and countries from different federations.

We planned the tour for more than a year. I flew to America at my own expense to hold meetings. We wanted to go in July but moved it to August, to make it easier to organise friendlies.

The idea was to play three or four games across two weeks. Sacramento Republic were confirmed, we were talking to the MLS side San Jose Earthquakes, and we hoped to play one or two friendlies against Caribbean countries. The crowds would have been huge, as there's a big Indian population in California, and our players would have been in the shop window. An Indian had never played in the MLS –

Sunil appeared in a cup game for Kansas City Wizards – but one or two were ready.

Ranbir and Graham made the arrangements. They would pay for hotels and we would buy our flights. It was a win-win situation, but the ISL weren't happy: they wanted the players back by mid-August in order to start pre-season. I thought that was unreasonable: the tour was a massive opportunity for both the players and the national team.

By the time we confirmed the dates, it was too late to get US visas for the squad. I was hugely frustrated. Two weeks' hard work in California would have improved the team, as well as being fun. Instead, we went to Bhutan, which wasn't quite the same.

We arranged a friendly at short notice in Thimphu and held a camp in Delhi beforehand. Two clubs wouldn't release their players. East Bengal were going for their seventh Calcutta Premier Division title in a row – the state league is a big deal – while Bengaluru were preparing for an AFC Cup quarter-final against Tampines Rovers of Singapore. The first leg wasn't until a month after Bhutan, but we couldn't force their hand as August wasn't a FIFA date.

Bhutan's Changlimithang stadium is one of the most beautiful in the world. An ornate, palace-like pavilion runs down one side. Hills loom over the terraces and, in the distance, mountains poke into the clouds. I would rather have been in the StubHub Arena, home of LA Galaxy, but I enjoyed the view. The air was fresher than Delhi, too. Thimphu is the third-highest capital city in the world.

Bhutan had improved since losing 7–0 to Nepal in my first international in 1999. They knocked Sri Lanka out of the World Cup in 2015 – a result that made headlines around the world – but they remained a level below India.

Sumeet Passi, a 21-year-old striker who made his debut against Laos, scored after two minutes. It was 3–0 within twenty. There was no point taking the piss so we left it there. I wasn't getting carried away – Bhutan were ranked 192nd – but it was three wins out of three. Going back to Guam at home, we had eight wins from ten.

We were due to play Puerto Rico in California so, when our American tour was cancelled, we invited them to India instead. We paid their expenses, so one of football's least-likely friendlies was on.

The AIFF asked if I was interested in holding the game in Mumbai. The last time India played there – February 1955 – they lost 3–0 to Lev Yashin's USSR. A lack of stadiums meant they hadn't returned, but the Andheri Sports Complex was newly refurbished. At least, that's what I was told.

In the week before the game, I flew to Mumbai to inspect the ground. It was poor. The pitch was hard and there was rubbish behind both goals. Puerto Rico couldn't fly halfway round the world to play there: it wasn't fit for international football. If it didn't improve the game would be moved.

I went back to my hotel and, at 11 p.m., got a call from a young politician called

Aditya Thackeray. His family had dominated Mumbai politics for decades. He was leader of Yuva Sena, the youth wing of a right-wing party called Shiv Sena, which his grandfather, Bal Thackeray, founded in 1966. More importantly, he was president of Mumbai's district football association.

'Can we meet to discuss the problems at the ground?' he asked.

'No problem,' I replied. 'I'll see you tomorrow. I leave at midday.'

'Can you come now?' he replied.

'But it's eleven p.m.,' I pointed out.

'I'll meet you at the ground,' he said, and hung up.

When I arrived Mr Thackeray was waiting with 25 people: groundsmen, labourers, the lot.

'Tell us what you need,' he said.

I stayed until 1 a.m. and by match day, the ground was outstanding. I can't thank Mr Thackeray enough.

More than 7,000 fans turned up but it felt like 20,000. The lights were on and the atmosphere was electric. Mumbai FC's fan group, the Yellow Brigade, sung nonstop. Mumbai is better known for cricket but the football fans are special. Even Puerto Rico taking the lead after seven minutes didn't stop them. We equalised after seventeen minutes and by half-time were 3–1 up.

Puerto Rico were 114th in the world but they couldn't handle us. Jackichand scored a fourth after 56 minutes and we could have scored more. The match finished 4–1 but the best moment came after full time: the Indian fans chanted for Puerto Rico and gave them a standing ovation. Their players responded with a lap of honour. It was a reminder of how football brings people together.

'One of the most impressive moments in the Puerto Rican national team's history,' said their general secretary Ignacio Rodriguez after the game. Mumbai won't wait 61 years for another match.

The match was extra-special for Gurpreet Singh, who I made captain. I can't praise him enough. When I first saw him in 2015, he wasn't ready. But let me tell you, he has worked his socks off in Norway. He's not on big money, he lives in a small flat, and he's spent months as understudy to Sayouba Mande, Stabaek's Ivorian keeper. But he was brave. He stuck it out. Now, he's good enough to have a career in Europe. I hope other Indians follow his example. The whole country will benefit.

We had won nine in eleven and the bandwagon was rolling. As always, people wanted to jump on. Michael Chopra – who I asked to play for India in 2002 – was seeing out his career with Kerala Blasters in the ISL. After the Puerto Rico win he told the press he had 'ambitions to play for India' and was 'speaking to lawyers'. Unfortunately for Chopra, lawyers don't pick the national team.

I already knew of Chopra's interest. In 2015, six months after I was appointed, I got a call from an agent claiming to represent him.

'Michael wants to represent India,' the agent said. 'He did well in the ISL last year.'

In 2014, Chopra played nine times for Kerala Blasters and scored no goals.

'I'm not sure he did well,' I said. 'I also think he looks overweight.'

Some time later, Chopra himself called.

'I will get hold of a passport, but I need to know if you'll pick me,' he said.

'I can't make promises before you have the passport,' I replied. 'But as things stand I don't think you can help us. You don't fit in with our style of play.'

Chopra was a decent player but his best days were long gone. In his last season in Britain, he scored two goals in 23 league games for Alloa Athletic in the Scottish second tier. Jeje, Sunil and Robin Singh were streets ahead: fitter, quicker and more hard-working. After Chopra spoke to the press, I was asked about him.

'It's not going to happen,' I told reporters. 'He's thirty-two now. Even if he decides to apply for Indian citizenship, the entire process will take at least two years. He's already well past it.'

I didn't mean to be rude. But Chopra can't say 'I want to play for India' and waltz into the team. I won't let a Premier League has-been use the Indian national team for a swansong. The country, and the fans, deserve better than that. A week later, Chopra was asked about my response.

'Constantine can say whatever he wants,' Chopra said. 'He was nothing as a player.'

How to win friends and influence people, the Michael Chopra way.

After beating Puerto Rico we moved to 137 in the FIFA rankings, our highest position since August 2010. We had risen 34 places since I arrived in 2015. It was a good achievement but I wasn't getting carried away.

Being 137 in the world – behind the likes of Tajikistan and Palestine – isn't good enough. Above all, Indian football must be ambitious. We should be a top-100 country that aims for the World Cup. We should have players in the top leagues in Europe. We should be selling out stadiums across the country. In years to come, we should be embarrassed about being 137th.

The AIFF was doing its bit. In December, the Asian Football Confederation named the federation as its 'developing member association of the year'. According to the AFC, the award is for 'professional administration and governance as well an exceptional contribution to the development and promotion of the game at all levels within the country'.

It was a big deal – the president, Praful Patel, picked up the trophy at a ceremony in Abu Dhabi – and in my opinion it was fully deserved. They have improved hugely since 2002.

I look back at my first training camp in Jamshedpur and laugh. The bunk beds, the bad food, the two-dollar kit . . . it was amateur. To go from that, to an AFC award, is fantastic. Praful Patel and Kushal Das deserve huge credit, as does the team manager Shantha Gopinath and all the backroom staff, from Venky and Ramos to Danny and Lee. But we're not even halfway there.

Mainly because of the ISL, we had no games between September 2016 and March 2017. While the rest of the world played, we missed two FIFA dates in October and November. India needs to play whenever we can. If we don't, the team goes backwards. The sooner we have one league, with breaks for internationals, the better.

We also need a national training centre – at the moment, we travel all over the country – and massive investment in youth football. Most Indian players don't see a proper coach until they're thirteen or fourteen. We need regional academies, better coach education, and state leagues at youth level … the list goes on. It will take time, but we need to think long-term.

Picking foreigners of Indian origin is unlikely to happen. The government won't change the law for us. But, after a brilliant idea from Abishek, we have a portal where young players living abroad with Indian passports can upload footage. If they're good enough, they're invited for a trial. At the moment it's for under-17s but we'd like to extend it. So far, we've found three players to train with the under-17 squad. Improving Indian football is like building a mansion. The portal is another brick.

In November, I was offered a fourteen-month contract extension, which runs until the end of the Asian Cup qualifiers. I was delighted to sign. Partly because Indian football is going places, and partly because I love the place.

If England is home, and Cyprus my second home, then India is my third home. In total, I have been here five years. I wouldn't have stayed five minutes if it weren't for the people.

Indians are easy-going but hard-working. Smart but humble. Serious but funny. The country isn't perfect: the poverty is shocking and the red tape is maddening. But, when Indians put their minds to something, they succeed. The country, and the football team, will be a super-power one day.

My contract runs until March 2018. By that time, I will have been in continuous employment for almost five years: from Apollon Smyrnis with Lawrie Sanchez, to Rwanda, to India. In football, that's an achievement. It feels a long time since I borrowed money to survive. It feels even longer since I slept in an abandoned car in a field in Limassol, a scared boy with no mother and no home.

When I left home in Cyprus aged 16, walking along a pitch-black, half-built road, I started a journey. It has taken me to Khartoum and Kathmandu. New York and New Delhi. Brighton and Blantyre. Almost forty years on, I am still walking.

The journey isn't over. But now, the road is better lit.

IN MAY 2016, SIX WEEKS AFTER LOSING AT HOME TO TURKMENISTAN, I did something I thought I'd never do. I turned down a Football League job.

Port Vale had just finished twelfth in League One, the English third tier. Their manager – the former Wales international Rob Page – was joining Northampton. It was years since I'd applied to an English club, but I knew the Vale chairman, Norman Smurthwaite.

Before I went to India, the agent James Garley – who got me the Gillingham interview – put me in for Port Vale. Nothing happened, but Norman kept in touch. When Page left in 2016, he called.

Five years earlier, I would have bitten his hand off. I'd spent years dreaming of the Football League. I'd spent years faxing my CV to clubs, the second I saw someone sacked on Ceefax. But those days were over. I was coaching a national team for the sixth time. England wasn't everything.

Of course, I would move for the right job. But Port Vale wasn't it. The money was less than half my Indian salary, the club had seven contracted players, and I wasn't allowed to bring in my own staff. The assistant manager, the former Sheffield United midfielder Michael Brown, was already in place. I'm sure Michael's a good coach, but what if we didn't get on? I'm only going to get one chance in England. It has to be right.

Norman said there were 77 applicants for the job. According to him, only fifteen were good, and only three met his criteria. I can't thank him enough for thinking of me – appointing an unknown takes balls – but I didn't need England any more.

I had worked all over the world. I had done things that most coaches only dream of. I didn't need a Football League job to validate my career.

I had spent years begging for a chance. Now I was turning one down. But whichever way you dice it, India is bigger than Port Vale. Finally, I was happy where I was.

15
EPILOGUE

I AM OFTEN ASKED TWO QUESTIONS:

1. When you started coaching, did you expect to be successful?

2. Are you happy with what you have achieved?

The answers:

1. Yes. It sounds arrogant, but I believed in myself. I am 100 per cent sure of my ability.

2. No. I am never satisfied. I always think I can improve.

I remember beating Vietnam in the LG Cup final in 2002, when Abhishek's late header gave India their first trophy since 1970s. On the bus afterwards, part of me was pleased. But another part was pissed off that we conceded two before we started to play. It's the same every time I win. I find it hard to enjoy the moment. I'm always worried about what comes next.

I have a wonderful career, which I've worked hard to get. But I'm scared I'll lose it. That fear makes me work harder. If I'd been a big-name player, it would be different. I would get second chances. Third chances. Fourth chances. But I'm only as good as my last job. If I failed at Nepal, that was it. My international career was over.

I have improved every team I had. The results don't always show it – in Sudan I didn't win a game – but I know what I've done, and so do people I've worked with. I get the best out of my players. I lay the foundations, even if I don't always get to finish the job.

My mind is filled with special memories. Being decorated by the King in Nepal will take some beating. I arrived in Kathmandu a nobody and left with a medal round my neck. Hearing 10,000 people sing my name at Calcutta airport was wonderful. And the minibus in Kigali, with the Rwandan squad singing their hearts out, will live with me forever.

Some memories are less obvious. Playing in the FA Cup at Goodison Park with Millwall, doing the warm-up in the rain under the floodlights, was inspirational. Meeting Glenn Hoddle in the dugouts at Molineux, before big Barry Hayles scored his last-minute winner, was fantastic. That was the sharp end. That was where I wanted to work.

But I've also seen bad things. In India, people lie in the street with nothing to eat. Watching Zimbabwe fall apart was horrible. The poverty across Africa – especially in Malawi – was heartbreaking. I will never forget taking the players to the orphanage in Mulanje.

When I look back, I feel very fortunate. I have been to amazing places, and met some wonderful people. It hasn't been easy – I have been turned down for thousands of jobs – but nothing worthwhile is. I have given my life to football. It has given me life back.

Every day, I receive emails from young coaches. I reply to them all. Some people want a job, which I can't give them. Some want advice, which I can. Here's what I tell them. You are as good as you want to be. And only you know how good you want to be.

16

MY DAD, THE FOOTBALL MANAGER

MY DAD'S JOB IS ALL-CONSUMING. FOOTBALL, TACTICS AND teams are part of daily dinner conversations and, more often than not, I don't understand a word of it.

It is hard to say exactly what it's like when your Dad is a football manager, because it has always been a part of life. My sisters and I have never known anything different. If I had to choose one thing, I would say the biggest impact is the travelling he does.

There have been many times when I felt like Dad was abroad more than he was at home. It has always been that way. His job has taken him, and us, to many different parts of the world, and sometimes to very separate parts of the world. His job has provided a lot for us, and has given us experiences. We have been to countries that, had it not been for his work, we wouldn't have seen.

Being educated in India was the most unusual time in my school life. Everything – from the lessons to the people – was different, especially in comparison to England. It felt like my Dad was famous there. When he took us to school, people would gather round and ask for his autograph!

The children were shocked by how pale I was. I didn't understand much of what was being said around me, which made me feel like an outsider. That feeling stuck whenever I started a new school, and there were four in total.

The experiences we had were amazing, and as a result I truly love travelling and seeing new countries – although maybe not as many as Dad. But I could never do a job like his. We see how hard it is to come home for three weeks, settle down, and then leave again. I prefer to stay in one place!

It was always sad, my Dad saying goodbye. Not seeing him for weeks on end became expected and that made it harder, especially as we got older. We knew that every time he came home, it was inevitable he would leave again. Being in a strange country where you don't speak the language will always be scary. Without Dad, Mum and I were that little bit more scared, particularly when we woke up to frogs leaping around the kitchen with no one to chase them away. That task did ultimately fall to me as a result of my mother's terror for anything that hops or scurries!

When we left India for England, my Dad still commuted to work (at Millwall). But he was home every night, which did feel more 'normal'. It seemed to make Mum a lot less stressed having him around. I know now how hard it was for both my parents being apart, my Dad not seeing his children and my mum looking after us by herself. It's clear how different things are when everyone's together, but they both did what they had to. As my sisters and I got older, we appreciated that more.

Although many people dream of having my Dad's job, it is a very hard one to have (and to get). We always knew how volatile his work was. Travelling, wins and losses, criticism, and publicity meant his job was never left at the door. When my Dad worked in Cyprus, whatever happened in his games could be felt at home. The nerves beforehand; the excitement when he won; the anger and disappointment when he lost.

We always knew when it had been a bad game from the look on his face. We definitely got on his nerves a lot more when his team lost. Having Dad back home in Cyprus was a lot better, if a lot stricter. No party could be attended without a precise location, guest list and curfew! There were also the countless football games on TV, with shouts of joy or rage when Arsenal won or lost. And no, I wouldn't watch the games with him.

Football is part of life for us and a way of life for my Dad. He plays, talks, watches and coaches football, and has tried countless times to explain the offside rule to me. Despite the fact that football is not a career I would pursue, and that my Dad didn't get his job the conventional way – A levels, university, etc. – his love for his work has shown how important it is to pick a career that you enjoy.

Dad's career has affected the whole family, in terms of travel, new schools, bad results and good ones. I don't really know exactly how it is for my Dad, but a lot of the time his work hasn't been glamorous or easy. It's been nerve-wracking for everyone, and very uncertain. There were times when he couldn't tell us when his next chance to come back was, or where his next job would be.

I always thought it would be easier for him to have a normal job, but I wouldn't have preferred it. Football is what he enjoys and it has definitely given me and my sisters some amazing opportunities. It has taught us to find something that we are good at and something we can be excited about. His love for football is what has kept him there and made him successful. That is something we aspire to.

Paula Constantine
Aged nineteen
December 2016

17
ACKNOWLEDGMENTS

I REMEMBER MEETING MARK HUGHES, WHO I RATE HIGHLY, ON a course. He told me to get the best people around me. I have tried to follow his advice, so to everyone who has helped me, thank you. Without you, I am nothing.

Nick and Deme Gregoriou are like brothers to me. Life has taken us in different directions, but every time we meet it's like we've never been apart. They are godfathers to Paula and Christiana and I am proud to call them my friends. I've had dark moments. I've needed help. Nick and Deme have always given it. I will be in their debt for the rest of my life.

Nikos Andreou – who I have known since living in the US in the 1980s – is another special person. We played together in New York, and coached together at Nea Salamina. He's been a huge help.

My biggest supporter, though, is my wife Lucy. I remember meeting her as if it were yesterday. Truly, it was the luckiest day of my life.

To this day, I'm not sure why she has stayed so long. I have dragged her halfway across the world and, more often than not, left her to handle the house and three young daughters. She is amazing. Her sacrifice is incredible. She gave up everything to be with me.

Lucy is the polar opposite of me. She is the nicest, most polite person I know. Without her, I would have nothing. The first house we rented in Cyprus had rats. We have come a long way since then, and we have Lucy to thank for that.

I also want to mention my daughters, who've put up with me not being around. They are amazing, hard-working girls, who will succeed in everything they do. I am hugely proud of them. Forget football: they are my biggest achievement. Thank you, girls.

One person who would be proud of me, I hope, is my mum. It is more than forty years since she died. I still miss her terribly.

When she passed away, I was a twelve-year-old boy who played Subbuteo on his dad's snooker table and broke windows in the back garden. She would be so pleased that I followed my dream. My Aunty Rose would also be proud. Those two made me what I am today.

Finally, I need to thank my northern friend Owen Amos, who had the bright idea to write the book in the first place. Your determination to see my story published, and the hours, days, weeks and months you have put into this book has been immense. It has been a pleasure working with you.

Thank you for reading. Enjoy the game.

FROM CO-AUTHOR, OWEN AMOS

Thanks to: Mum and Dad for the proof-reading; Timothy Abraham for the ideas and the groundhops; Andrew Mollitt for the encouragement and the tours; and Stephen Constantine for the stories.

And to my wonderful wife Samantha and son Freddie: thanks for your patience and support while I watched old matches on YouTube. It was research – honest.